Reading
People

Reading People

People

HOW TO UNDERSTAND PEOPLE
AND PREDICT THEIR BEHAVIOR—
ANYTIME, ANYPLACE

———

Jo-Ellan Dimitrius, Ph.D.,
and Mark Mazzarella

BALLANTINE BOOKS • NEW YORK

A Ballantine Book
Published by The Ballantine Publishing Group

www.randomhouse.com/BB/

Ballantine and colophon are registered trademarks of Random House, Inc.

Library of Congress Catalog Card Number: 99-90259

ISBN 0-345-42587-1

Manufactured in the United States of America

Cover photo by Benoit

First Ballantine Edition: June 1999

10 9 8 7 6 5 4 3 2 1

To my father, Harlan Huebner, whose love of people was contagious; to my mother, Joan Huebner, who continues to inspire me with her passion for people; to my wonderful children, Nikki, Francis, and Stirling, who bring me love and joy every day of my life; and to Mark, whose intellect, humor, compassion, patience, and devotion made this book possible.

—JO-ELLAN DIMITRIUS

To my mom, Carol, who is with me in spirit always; to my children, Eve, Laurel, Joel, Michael, and Cody, who give me strength—and lots of practice reading people; and to Jo-Ellan, who has taught me to see people, and the world, through different eyes.

—MARK MAZZARELLA

Acknowledgments

No one ever achieved much without the contributions of others, and creating this book was no exception. From the time we first decided to write *Reading People,* through its many drafts, and finally during the process of editing, publishing, and promotion, we have been blessed with the encouragement and assistance of so many wonderful and talented people that we could never thank them all. But we would like to publicly acknowledge a few to whom we are particularly indebted.

We owe a special debt of gratitude to Dr. Spencer Johnson, who first suggested that we write this book together. His vision of a book that would help others live more enjoyable, meaningful, and fruitful lives took root and grew into *Reading People.* Thank you also, Spencer, for introducing us to our agent, Margret McBride, who has been a vital and enthusiastic supporter since the inception of this project.

This book could never have been written without the assistance as well of Jack Dunn, the CEO of FTI Consulting, who encouraged Jo-Ellan to take as much time as she needed away from her duties at the office; and without the support of the partners, associates, and staff of the law firm of Mazzarella, Dunwoody, Wilson & Petty, who pitched in to free Mark up to spend the many months required to put our thoughts on paper.

We'll never be able to thank Lynn Randall enough for her twenty years of support and friendship to Mark, and her help and encouragement with this book. Thanks also to Diane Anderson and Melinda Lewis, who transcribed draft after draft of the text. Their diligence, talent, and phenomenal ability to understand Mark's dictation and read his handwritten edits kept us on schedule. We are also grateful to John Wexo and Michael Rondeau, good friends and gifted writers, who took time out of their busy lives to brainstorm and edit this book. A special thanks to you, John—you showed us the way.

Our thanks also go out to all the great people at Random House, especially Deb Futter, our editor, for believing in this project and helping make our dream a reality; and Jolanta Benal, our copy editor. We also want to recognize Lynette Padwa for all her hard work on the early drafts of the text.

Most important, we want to thank our families, friends, and loved ones, whose quiet contributions will never be known, except by us.

Thank you all.

Contents

Introduction:
A Passion for People

When I was a child, I'd peer down from my perch at the top of the stairs above my parents' living room during their frequent dinner parties. I'd watch as my mother scurried around, carefully ensuring that no glass was empty. I remember the chubby, bald man whose booming laughter resonated throughout the house, and his rail-thin wife, who shook her head and rolled her eyes as he launched into an only slightly modified version of a story he'd told dozens of times before. I would laugh to myself as my father's friend John reached out casually for another hors d'oeuvre to add to the scores he'd already inhaled, while my dad playfully poked him in the stomach, and said, chuckling, "Make sure you save some room for dinner, little boy." I loved those Saturday evenings, when the house filled with the laughter and conversation of a dozen people—all so different, and yet so alike. Even when I was a child my passion was people.

Twenty-five years later, armed with nothing more than my lifetime of experiences, paper, and a pen, I sat nervously in court watching several dozen prospective jurors file into the courtroom for the first time. From among them, I would have to select the twelve who would decide whether my client would live or die. Every other decision I'd ever made about people suddenly seemed insignificant. Should I have trusted the salesman who sold me my first used car? Was I right to confide in my best friend that I had a crush on her big brother? Had I chosen a good baby-sitter for my young daughter? I had been reading people for over thirty years, but this time a man's life was at stake.

For fifteen years since then, I have made my living reading people. I have sized up more than ten thousand prospective jurors, and evaluated thousands of witnesses, lawyers, and even judges. I sat for weeks next to "the Night Stalker," Richard Ramirez, peering every day into the coldest eyes I have ever seen. I shared Peggy Buckey's anguish at her unwarranted prosecution for child molestation in the McMartin Preschool case. I watched in horror as rioting spread through Los Angeles after the defense verdict in the Rodney King Simi Valley trial. In the Reginald Denny case, I tried to comprehend why four young men would mercilessly beat a complete stranger, and struggled to select jurors who would understand those motives and respond leniently. I strained to comprehend the internal torment that led John DuPont to shoot and kill Olympic wrestler David Schultz. And I endured the world's scrutiny, and often its harsh criticism, because I helped select the jury that acquitted O. J. Simpson.

It has been a wild, sometimes exhilarating ride, but not as glamorous as some might think. I have worked agonizingly long hours, and while I have been applauded by some for my involvement in unpopular cases, I have also been criticized by others for the very same involvement. My efforts to explain my deep commitment to the American system of justice and the principle that no one should be denied his liberty, let alone his life, by anything less than a truly impartial jury, have often fallen on deaf ears. My life has been threatened. I was even blamed by some for the L.A. riots in 1992 because I helped pick the jury that acquitted the four police officers charged with beating Rodney King.

Through it all, I have watched and listened. I have done my best to apply my education, my powers of observation, my common sense, and my intuition to understanding those who have passed through the courtrooms where I have worked. Mostly, I have learned. And if there's one thing I have learned, sometimes the hard way, it is how to read people.

From the day I was chosen by "the Dream Team" to become the jury consultant in O. J. Simpson's criminal trial, I have been approached from seemingly every angle to write a book. Not a book about what I do best—reading people—but about the dirt on the Los Angeles District Attorney's Office, or how the O. J. Simpson case compared with my other high-profile cases, or (and this was far and away the most popular topic) the inside scoop on the Dream Team. But writing an exposé never interested me. It was not until a very wise friend, the writer Spencer Johnson, suggested, "Write about something you know best, something that will make a difference in people's lives," that we were inspired to write *Reading People*.

No matter with whom you interact, no matter where or when you interact with them, the quality of your life will depend to a large extent on the quality of your decisions about people. Salesmen will sell more, and customers will make better purchasing decisions. Employers will make better hiring choices; prospective employees will improve their chances of landing the best jobs. You will choose your friends, lovers, and partners better, and understand your family members more. As a friend you will be more sensitive and as a competitor you will be more alert.

Some of those who read people for a living, as I do, rely almost exclusively on scientific research, surveys, studies, polls, and statistical analysis. Others claim to have a God-given talent. My own experience has taught me that reading people is neither a science nor an innate gift. It is a matter of knowing what to look and listen for, having the curiosity and patience to gather the necessary information, and understanding how to recognize the patterns in a person's appearance, body language, voice, and conduct.

During college and graduate school, I spent almost a decade studying psychology, sociology, physiology, and criminology, along with a smattering of statistics, communication, and linguistics. As valuable as my formal education has been, it is not what made *The American Lawyer* dub me "the Seer" a few years back. Rather, it is my near-obsessive curiosity about people—how they look, sound, and act—that has made me an effective people reader. The empathy I feel for others drives me to understand them better.

My most important skill is my ability to see the pattern of someone's personality and beliefs emerge from among often conflicting traits and characteristics. It is a skill I learned from the time I was a little girl, sitting at the top of those stairs during my parents' dinner parties, and refined through a lifetime of experiences and over four hundred trials. Best of all, it's a skill that can be learned and applied with equal success by anyone—anytime, anyplace.

Why am I so sure?

Because over the past fifteen years I have tested this method on more than ten thousand "research subjects." After predicting the behavior of thousands of jurors, witnesses, lawyers, and judges, I have been able to see whether my predictions came true. After the cases were decided, I spoke with the participants to explore what they thought and why. I did not always peg them correctly, especially in the earlier years. But by testing my perceptions over and over, I have verified which clues are generally reliable and which are not. I have also learned it is important not to focus on any single trait or characteristic: taken alone, almost any trait may be misleading. And I have found that the approach outlined in this book will help anyone understand people and better predict their behavior in the courtroom, the boardroom, and the bedroom.

People are people, wherever they are. The man on the witness stand trying to persuade the jury of the righteousness of his cause is no different from the salesman hawking his goods at the flea market. The prejudices shown by a prospective juror are the same as those that may surface in a job interview. A juror or witness will try to avoid answering a sensitive question in court in much the same way as he does at home or at work.

Each courtroom is a microcosm of life, filled with anger, nervousness, prejudice, fear, greed, deceit, and every other conceivable human emotion and trait. There, and everywhere else, every person reveals his emotions and beliefs in many ways.

In the first chapter, "Reading Readiness," we will explain how you can prepare yourself to read people more effectively. Chapter 2, "Discovering Patterns," will show you how to make sense of a person's often contradictory characteristics. In the succeeding chapters, you will discover how people reveal their beliefs and character through their personal appearance, body language, environment, voice, communication techniques, and actions. You'll also learn how to enhance your intuition and use it to your advantage. The final chapters will show you how to make a good impression on those who are reading you, and how to make wise and reliable snap decisions.

Throughout this book you'll be seeing what can be learned from how a person looks, talks, and acts. But the goal is not just to provide you with a "glossary" of people's characteristics and behaviors. Instead, *Reading People* aims to teach you how to evaluate people's complex characteristics and how to see the overall pattern those characteristics form—the pattern that truly can reveal and predict behavior. This method has been the secret to my success at reading people. Once you've mastered these skills, they will serve you just as well, at work and at play, today and for the rest of your life.

Reading
People

Reading Readiness:
Preparing for the Challenge
of Reading People

"I can't believe I didn't see the signs. They were right
there in front of me! How could I have been so blind?"

We've all said something very much like this, probably more times than
we care to admit. After we've misjudged our boss's intentions, a friend's
loyalty, or a baby-sitter's common sense, we carefully replay the past—
and usually see the mistakes we made with 20/20 hindsight. Why, then,
after living and reliving our mistakes, don't we learn more from them? If
reading people were like driving a car or hitting a tennis ball, we'd be
able to recognize our weak points and improve our performance with
every try. That rarely happens with relationships. Instead, we interact
with our friends, colleagues, and spouses in the same old ways, doggedly
hoping for the best.

In theory, thanks to the people-reading skills I acquired over the years,
it should have been easy for me to make better decisions in my personal
life—whom to let into it and what to expect from them once I did. Yet
for many years I failed to apply my courtroom abilities to my off-duty
life. Perhaps I had to reach a saturation point of pain and disappointment in some of my personal relationships before I was willing to ana-
lyze my mistakes and put my professional experience to work for me.

When I finally resolved to bring that focus and clarity to my personal
life, it made sense to start by comparing the courthouse with the world
outside. I was determined to figure out what I was doing in the court-

room that enabled me to read people in that setting with such consistent accuracy. I thought I should be able to distill that information into a set of people-reading basics that would work anywhere.

When I told my colleagues about the great difference between my people-reading successes on and off the job, I found I wasn't alone. Many of the best attorneys I knew confessed that, while they enjoyed great success reading people in court, the rest of the time they didn't do much better than anyone else. Why?

The conclusions I eventually reached led me to the keys of "reading readiness"—the foundation of understanding people and predicting their behavior. The first thing I discovered was that *attitude is critical.* In a courtroom, I was ready to focus fully on the people I encountered, to listen to them closely, to observe the way they looked and acted, and to carefully think about what I was hearing and seeing. I had a very different attitude in my private life. I rarely did any of those things. The fact is, you have to be *ready* to read people, or all the clues in the world won't do you any good.

In this chapter, you'll learn how to bring a courtroom state of mind—clear-eyed, observant, careful, and objective—into the emotional, subjective drama that is everyday life. Master the following skills, and you'll be ready to read people.

1. Spend more time with people. That's the best way to learn to understand them.
2. Stop, look, and listen. There's no substitute for patience and attentiveness.
3. Learn to reveal something of yourself. To get others to open up, you must first open up to them.
4. Know what you're looking for. Unless you know what you want in another person, there's a good chance you'll be disappointed.
5. Train yourself to be objective. Objectivity is essential to reading people, but it's the hardest of these seven skills for most of us to master.
6. Start from scratch, without biases and prejudices.
7. Make a decision, then act on it.

DISCOVERING THE LOST ART OF READING PEOPLE

Unless you've been stranded on a desert island for the past fifty years, you've noticed that the world has changed. Understanding people has always been one of life's biggest challenges, but the social changes and technological explosion of recent decades have made it even more difficult. Today, many of us don't enjoy close bonds or daily contact even with the most important people in our lives. We're out of touch and out of practice.

Unless you practice the skills you'll learn in this book, you won't retain them. But that's difficult today, because we live in a global society. We're in contact with people across town, across the country, or even on the other side of the world. But our contact usually isn't personal. The same technological advances that allow us such extraordinary access to others have exacted a toll—they have made face-to-face conversation relatively rare. Why meet with a client in person if you can phone him? Why have an actual conversation with Mom if you can leave a message on her answering machine? Why phone a friend if you can send an e-mail or a fax? As long as the message gets through, what's the difference? Most of us have even phoned someone, *hoping* to leave a message, only to be *disappointed* when she's actually there to answer the call. Some of us even bow out altogether, relying on our assistants, kids, spouses, or friends to do our communicating for us. Or we settle into cyberspace, meeting, doing business, sometimes even becoming engaged—all on the basis of the sterile, electronically generated word, without the benefit of seeing someone or even talking to him.

All forms of communication are not equal. If I want to ask a favor of my colleague Alan, I have several choices. I can walk down the hall and speak with him in person. In that case, I'll be able to gauge his response accurately. Maybe he'll gladly say yes. Then again, maybe he'll say yes while wincing. Or perhaps he'll say no, but will clearly show his reservations. There's an almost infinite number of reactions I might see if I'm there in the room with him. Now, if I phone Alan instead, I'll be able to sense some of his feelings from his voice—but I may miss the more subtle undertones and I won't get any visual cues. If we e-mail each other, effectively squelching almost all human contact, I'll get just the facts. And what if I simply send someone else to ask?

Making matters worse, most of us purposely avoid meaningful conversation with all but our closest friends and family. When we do get together, we may be more comfortable saying what is expected or "politically correct" than what we really believe. Self-revelation comes hard to most people; those who confess their innermost secrets on afternoon talk shows are the exception, not the rule.

The reasons we don't like to expose ourselves could fill a book, but undoubtedly the edgy, distrustful tenor of urban life is among them. From childhood on, those of us who live in or near big cities are urged to be wary of strangers; the concept is reinforced nightly on the local news. We urbanites often return from a visit to a small town marveling at how we were treated. Instead of the averted gazes we've grown accustomed to, we're met with a friendly "Hello, how are you?" from people who really seem to mean it! That level of spontaneous, trusting communication is hard to come by in the cities where most Americans live.

Most of us did not grow up in communities where our high school classmates became our dentists, our barbers, and our children's schoolteachers. Sure, we have friends and families, but the majority of people we see each day are strangers and therefore suspect. Because we fear them, we often avoid contact, and as a result we don't use our social skills as often as we could. Our people-reading muscles have atrophied for lack of exercise.

Making Contact

If you want to become a better people-reader you must make a conscious effort to engage other people. Even the most entrenched Internet junkie can learn the true meaning of "chat" if the desire is there, but you have to get off the couch and make it happen. Work those atrophied muscles, even if it makes you feel inconvenienced, awkward, or vulnerable.

To practice and develop your people skills, start by becoming aware of how and when you make personal contact. For the next week, each time you have the opportunity to communicate with someone, enhance the quality of that communication by moving up at least one rung on the contact ladder:

1. Face-to-face meeting
2. Telephone call
3. Letter/fax/e-mail/answering machine
4. Delegation

Instead of asking someone else to set up an appointment for you, contact the person yourself by letter, fax, or e-mail. Instead of e-mailing your cross-country friend, call, even if the conversation has to be brief. Instead of phoning your neighbor to discuss the school fund-raiser, knock on her door and talk to her in person. Step by step, you'll become more comfortable with the increased contact.

Try to improve the quality of your communication, too, by making a conscious effort to reveal something of yourself. It doesn't have to be an intimate secret—in fact, many people will be turned off if you inappropriately reveal confidences. But you can share a like or dislike, a favorite restaurant, book, or movie. And ask something about the other person—where she bought a piece of jewelry, or whether he saw the ball game last night. Warm them up, and the conversation will start rolling.

After a few weeks, you'll become more adept at these social skills. Test yourself on the person checking your groceries, the receptionist in your doctor's office, the mail carrier, the next customer who walks into the shop. Connecting doesn't have to mean a ten-minute discussion. It can mean simply looking someone in the eye, smiling, and commenting on the weather. These brief sparks of contact aren't superficial, they're sociable, and they are where trust and communication—and people reading—begin.

Learn to See the Sheep

The more time you spend reading people, the easier it gets. Just as the anxiety and awkwardness of your first time behind the wheel of a car disappeared after a few months of everyday driving, people-reading skills that may seem unattainable today will become automatic with a little practice.

With willpower and persistence, we can sharpen any of our senses. Nothing illustrates this more clearly than an experience a client of mine had several years ago. He'd been hired by the Big Horn Institute, a facility dedicated to preserving an endangered species of bighorn sheep that live in the mountains just southwest of Palm Springs, California. Development of neighboring land was disturbing the sheep and interrupting their breeding activity. The institute wanted to do something about it.

When my client visited the institute, the director took him outside, pointed to the massive, rocky hills that rose up behind the offices, and said softly, "There are a lot of them out today." My client squinted up at the brown hills, trying to hide his amazement—not at the beauty of the bighorn sheep, but at his inability to see even one of them. Obviously accustomed to this reaction, the director tactfully called his attention to a sheep just below a triangular rock, and another on the crest of a hill to the left, and then another—until he'd pointed out almost a dozen.

The director's eyesight was no better than my client's. But he had learned to see the sheep. He knew how their shape broke the subtle patterns of the hills. He could detect the slight difference between their color and that of the rock. He had learned where the sheep were most likely to gather at a particular time of day. He had experience. He had contact. He had practice. What was virtually automatic to him was foreign to my client—until he, too, learned to see the sheep.

STOP, LOOK, AND LISTEN

In the courtroom, I constantly watch jurors, witnesses, lawyers, spectators, and even the judge, looking for any clues about how they're responding to the case and the people presenting it. I listen carefully to the
words that are spoken, and to how they are spoken. I pay attention to
the way people breathe, sigh, tap their feet or fingers, or even shift their
weight in a chair. As the jurors walk by I notice any unusual smells—
heavily applied perfume, body odor, the scent of medication. When I
shake someone's hand I take note of the feel of his handshake. I use *all*
of my senses, *all* of the time.

Patience, Patience

Observing people properly takes time. Most people simply don't take
enough time to gather information and reflect upon it. Instead, they frequently make critical decisions about people in a hurry, as if life were a
game show in which quick answers scored more points. It's usually the
other way around in life: quick answers are often wrong—and lose
points.

Quick answers aren't necessary most of the time, anyway. You'll find
that you often have more time to make up your mind about people than
you think you do. Abraham Lincoln was once asked how long a man's
legs should be; he responded, "Long enough to reach the ground." Likewise, the question "How much time does it take to read people?" can be
answered: "As much time as you have." There is seldom a premium on
the speed with which we read people. Most deadlines for decision making are self-imposed. *If you take all the time you really have available,
you'll usually have as much as you need.* If you're offered a job, the offer
probably won't vanish if you ask for a few days to think about it. You
seldom need to make a decision about a doctor, lawyer, accountant, day-
care provider, mechanic, or purchase on the spur of the moment. So
don't! Ask yourself what information would help you make the best
choice, and then take the time to gather it. If you're still not sure, sleep
on it.

In almost every jurisdiction in the country, the judge cautions jurors at
the beginning of the trial that they must not decide the case until all the
evidence has been presented. This concept has been ingrained in the law
for hundreds of years, and for good reason. Just as you can't solve a riddle without all the clues, you can't make wise decisions about people if
you act prematurely. To be successful, you must be patient.

Pay Attention, or Pay the Consequences

Every interview with the neighbor of a heinous criminal seems to start with: "He seemed like such a nice guy." Further questioning usually reveals that the neighbor never really noticed the man. Ultimately the neighbor usually admits, "He kept to himself." In fact, there were probably many clues that Mr. X was not such a nice guy after all. It's just that no one ever paid much attention.

Decisions are no better than the information on which they're based. Incorrect or incomplete information can lead to an incorrect conclusion—garbage in, garbage out. So before you can effectively read people, you need to gather reliable information about them. You can do this by using your eyes, your ears, and at times even your senses of touch and smell. When people fail to be attentive and focused, the consequences can be regrettable. One of the more notable moments in the O. J. Simpson criminal trial illustrates the point.

Late in the trial, Laura Hart McKinny was called to the witness stand by the defense to testify about her audiotaped interviews of Mark Fuhrman, who used "the 'N' word" with alarming frequency. She was cross-examined by an obviously agitated Christopher Darden, and their exchange became more and more confrontational. Finally, Ms. McKinny asked, "Why are we having this adversarial conversation?" To me this was clearly a shot across the bow. Ms. McKinny was sending a message to Mr. Darden. Her tone and manner were saying, "Back off. I'm just telling you what I know. If you keep hounding me, you'll be sorry!" But Mr. Darden continued to bore in, either not understanding what Ms. McKinny was trying to communicate or choosing to ignore it.

Ms. McKinny was always truthful, but her early testimony had been calm and almost understated. As Mr. Darden attacked, Ms. McKinny—now apparently angry and frustrated—defended herself by providing more detail, using more descriptive and negative words, and adopting a more critical tone of voice. Her testimony quickly grew even more damaging to Detective Fuhrman—and to the prosecution.

It's not hard to recall occasions when we've been inattentive to important clues. We may hire a day-care provider without spotting the faulty latch on her backyard fence, noticing how she ignored the children under her care as she spoke to us, or paying attention to her poor grammar. Yet each of these factors could have a critical impact on our child's well-being and development. We may not notice the flushed face and ever-so-slightly slurred speech of an employee who returns from a long lunch, but these may be clues he's been drinking—maybe drinking too much. This type of critical information is usually available to you—if you just take your time and pay attention.

COMMUNICATION IS A TWO-WAY STREET

During jury selection, prospective jurors sit before the assembled clients and attorneys, where they are subjected to an onslaught of personal questions—which they swear to answer truthfully. They aren't allowed to ask anyone on the legal team any questions, and we have no obligation to reveal anything about ourselves. In short, the procedure is specifically designed to let one set of people, the lawyers, read another set, the jurors.

Outside the courtroom, few people will sit politely and answer a barrage of questions without wanting to ask you a few of their own. If you're reading them, they want some opportunity to read you. If you want candid responses to your questions, you usually have to give something in return. Unlike jurors, the people you engage in everyday conversation aren't required to open up to you, and they haven't sworn to be forthcoming or honest. To coax unguarded and honest responses out of them, you need to encourage them to trust you.

The best way to establish this trust is to reveal something of yourself. Let people read you to some extent, and they will feel more comfortable. As their comfort level increases, they will open up to you. It's simple—*if you want a clear view of another person, you must offer a glimpse of yourself.*

Good trial lawyers use self-disclosure effectively to develop rapport with jurors during the jury selection process and throughout the trial. They know that even though openness isn't required of them, they can take the jury selection process to a much more meaningful level if they disclose something of themselves during the questioning. If this consistently works in an intimidating setting like the courtroom, imagine how effective it can be at a casual lunch.

KNOW WHAT YOU'RE LOOKING FOR

Laurence J. Peter observed in *The Peter Principle:* "If you don't know where you're going, you will probably end up somewhere else." It's a good rule in general, but doubly important when it comes to reading people.

Long before prospective jurors enter the courtroom, the legal team and I prepare a "juror profile" that lists the personal attributes of jurors who will view our case most favorably. Sometimes we conduct mock trials or surveys of community attitudes to help us gauge the type of person who is most likely to be open-minded toward our client. I grade all candidates on their empathy, analytic ability, leadership, gregariousness, and life experiences, and on my gut reaction to them. Then I consider what other characteristics might be important in that particular case. If it's a death penalty trial, I also evaluate personal responsibility, punitiveness, and authoritarianism. In a contract dispute, I may be more concerned with prospective jurors' attention to detail or experience with legal agreements. In short, I know exactly what I'm looking for in the jurors for that particular case. If I didn't, how could I choose the right ones?

Outside the courtroom, we aren't usually so methodical. In part this is because it seems a little cold-blooded to create a checklist of desirable attributes. When it comes to romance, we like to think the fates will throw us together with the perfect mate. We rarely take the time to consciously evaluate even a casual friend's characteristics. By the time the bad news sinks in—"Hmmm. She doesn't keep her word"; "He's always late"; "She still hasn't taken her sick cat to the vet"—we've often become emotionally committed and find it hard to change the relationship. We devote even less forethought to people who appear less frequently in our lives—doctors, contractors, plumbers, and the like. Instead, we rely on a friend's recommendation—or, worse, an advertisement.

If we're not aware of our own needs and haven't decided what we want in a friend, a boss, or a paid professional, it's hardly fair to blame that person for disappointing us later. I recently watched a talk show in which a young man was complaining that his girlfriend of two years dressed like a streetwalker and blatantly flirted with other men. When asked, he admitted that she had dressed and acted exactly the same way when they first met. He loved it back then, when he was focused on the immediate prospect of a few fun nights on the town; but once he decided he wanted a committed relationship, his girlfriend's wild side was unacceptable. He had failed to evaluate her in light of his long-term needs.

Before you decide whether a person meets your needs, create a mental list—or, better, a written one—of everything that is truly essential for a successful relationship of the type you're contemplating. And then don't hesitate to regularly compare your real-life candidate with the ideal one.

Whether you're looking for a husband, a business partner, or a gardener, reflect on the experience and qualities you'd like this person to have. If you're a divorced woman with two young children, it might make sense to date men who also have kids: they'll understand the demands of a family. If you're looking for a business partner, ask yourself exactly what skills your enterprise will need that you don't possess—and look for someone who has them. If you need a gardener, decide whether you want a master of topiary art or someone to reliably mow the lawn and rake the leaves once a week.

Whatever you do, approach the task with absolute honesty. You won't be doing anyone a favor by pretending to have different needs and priorities than you really have. Once you know what to look for, you'll be much more likely to know whether you've found it.

OBJECTIVITY: THE ESSENTIAL INGREDIENT

During jury selection, I have only one goal: to assemble a group of people who will listen with an open mind to my client's side of the story. It's easy for me to be completely objective about this, since I have no vested interest in any particular juror serving or being excused from the jury. They aren't friends, family, or even acquaintances. Odds are I'll never see them again.

When I first tried to apply my people-reading methods to my personal life, I quickly found that the objectivity I took for granted in the courtroom was my greatest weakness. In real life, I cared very much what others thought of me. I agonized over how I'd feel if I said, "Yes," "No," "You're not right," or "You're not good enough." In order to translate my courthouse skills to the outside world, I'd have to transfer my objectivity as well. *You can't read people accurately unless you view them objectively.*

Unfortunately, as a general rule, the more important a decision is in your life, the more difficult it is to stay objective. It's easy to be objective about whether a casual acquaintance might be a good blind date for your brother. If she's a co-worker, there's more at stake. If she's your boss, there's even more. If she's your best friend, all bets are off.

We all have a tendency to make decisions based on what will be painful or pleasant for us at the moment. All too often, we pick the easiest, least confrontational solution because our emotions blind us to the big picture or the long-term reality. If a woman's boyfriend constantly flirts with other women, she'll probably notice it. But if she's in love and doesn't want to admit to herself that her boyfriend has wandering eyes— and that the rest of him is probably not far behind—she may choose to think his behavior is innocent. Odds are, if he were somebody else's boyfriend, she wouldn't be so charitable. A businessman who is having trouble with a new employee may prefer to write off her mistakes to new-job jitters, rather than admit he needs to replace her. And the daughter of an elderly woman suffering from Alzheimer's disease may explain away her mother's bizarre behavior rather than face the painful truth.

Whenever the truth is threatening, we tend to reach for the blinders. Just a few years ago, a friend confided to me that her teenage daughter must be lovesick, although as far as she knew the girl hadn't been seeing anyone in particular.

"How can you tell she's in love?" I wanted to know.

"Well, her grades have really started to slip. She seems to have lost her interest in everything, sleeps late all the time, stays out till all hours without calling. She just seems to be very distracted."

To me this behavior screamed "drugs," not "young love." My heart went out to my friend as I gently suggested this possibility, which she briefly considered, then rejected. It took her another six months to confront her daughter, who by that time was prepared to acknowledge her drug problem and accept help.

It is human nature to close our eyes—and minds—to things that are uncomfortable or disturbing. Leon Festinger coined the term "cognitive dissonance" in 1957 to describe the phenomenon. One symptom of cognitive dissonance is a person's refusal to accept the obvious, as my friend did with her daughter. This is a form of delusional thinking. The word "delusional" usually brings to mind someone who has completely lost sight of reality and who babbles meaninglessly or lies without any perception of the truth. But most delusional activity takes place in the minds of ordinary people like you and me as we make day-to-day decisions that may have tremendous impact on our lives. The truth is hard to see, especially when we don't want to see it.

Most lapses in objectivity are due to some degree of cognitive dissonance or delusional thinking. Even though it's difficult, we can overcome our tendency to ignore facts we don't like. First, we have to understand what it is that upsets us so much that we're willing to ignore or distort reality instead of acting on it. I've found that four states of mind most often lead to the loss of objectivity:

1. Emotional commitment
2. Neediness
3. Fear
4. Defensiveness

If you avoid making decisions about others while under the influence of these four mind-sets, you are far more likely to stay objective, and make better choices.

Emotional Commitment: The Tie That Blinds

We all feel love, friendship, contempt, and even hatred for some people in our lives. These feelings all tend to compromise our objectivity. We don't want to think ill of those we love, and we don't want to see anything good in those we hate. To further complicate matters, most of us dislike change. For our own security and convenience, we have an emotional commitment—to ourselves—to keeping things just as they are. The same emotional undercurrent that pulls us toward the status quo also warps our objectivity when we're deciding whether to change it.

Once you're emotionally committed to a particular outcome, it can be very hard to maintain your objectivity. The stronger the emotional commitment, the greater the tendency to behave irrationally. This is why counselors usually advise against sexual intimacy until mutual respect, trust, and friendship have been well established. Once the powerful and pleasurable ingredient of sex has been added to a relationship, we tend to overlook even basic flaws until the passion subsides. By then we may be well down the road toward emotional disaster.

You can't always avoid making decisions when you're emotionally vulnerable, but if you're aware of the pitfalls, you can sidestep many of them. To begin with, try to avoid situations in which you may feel pressured to arrive at a particular answer. In those circumstances, you'll lose your objectivity. The result may be that you'll make a bad decision in the first place, then be reluctant to acknowledge your mistake even when it should become obvious later on. If you interview the daughter of a friend for a job, you may overlook her fundamental deficiencies, because you're not going to want to tell your friend his daughter doesn't measure up. If you hire your neighbor as your accountant, or your golfing buddy as your lawyer, you'll tend to overlook what would otherwise be unacceptable performance because of your friendship. Whenever your worlds collide, you bring the emotional commitments of one to the other. If you mix business with pleasure, the result might turn out fine, but more likely your desire to keep everyone happy and avoid confrontation will lead you to misread people.

Another common way we create emotional commitment is recognized in a typical jury instruction. On beginning their deliberations, jurors are told not to announce their feelings about the case until after they've discussed it together. Once people publicly commit themselves to a particular viewpoint, they are reluctant to change it. Pride, stubbornness, or fear of admitting we made a mistake gets in the way. If your goal is to be objective when evaluating other people, don't hamstring yourself by announcing your feelings about someone to your friends, family, or co-workers before you've had time to gather pertinent information and carefully think it over.

If you do find yourself evaluating someone to whom you have an emotional commitment, at least be aware that your objectivity is probably impaired. Be conscious of your emotions, and thoughtfully employ the people-reading techniques discussed in the chapters that follow. Take as much extra time and effort as possible before you form any lasting conclusions. Consider whether a trusted and respected friend who is more objective may be able to add perspective. Play devil's advocate by asking yourself how you would view the person if you weren't so close to the situation. Even if you can't eliminate the influence of your emotional commitment, you can minimize it by using one or more of these techniques.

Don't Shop When You're Hungry

Negotiators have a saying: "The person who wants the deal the most gets the worst deal." This rule applies to relationships, too: the person with the greatest need is most likely to fill it with Mr. or Ms. Wrong. Only after he's felt the sting of his mistake will he recognize his decision for what it was—a compromise.

We first learn to compromise as children, when we fall victim to the lure of immediate gratification. We'll take the bicycle with a scratch on the fender rather than wait for an undamaged replacement to arrive, because we are afraid that Dad may change his mind if we don't act quickly. As teenagers, we may accept the first offer of a date to the senior prom because we worry that no one else will ask. As adults, we continue to make bad decisions about people out of neediness. The most familiar example of this is the inevitably disastrous "rebound relationship." But neediness also drives the employer who's desperate to fill a position and hires the first passable applicant, only to find himself flipping through résumés again two months later; or the parent who settles for substandard child care rather than miss another day of work.

My mother used to say, "Don't shop when you're hungry." Good advice. When you're hungry, everything looks tempting, and you end up bringing home items you don't really need, plus some that may even be bad for you. The key is to slow down long enough to write a shopping list and maybe even have a healthy snack while you write it. Just don't let your unchecked cravings rule the day, whether you're shopping for dinner or a wife.

One crisis that has erupted throughout the country as a result of the increase in two-wage-earner households is the day-care scramble. Good day care is hard to find and often hard to keep. When the child-care provider leaves without giving her employers much notice, they're thrown into a frenzy looking for a replacement. It's hard to imagine a more stressful situation: you need a very special person to care for your child, and until you find that person, you can't go to work, which jeopardizes your livelihood. Choosing a long-term child-care provider under these circumstances is a terrible idea. Don't fool yourself into believing you can be objective under these conditions.

Whenever you find yourself reacting differently than you would if you had unlimited time, you're acting out of neediness and won't be reading people clearly. Stop and consider alternative courses of action before you go forward. It's often best to find a temporary solution to begin with, and decide on a permanent one later. The parents urgently seeking child care could put their immediate efforts into convincing a friend or family member to pitch in for a week or two, buying them time to look for permanent help. If they can afford it, they can hire a professional nanny for a while. Temporary solutions may be more expensive or inconvenient in the short run, but they'll give you the time you need to make a wise choice about your long-term selection.

Fear: The Great Motivator

Many psychologists believe our primary motivator is fear—fear rooted in our instinctive desire to avoid loss, pain, and death. With such a powerful emotion at work, it's little wonder that objectivity usually gets pushed aside.

It is hard to overestimate the influence of fear on our ability to read people. And it is impossible to remove fear from the equation entirely. We fear ending a relationship because we're afraid we won't find anyone better. We fear turning down a job: what if it's the best offer we get? We may even avoid disciplining our children because we're afraid we'll alienate them.

There's no magic pill to eliminate our fear and clear our vision while we evaluate people. Our viewpoint will always be somewhat skewed by our desire to avoid pain. But we *can* diminish our fear—and even use it to help us better read the people in our lives. If we understand *why* we are afraid, and *how* other people can either cause or eliminate the pain we fear, we can use fear to our advantage.

To repeat a point made earlier, the more important a decision is, the harder it is to stay objective. Fear is a major reason—fear that can develop into mental paralysis when a great deal is riding on a decision. For example, suppose you find yourself in a dead-end job. After several years, you get the uneasy feeling that your days there are numbered and consider leaving. Perhaps you feel that your boss is treating you differently than she used to. You've been trying to evaluate what she thinks of you and whether she is looking for a reason to fire you. No matter how hard you try to be objective, you can't help but be influenced by your fear.

To help neutralize the fear and become more objective, you should make two lists: one of all the painful experiences you might have if you stay at the job; another of the painful experiences you might suffer if you chose to leave. The first list might include ongoing stress, humiliation or ridicule by your boss, lack of promotion or raises, and, most terrifying of all, being fired. The second list might include landing another job that is even worse, loss of seniority that could make you even more vulnerable in the new job, being unable to find a new job, and failing at your new position, so that you lose it, too.

By making these lists, you start getting a grip on your fears. At least now you know what you're afraid of. If one set of fears is clearly worse, in most instances you'll choose the less painful option. But if both routes have comparable risks, you should at least be able to put your generalized fear aside and focus on gathering specific information with which to objectively evaluate your real concerns.

The best weapon against fear is knowledge. When you list your fears, you gain knowledge of yourself and your motivations. After you've gained that insight, you can go on to gather more objective information about the people who will ultimately influence your decision. If you carefully watch your boss as she relates to you and to others, perhaps you'll find she bluntly criticizes *everyone.* Or maybe you'll find she's complimentary to others and harsh only with you. From observations like these, you will eventually be able to correctly read your boss's intentions, reliably predict her behavior, and choose the best plan of action.

This is exactly the process I have found so helpful when selecting a jury. Frequently we must decide if we should keep Juror Number One or reject her in favor of Juror Number Two. Each may present very different combinations of potential benefits and dangers. It may be more probable that Juror Number One will be critical of the prosecution's case, and therefore more likely to find the defendant not guilty—but she takes a hard line on the death penalty, so she'll probably be tough on the defendant if there's a conviction. Juror Number Two, on the other hand, may seem more likely to accept the prosecution's case and convict the defendant; but less likely to impose the death penalty. Both options present risks and thus give rise to fear. After a trial is over, I don't want to wonder whether my client would be free if I'd picked Juror Number One or, even worse, if he'd be alive if I'd picked Juror Number Two. The only way I can sleep at night is to know that I have made the best, most objective, most rational decision possible.

By mentally listing the specific consequences I fear most about each choice, I force myself to focus on them clearly. This helps me form questions for the prospective jurors that will help me gain insights into their attitudes about those issues that are troubling me. I then discuss my observations and the risks associated with choosing each juror with the defendant and his lawyer. Ultimately, it's the lawyers and defendants who must choose if they will risk a possible death sentence in exchange for a better chance of an acquittal—but it is my job to bring as much objectivity as possible to the process. You can use the same process to make better decisions in your own life.

Defensiveness: The Fastest Way to a Closed Mind

No one likes to be attacked or criticized. We often respond by shoring up our defenses like a fort under siege. We see red and quit listening. We lose objectivity, and along with it our good judgment.

I've seen it a hundred times in court. A lawyer is cross-examining a witness and hits a nerve. The witness tenses, sets his jaw, and leans forward; he becomes confrontational, sarcastic, or argumentative. Intent on defending himself, he completely loses sight of the way he looks to everyone in the courtroom, including the jury. He doesn't see the jurors shake their heads or hear the comments they mutter under their breath. He no longer knows or cares whether he is answering the lawyer's question, and everyone sees it.

I remember a vivid example of this from a trial a few years ago involving a dispute over the ownership of a large piece of real estate. The defendant, a successful real estate developer, came to hate the lawyer who represented the investor who was suing him. The investor's lawyer quickly learned how to push the defendant's buttons, and the defendant became argumentative and confrontational. He wouldn't concede even the most minor, obvious points to this man whom he loathed. To the simple question "Isn't it true you told my client you had approval from the city to build a golf course on the property?" he snapped back, "I didn't *tell* him anything, I only wrote him letters." When the investor's lawyer continued, "Well, when you *wrote* him, didn't you say that in your letters?" the defendant responded sarcastically, "You tell me, you have copies of all my letters." After just a few moments of this, the jury was ready to throttle the man. And when the trial was over, they did—with their verdict.

As hard as it is to keep your eyes and ears open under ordinary circumstances, it's even more difficult when you're under attack—but that is exactly when you need to be most clearheaded and objective. If your boss or best customer is criticizing your performance, you should listen and learn if you want to keep your job or your key account. The last thing you should do is to misread your critic because you're focusing solely on what you're going to say to defend yourself. If your husband tries to explain to you why he's unhappy in your marriage, watch and listen carefully; don't withdraw or respond with a defensive tirade—at least, not if your marriage is important to you.

Remember, there will almost always be a time and a place for you to respond, and your response will be much more effective if you thoroughly understand what you're responding to. The only way to gain that understanding is to stifle your defensiveness and open your ears and your mind. They say "success is the best revenge." And the best way to be successful in any relationship is to keep a clear head so you can read the other person effectively. As we tell witnesses before they are cross-examined by the opposing lawyer: "Just listen carefully to the questions and do your best to answer them. Don't argue. You'll have a chance to explain your side of the story later." Good advice, inside the courtroom and out.

START FROM SCRATCH

The next step toward reading readiness is to clear your mind of the stereotypes and other forms of mental laziness that so often substitute for careful reflection. *You can't pour a hot bath if you start with a tub that's half full of cold water.* And if you want to evaluate people accurately, you must start from scratch, without preconceived notions of where you should end up. Think of yourself as a pipe clogged with years of deposits from an assortment of biases and prejudices. You need to scrape off those deposits and let information flow freely.

Most of us are somewhat aware of our own prejudices. Although we don't like to admit it, we often judge people by their race, sex, age, national origin, economic status, or appearance. As this book stresses throughout, hundreds of characteristics can have a significant influence on how someone thinks and behaves. But no trait exists in isolation, and no single trait takes precedence over others in every situation. It's a mistake to base your evaluation of anyone on a bias you may have about people with a particular single characteristic. This sort of stereotyping can derail your efforts to predict behavior even before you get started.

I've found that forcing yourself to recognize your biases is the first step to overcoming them. As soon as you're aware that you're making a snap judgment about a person on the basis of some bias, you can stop yourself. You can identify your prejudice and remind yourself that you can't evaluate a person when you have so little to go on. You need to evaluate a great deal of information about people before you can see patterns that will enable you to understand them. Force yourself to look for more details.

I often do this myself in jury selection. After interviewing thousands of people, I've noticed that people who share certain characteristics often think and act alike. Consequently, I have become biased. I tend to expect that the wealthy will be tougher on crime than the poor; that men with long beards will be less conservative than those who are clean-shaven; and that young people will respect authority less than older people do. Whenever I'm evaluating someone who falls into one or more identifiable groups—which means just about everybody—I make a conscious effort to put aside preconceptions as I gather and evaluate information about the person. Otherwise I can't say I'm reading ready.

Less obvious than stereotyping is shortcut thinking—taking the easiest route to a conclusion. This tendency is so common that advertisers take advantage of it all the time to sell us things. The ad that touts a car as "the best-selling vehicle on the market" appeals to us because we naturally conclude that if "everyone else" is buying the car, it must indeed be the best. Jumping to this conclusion is easier than poring through a stack of *Consumer Reports* and making an informed decision for ourselves. In fact, the car may be the worst vehicle on the market, selling so well only because it is the most heavily advertised. This kind of shortcut thinking can also interfere with reading people. We tend to assume that a person who uses big words is knowledgeable and reliable, or that a person who wears sunglasses indoors must be a shady character. But if we don't go further and test our snap judgments, we could be wrong.

The point was illustrated during jury selection in a murder case in which a middle-aged African-American man, conservatively dressed and articulate, wore sunglasses to court three days in a row. The legal team couldn't help but wonder why. What was going on? Was he bleary-eyed from night after night of partying? Was he making a fashion statement, or a political one? Could he be hiding bruises from a fistfight? Surely the sunglasses reflected on his character in some way—don't they always?

There were as many theories as there were lawyers in the courtroom. Finally, the prosecutor asked the question that was on all of our minds. The prospective juror took off his glasses and revealed an injury that made one of his eyes hypersensitive to light.

If a decision is not terribly important, you may choose to take the easy route when judging somebody, just to save time. But whenever your conclusion is critical to your personal or professional success, shortcut thinking simply isn't good enough. In these circumstances, you must ask yourself whether you have started with a clean slate and validated your conclusions independently. You can't afford to jump recklessly from A to Z without stopping anywhere in between.

MAKE A DECISION, THEN ACT ON IT

We've all complained about someone: our dentist, doctor, day-care provider, tax preparer. We've figured them out. They're sloppy, lazy, uncaring, incompetent, or dishonest—yet we keep going back to them like lambs to the slaughter. Why bother reaching the right conclusion in the first place if we're not going to act on it? Why don't we just go ahead and do the right thing?

There can be several reasons. Sometimes we hesitate out of misplaced charity or a lack of confidence in our own judgment. We may still have some doubt about our impression and feel that if we just dig a little deeper, we'll find the missing clue that will explain the person's behavior. If you're not convinced that your evidence is solid, it makes sense to go back and gather more. But remember, there's no guarantee you'll ever understand anyone completely no matter how much information you gather. And at some point you have to make a decision, or you'll be trapped in "analysis paralysis."

Some people fail to act because they simply can't bear the emotional pain or uncertainty of a difficult decision. *If you have this problem, remember that maintaining the status quo is a decision.* If a relationship isn't working, the decision not to change it is a decision to stay in it.

When you're stuck in a situation and unable to act on the information you've gathered, try a little trick. Pretend you have several choices, one of which is just exactly the way things are. For instance, if you are questioning whether your current romantic relationship is right for you, ask yourself: If I were single and I met someone exactly like the person with whom I'm currently involved, would I want to settle into a relationship with the new person, or would I keep searching? Objectively evaluate all the available information. If you find yourself recoiling from the prospect of jumping into a new relationship just like the one you're in, it may be time for a change.

I tried this very exercise a few years ago when I was unhappy with my secretary. I asked myself whether I'd hire her if I needed a secretary and she applied. I had to answer with a resounding "no". As simple as it might seem, it took this exercise to help me make the right decision.

Sometimes we delay decisions because we fool ourselves into believing that the person who has disappointed us will change. This doesn't happen just between lovers, spouses, and friends. For example, attorneys should know better, but I've seen many a lawyer accept a juror who is openly hostile to his case because he believed the juror would be swayed by his eloquence. But I've seldom seen that transformation take place. After watching thousands of people make decisions, I've learned *it's a lot easier to change the way you think about a person than to change the way a person thinks*!

Finally, there will undoubtedly be times when you've gathered and objectively evaluated all the available information, yet still find that the best choice isn't clear. In those cases you just have to make the best decision you can. You may have made a bad choice, and you may be sorry later, but you can take some comfort in the knowledge that few decisions are irreversible. If you make the wrong call about someone, you usually won't need to live with that choice forever.

One final word about reading readiness: as you go on to acquire the more specific skills described in the rest of this book, *keep practicing* the basic skills outlined in this chapter. They are the key to getting the most out of this book, because they will put you into the proper state of mind to understand people better. They will help you stay receptive and alert—the very qualities you need if you're to make rapid progress.

KEY POINTS

Make contact: Communicate personally or by phone if possible; and don't forget—if you want a clear view of another person, you must offer a glimpse of yourself.

Know what you're looking for: "If you don't know where you're going, you will probably end up somewhere else." By clearly defining what you truly need, want and, expect from others, you can focus more clearly on their ability to deliver.

Stop, look, and listen: Be both attentive and patient. Don't rush to judgement. Remember, if you take all the time you *really* have available, you'll usually have as much time as you *really* need.

Don't fall victim to "short cut" thinking: Keep an open mind; not one filled to the brim with either your or other people's biases, prejudices, or stereotypes. Remember, you can't pour a hot bath if you start with a tub that's half full of cold water.

Don't shop when you're hungry: Avoid decisions when you're emotionally blinded, needy, afraid, or defensive.

If you can't be objective, at least be thorough: Make sure you've gathered as much information as possible. Play the devil's advocate and ask what you would think if it was someone else's decision; consult a trusted friend; and make lists of the possible positive and negative consequences of your more important choices.

Make a decision, then act on it: Don't let your own indecision, or the actions of others, control your fate.

Discovering Patterns:
Learning to See the Forest,
Not Just the Trees

In 1939, Sir Winston Churchill called Russia "a riddle wrapped in a mystery inside an enigma." He could have been describing any of us. Even saints have a darker side, and the devils we encounter may reveal elements of honesty and charm. No one is entirely consistent, and most of us are a hodgepodge of often conflicting thoughts, values, and behaviors. But no matter how complex a person may be, patterns of behavior emerge from their seeming inconsistencies. Once you learn to identify those patterns, you'll be able to understand others and predict their behavior.

Collecting a mountain of miscellaneous data about somebody by scrutinizing her looks, body language, environment, voice, and conduct will do little good unless you know which traits can be important indicators of character and which are relatively inconsequential. Even more important, after you've identified someone's potentially revealing characteristics, you then have to sort through them and find out how the pieces fit together. You need to learn to see the big picture—the forest, not just the trees.

IT'S ALL ABOUT CHARACTER DEVELOPMENT

We can learn a great deal about reading people by analyzing the techniques gifted storytellers use to develop a character and bring him or her to life. Think about how the creators of Walt Disney's *Beauty and the Beast* transformed the Beast into a sympathetic hero. A huge brute with fangs and thick fur is frightening, not sympathetic. But the filmmakers found ways to make the audience see that there was more to the Beast than first meets the eye. First they dressed him in princely clothing, a clear sign this is no ordinary monster. Then they used body language to reveal additional aspects of his human character. To this they added dialogue and actions which imply that the Beast may be a sheep in wolf's clothing. The central clue to the creature's real identity comes from an outside source, the narrator, who explains that the Beast is really a prince who has been transformed as a punishment for his uncaring actions years earlier.

By the movie's climax, the pattern is complete. The audience sees not a Beast but the kindhearted hero who lives within. The gradual revelation of the Beast's true character, layer by layer, is what makes the movie a masterpiece. The audience doesn't have to work to develop the pattern that reveals the Beast's nature. The writers and animators make it unfold before our eyes. But in real life, we have to search for the pattern of traits that divulges each person's character.

Discovering a predictable pattern is more than just gathering information by following steps A, B, and C. Once you have all the available information, you must sift through it and weigh it until finally you can step back and look at the whole person. It's not unlike the process a physician goes through when trying to diagnose an ailment. If you come into the office with a painful wrist, he might ask to see how much you can move it. He'll probably feel it and manipulate it himself; ask what recent activities might have hurt it; and then take an X ray. Each of these diagnostic techniques provides a different piece of information and each individual piece of information could mean many different things. But when all are considered as a whole, he is able to make an accurate diagnosis.

In the same way, you should look at as many different clues as possible when you evaluate someone. Which ones are most influential depends on the circumstances and on what you need from the relationship. If I'm hiring someone to tile my patio, my needs are simple and clear-cut: he should be good at his craft, honest, and reliable. I don't have to spend hours contemplating whether he'll be good with children. But if I'm deciding whether to enter into an intimate relationship with someone, I should put a lot more energy into determining what my needs are and carefully consider all the information available about the man.

The following section describes the process I generally follow when I'm trying to get to know and understand someone. The process is the same whether I'm in or out of the courtroom: people are people, whether in the jury pool, the office pool, or the car pool. Although the material is presented in the order that works best for me, it usually won't matter which area you reflect on first, as long as you keep all of them in mind when you're sizing someone up. With a little practice, you'll develop your own approach. Eventually much of this process will become second nature to you, as it has to me.

To discover meaningful and reliable patterns:

1. Start with the person's most striking traits, and as you gather more information see if his other traits are consistent or inconsistent.
2. Consider each characteristic in light of the circumstances, not in isolation.
3. Look for extremes. The importance of a trait or characteristic may be a matter of degree.
4. Identify deviations from the pattern.
5. Ask yourself if what you're seeing reflects a temporary state of mind or a permanent quality.
6. Distinguish between elective and nonelective traits. Some things you control; other things control you.
7. Give special attention to certain highly predictive traits.

YOU HAVE TO START SOMEWHERE— BEGIN WITH THE MOST STRIKING TRAITS

The amount of information I'm able to gather about prospective jurors is trivial compared with what's available in everyday life. We often see people in many different settings: casual, formal, business-related, social. And we often get to know them over the course of months or years. In fact, we have access to so much information it's easy to feel overwhelmed, unless we have a game plan designed to keep us focused.

Anyone who has assembled a jigsaw puzzle has learned that without some logical approach, one can fumble endlessly with the hundreds of pieces on the table before finding a single match. To get started, most people begin by putting together the edge pieces—not because they show what the finished puzzle will look like but because they are relatively easy to identify and assemble. Once the edge of the puzzle has been completed, we have a framework to help us determine how the other pieces fit into place.

Within the first few minutes, or even seconds, of meeting someone, I've usually gathered a tremendous amount of readily observable information about age, sex, race, physical characteristics, vocal mannerisms, and body language. With a few questions I can quickly learn about my new acquaintance's education and marital status, the number, sex, and age of his children, what he does for a living, and his family history, hobbies, club or organizational memberships, and favorite television shows. This represents just the first layer of information available to those who are trying to read people.

A second, more subjective level of information is based on physically observable traits that require interpretation: the meaning of body language and mannerisms, the significance of vocal qualities, and the importance of specific actions, to name but a few. Here, you need some understanding of the possible meanings of each of the person's observable traits.

And there is a third level of information, which reflects conclusions about the person's character based on analysis of the information revealed at the first two levels. Is a person considerate or rude? Stingy or generous? Violent or passive? Hardworking or lazy?

After years of trying, I still can't read and interpret all this information at once, and I have never met anyone who could. Yet all of this information goes into the recipe for reading people. To bring order to the chaos, *when I meet someone new I usually take note of the two or three characteristics that stand out most clearly:* his size, clothing, voice, mannerisms, speech quality, or actions. Or I may even have a sense of his emotional and mental state. From these most striking characteristics, I form a first impression. But I never forget that first impressions are just that—*first* impressions.

People often try hard to make a good first impression. The challenge is to continue to examine your first impression of someone with an open mind as you have more time, information, and opportunity. Otherwise you may overlook essential clues that lead in a completely different direction.

I constantly test additional information against my first impression, always watching for patterns to develop. Each piece of the puzzle—a person's appearance, her tone of voice, hygiene, and so on—may validate my first impression, disprove it, or have little impact on it. If most of the new information points in a different direction than my first impression did, I revise that impression. Then I consider whether my revised impression holds up as even more clues are revealed—and revise it again, if need be.

Stay particularly alert to new information that does not match your first impression. As mentioned in the last chapter, once people have formed an opinion about someone, they resist changing their minds. If you yield to this temptation, you'll often end up with the wrong impression of people. Every relationship deepens and evolves. It sometimes

takes months or even years to get past a first impression and more accurately see the complex patterns of a person's behavior.

EVERYTHING MUST BE SEEN IN CONTEXT— NOT IN THE ABSTRACT

As William Shakespeare aptly noted, "All the world's a stage, and all the
men and women merely players. . . . One man in his time plays many
parts." *To accurately identify patterns in people's traits and behaviors,
you need to consider the stage upon which they appear.* If you told me
simply that a young man wears a large hoop earring, you couldn't expect
me to tell you what that signifies. It might make a great parlor game, but
in real life I would never hazard a guess based on so little information. If
the man is from a culture in which most young men wear large hoop earrings, it might mean he's a *conformist.* If, on the other hand, he's the son
of a Philadelphia lawyer, he may be *rebellious.* If he plays in a rock band,
maybe he's *trendy.*

Think again about the jigsaw puzzle. A single blue puzzle piece could
be part of the sky, a pool of water, a building, the side of a truck, or a
man's shirt. Relying on a single trait to predict the beliefs, character, or
probable actions of a complex human being is like picking up that one
piece and proclaiming it to be the left side of a blue 1982 Ford pickup.
Good luck!

To illustrate the point, I'll describe some characteristics of a man I
knew almost ten years ago. When I first met him, he was sitting at a
table. He was thin and somewhat hunched over; he looked like a bird
with a broken wing, afraid and isolated. He had a nervous smile and an
awkward way of doing just about everything. Soon after, when he got to
know me better, he began drawing pictures for me, usually of small animals. Rabbits were his favorite. He was quite a good artist.

You probably imagine a small, timid man who wouldn't hurt a fly—
but I'll add a few more pieces to the puzzle: The table this man was
hunched over was the defense counsel's table in the courtroom where he
was on trial. He was handcuffed at his wrists and ankles. He was afraid,
isolated, and nervous because he was facing the death penalty for killing
thirteen mostly elderly women. And why did he draw me pictures of
small animals? I don't know. I suppose it was because he liked to draw
and it kept his mind off the trial. He was Richard Ramirez, "the Night
Stalker," who remains on death row today.

Always bear in mind, there are many interpretations of almost every
aspect of a person's appearance, body language, environment, vocal in-

tonations, words, and actions. Unless you consider them in light of all the available information, your effort to interpret them will be little more than a shot in the dark.

LOOK FOR EXTREMES

I recently overheard an amazing conversation between two women at the coffee shop I frequent on Saturday mornings.

"My daughter came home last night with a tattoo," said the first woman, almost sobbing.

"You're kidding!" her friend said quietly, leaning closer.

"No, I'm not. I can't believe it. I'm not sure what I'm supposed to say. At this point, I guess there's not much I can do."

"I'm so sorry. But I'm sure it'll be okay," her friend said as she grabbed the first woman's hand to console her.

They went on like this for at least ten minutes. It was impossible not to eavesdrop—they were sitting at the next table. I was having a hard time not turning around and blurting out: "Okay, I give up. Where the heck is this thing? How big is it? And, for Pete's sake, what does it look like?" Were they assuming, because the young woman got a tattoo, that she was doing drugs or hanging out with a motorcycle gang?

Tattoos are revealing, but a small butterfly on the ankle is very different from a large rose on the breast. The woman in the coffee shop may have been agonizing over nothing. In fact, *the significance of nearly every trait depends on how big, small, intense, or subtle it is. In other words, it's a matter of degree.*

An excellent illustration is the shoe-shining obsession of a lawyer I knew. I'm used to the pricey, clean-cut, conservative clothes attorneys wear—they want to make a particular kind of first impression—but this fellow went to extremes when it came to his shoes. The merest scuff, and he'd be off in search of a shoe-shine stand. Was he a neat freak, or incredibly vain? Did he suffer from obsessive-compulsive disorder? Perhaps he came from a family in which he was taught from a young age to keep his clothing perfectly neat. Or maybe he had a military background: servicemen are trained to keep their shoes spotless, and many never lose the habit.

Without knowing more about him, it would have been impossible to attribute a particular meaning to his remarkable quirk. But whatever the truth was, I knew it would provide an important clue to his character. And it did. As I got to know him, I learned he'd grown up so poor that his parents could afford to buy him new shoes only once a year, at the beginning of school. He was self-conscious about his poverty and learned to take extraordinarily good care of his shoes so they wouldn't reveal his family's financial plight. It was a habit he retained into adulthood, and it enabled me to understand him much better. It explained his extremely frugal nature as well as his insecurity and obsessive drive for success.

The significance of any trait, however extreme, usually will not become clear until you learn enough about someone to see a pattern develop. As you look for the pattern, give special attention to any other traits consistent with the most extreme ones. They're usually like a beacon in the night, leading you in the right direction.

FOCUS ON DEVIATIONS FROM THE NORM

Anything unusual is usually important to understanding people. That certainly applies to deviations from what you may have come to recognize as someone's normal pattern. There are two types of deviations to watch for. The first is a trait that clashes with a person's other characteristics—call it a "rogue trait." The second is conduct inconsistent with a person's normal habit or routine. Call this a "rogue action."

Your initial reaction might be to dismiss rogue traits, because, by definition, they're "out of character." But most often that's a mistake. The rogue trait is usually worth examining closely. In rare cases, it reveals the true nature of a person who has managed to disguise every other clue to her personality. More frequently, the exceptional trait simply provides you with valuable insight into the complexity of her character.

If you saw my brother-in-law, Amal, and his conservative attorney, you would know exactly what I mean. Amal is from Morocco and makes leather clothing and jewelry, much of which he sells to rock musicians. The hoop earring he wears fits in well with his trendy clothes, long hair, and casual manners. But what if his lawyer sported the very same earring along with his Brooks Brothers suit, wing tips, and erect posture? You would certainly want to look for more clues to explain this unusual feature.

Even a small deviation in someone's pattern can expose his priorities. A very small but distinctive rogue trait provided me with great insight into the character of the chairman of the board of FTI Consulting, the company I work with. As the head of a successful, publicly traded company, Dan dresses well and very conservatively. He is poised, confident, and always professional. There's clearly a pattern. What sticks out on

Dan, and reveals a different side of his personality, is that he always wears "friendship bracelets" braided by his children—whether he's at a casual gathering or presiding over a board meeting. When I got to know Dan better, I realized that this choice to wear his children's bracelets wherever he goes is a sign of how important his family is to him. Not only is he a proud father, but he also wants to make his children happy by wearing their gifts, even if they clash with his wardrobe. This rogue trait turned out to be highly predictive of Dan's caring, compassionate nature, which might not have been otherwise obvious.

The significance of rogue traits can be illustrated a thousand ways. The young woman in a tight dress and spiked heels reveals that this isn't her usual attire when she wobbles across the room like a toddler taking her first steps. The socialite dressed in a thousand-dollar gown who proudly wears the simple engagement ring her husband gave her when they were struggling students thirty years earlier shows her traditional values and self-confidence by her decision not to "upgrade" to a five carat rock. And the man who appears calm and poised during an interview but whose fingernails are chewed to the nub is probably less tranquil than he appears.

Rogue actions can be even more revealing than rogue traits. Most people are creatures of habit. They love routine and stick to it unless something specific causes them to change. If your normally talkative child is suddenly quiet as a mouse at dinner, you know something's up. If your typically upbeat and friendly employee shows up one day quiet and sullen, you should wonder why. And if your boyfriend calls you like clockwork every Thursday night to make plans for the weekend, then one week doesn't phone until Saturday at noon, it's behavior worth investigating.

One isolated lapse from a routine shouldn't automatically shake your belief in the accuracy of the pattern you have seen develop. But it should get your attention. Even if you're confident that your child is happy, your employee friendly, and your boyfriend faithful, rogue actions deserve exploration. Whatever the explanation, it probably will help you understand the person better.

ARE YOU SEEING A STATE OF MIND OR A STATE OF BEING?

An occasional outburst of anger does not make someone an angry man. You're not introverted because sometimes you don't feel like talking, or fundamentally selfish because last Thanksgiving you took the last piece of pumpkin pie, or insecure because you asked your boss if he was happy with the last project you completed.

Child-rearing experts always caution parents not to tell children they're bad when they misbehave, but rather to scold them for doing *bad things*. This concept applies to adults, as well. Good people occasionally do bad things, and bad people sometimes behave like angels. In looking for patterns, it is critical not to confuse occasional behavior or feelings with a more permanent personality trait or quality.

If you're considering rehiring someone who worked for you a few years earlier, you'd be wise to recall your past experiences with him. But you'd be ill-advised to base the decision on a single occasion when he disagreed with you, unless you saw other behavior that indicated he was argumentative by nature. Isolated episodes don't usually reveal a permanent state of mind. As you search for patterns, ask yourself whether the clue you are evaluating is just an isolated event. If it is, don't give it too much weight unless it can be characterized as truly extreme.

SOME THINGS YOU CONTROL, SOME THINGS CONTROL YOU: ELECTIVE AND NONELECTIVE TRAITS

The perspectives most people have on life are shaped to some degree by the way their bodies look and function. A man who is six feet tall will probably have a very different take on the world than his five-foot brother. That foot makes an incalculable difference that neither man can control entirely, and it's not just about reaching the top shelf in the closet.

Physical characteristics fall into two main groups: elective and nonelective. Elective traits include things that can be controlled: for instance, clothing, tattoos, makeup, and accessories. They tend to reveal who we would like to be, or at least what we want to project to others. Nonelective traits are those that cannot be controlled—height, race, body proportion, complexion, coloring, facial features, physical handicaps, and, to a lesser degree, voice. These nonelective traits that significantly affect someone's experiences in life tend to reveal much about his or her character, way of thinking, and behavior. This is especially true of traits we've had since birth.

Nonelective Traits

Traits people were born with, particularly those that present physical challenges or make it more difficult to be included in normal social settings, usually have a deep-rooted and permanent effect on personality and behavior. For that reason, I rely heavily on such traits for clues to the core of a person's character.

Someone confined to a wheelchair from birth has spent a lifetime compensating for what the able-bodied take for granted. He has suffered discrimination and been pointed at, laughed at, and talked down to as if his mind functioned no better than his legs. In most cases, such experiences can't help but cause his handicap to become central to his life. The same can be said of the attitudes of many minorities, the obese, the physically deformed, the mentally and emotionally challenged, and those who suffer from debilitating diseases.

When searching for patterns among the traits of those whose life experiences have been drastically affected by their nonelective traits, I first focus on what the effects have been, and on what the people have done to try to overcome the obstacles they face. Are they fighters, who struggle with a walker rather than yield to a wheelchair? Are they independent? Do they choose to read Braille, rather than rely on a helper? Are they confident enough to venture out in public without hiding their deformity? When they go out in public, are they self-assured, or do they avert their eyes to avoid the stares of young children and insensitive adults?

Some people meet with enthusiasm, resolve, and good nature whatever challenges the fates have thrown their way. Others retreat, defeated and bitter. Most find a path somewhere in between. The course they choose may reveal much about their personalities.

Most nonelective traits are less significant than those just discussed. If they aren't extremely unusual, facial features, height, body proportion, and the like generally don't warrant special consideration—unless someone decides to alter what would be a permanent nonelective trait but for the miracles of modern medicine. Whenever I meet someone who has invested the time, energy, and money required to permanently alter some aspect of her physical appearance, I look particularly hard at what that says about her desires and priorities. Whatever significance a trait might normally have will apply twofold if someone wanted it badly enough to go shopping for it.

Not all nonelective traits are physical. Financial status, for example: the average person can't wake up in the morning and decide, "Today I think I'll move into a million-dollar home and drive a Porsche to work." Like someone with a physical handicap, a person with a limited income will learn to cope in some way. How people choose to spend whatever money they have can speak volumes about their beliefs and values. If someone on a fixed income dresses in expensive clothing, it might suggest she's impractical and insecure and longs to gain social acceptance. If there's little money left over for the kids' clothes, she's also selfish and self-centered. If a wealthy woman purchases the very same clothing when she can afford to spend more, it *might* reflect the exact opposite: confidence, frugality, security, and no particular concern about how others view her. However, I would also look for other clues. Maybe she dresses down because she *does* care about how others perceive her, and wants to be seen as down-to-earth. Only after completing the pattern-building process would I feel comfortable deciding which is the case.

Elective Traits

Because people can change elective traits from day to day or minute to minute, I view them very differently. A person's clothing, jewelry and accessories, and even many mannerisms, can be altered almost at will. They change as we change settings and circumstances. Most of us don't dress for work the way we do when we're lounging around the house or going to a party. We speak differently when talking with old high school friends than we do with our boss or a customer.

When you're identifying patterns, it is particularly important to keep in mind that elective traits often fluctuate. If you rely on them in isolation, you may not see the truest picture of someone's personality. If you saw me in my sweats at the market on a Saturday afternoon, you would draw very different conclusions about me than you would if you saw me in business dress, entering the courthouse. Either set of conclusions would miss the mark to some degree. Don't assign too much significance to someone's elective traits, unless you've seen him enough times and in enough different circumstances to form a well-rounded picture.

Remember, also, that we alter our nonelective characteristics as we mature. The woman who gets a nose ring as a fashion statement or a form of rebellion when she's nineteen may have forgotten it completely by the time she's thirty-five. The nose ring may be more a reflection of youthful experimentation than of her core character. Of course, if she's fifty-five and still sporting a ring in her nose, I would consider it an extreme trait and pay it much closer attention.

ALL TRAITS ARE NOT CREATED EQUAL

He's short, dark-haired, slightly overweight, well-dressed, smiles a lot, has a college degree, is married with two young children, teaches high school history, belongs to the Rotary Club, loves gardening and old movies, speaks with a slight Southern accent, and comes from a large, close family. And he has a thousand other characteristics. I have five minutes to decide whether he can give my client a fair trial. So many clues, so little time!

I often face this type of pressure in the courtroom. A wrong decision could literally be fatal to my client. I usually have more time in life outside the courthouse. But I also accumulate even more information in which to look for patterns. With so much to look at, the only way to ever reach a meaningful conclusion about someone's personality or beliefs is to focus on those traits and characteristics that will most likely predict how a person thinks and behaves.

Over fifteen years, during which I've evaluated thousands of individuals at hundreds of trials and focus groups, I've learned that while every case and every person is different, some characteristics are consistently more telling than others. Bear in mind that these are generalizations and can sometimes be entirely off the mark. Usually, though, you'll find them to be accurate guides.

Before a legal team selects a jury in a big case, we often conduct research designed to identify "predictive traits," characteristics likely to have the greatest influence on a juror's beliefs about the issues in the case. We conduct community attitude surveys over the telephone and live mock trials with people who fit the profile of the typical juror who might be called to serve in the upcoming trial. We ask these people everything we can think of that will provide clues about how they might feel about our case. We record their age, sex, and race, and we question them to gather information about their employment history, hobbies, education, marital status, what they read, what TV shows and movies they watch, what political, social, or fraternal organizations they belong to, and so on. We also ask them about their life experiences: where they were born and grew up, what their parents did for a living, how many kids were in the family, whether they have been involved in a lawsuit, and much more. Then we gather even more information about their attitudes. How do they feel about the death penalty? Do they think people sue too much or are awarded too much money? Should oral contracts be treated differently from written ones? If someone lies once, is he likely to lie all the time?

Next, we tell our mock jurors the key facts about the case and ask for their initial reaction to the principal issues. From their replies, we determine which traits most frequently appear in people who view the case in a particular way. In one case we may find that young, single, college-educated women with high incomes tend to favor the defendant, while older married men in blue-collar jobs favor the prosecution. In another, with different facts, it may be just the opposite.

After studying the information obtained from the mock jurors, we prepare questionnaires for the real prospective jurors. These questionnaires help us determine which traits each prospective real juror has. We can't ask them in advance how they would decide the case, but if we know how others with similar traits would have decided it, we can make an educated guess.

Next, when the lawyers are questioning the jurors face to face, we focus on the traits we've found to be the best indicators of how someone would decide the case. We also focus our questions on individual jurors' unique characteristics; this is usually the most critical aspect of the process. The fact that most older married men in blue-collar jobs favor the prosecution doesn't mean the one in the jury box will. We may find during the oral questioning that he was once wrongly charged with a crime and is likely to be very suspicious of the police and the prosecution.

I have worked through this process hundreds of times in every conceivable type of case—not only criminal cases but also civil lawsuits involving personal injuries, breach of contract, employment disputes, fights over movie rights, family quarrels, and more. Almost no issue has escaped scrutiny, from attitudes toward the police and other authority figures, to views about when individuals should take responsibility for their own actions, to biases against large companies, to employers' responsibilities to their employees and vice versa.

The traits and beliefs I evaluate at work are no different from those you will see in every company, household, street, and neighborhood. And the lessons I've learned have proved equally applicable wherever I am. First among those lessons is one we've already emphasized and will continue to stress throughout this book: no trait or characteristic means the same thing in every person or in every circumstance. However, I've identified three key characteristics that provide consistently reliable insight into almost everyone, almost all the time:

1. compassion
2. socioeconomic background
3. satisfaction with life

As I try to identify patterns in someone's characteristics, I always focus intently on these traits, because they are blind to race, gender, age, sexual orientation, and other characteristics by which we often stereotype those who belong to an identifiable group. Concentrating on these three traits forces me to look through any stereotype and to the person's underlying qualities and experiences. We'll illustrate how the process can be used to cut through gender, age, and racial stereotypes, but the same analysis can be applied to any bias.

I have found women much less likely to vote for the death penalty in murder cases than men. But it would be a critical mistake for me to tell my client to select a woman over a man to sit as a juror in such a case on the basis of her sex alone. Sex isn't the real issue—it's the juror's level of compassion for others. Women, as a group, tend to be more compassionate than men, because women are more frequently raised to be care-givers. A man who grew up in a compassionate, loving home and acquired those traits himself would be a much better choice as a juror in a capital punishment case than a bitter, hardened woman. The relevant question isn't "What is the juror's sex?" but "Is he *or* she compassionate?" or "How was he *or* she raised?"

Similarly, should you consider only women candidates when hiring a nurse for your elderly grandparent? Of course not. Even if you were able to prove that two out of three women are more caring and attentive than the average man, a decision based on gender alone would still be wrong a third of the time. That's certainly not good enough for me in the courtroom, and it shouldn't be good enough for any of us outside of it.

Elderly people often tend to be more conservative than the young. But it's not because they're old; it's because *most* elderly people were raised during more conservative times and usually in more conservative house-holds than *most* young people. Many elderly people vividly recall struggling through the Great Depression, and their beliefs and values have been affected by that aspect of their socioeconomic background. But if I wanted to select a conservative jury, I wouldn't just pick the twelve old-est prospects. One of them might have been raised by a free-spirited vaudevillian and be the most liberal of the lot. To identify those who will think and act conservatively, I need to know their backgrounds, not just their ages.

Of all stereotypes, those based on race are undoubtedly the most prevalent. And once again, it's foolish to act on such a bias rather than gather information upon which to base an informed decision. A person's experience, not the color of his skin, dictates his view of the world. Until we become a truly color-blind society, racial background will undoubtedly impact our experiences. Even so, the son of an African-American Beverly Hills doctor will usually have more beliefs in common with his white neighbor than he does with an African-American man raised in the projects.

Of course, there are exceptions, but they are typically based in significant part upon shared experience, not just shared skin color. For example, almost to a man, the hundreds of young African-American men I've seen asked about their attitudes toward the police have expressed hostility. But the origin of their attitude can almost always be traced back to an experience in which either they or someone close to them had an insulting or frightening encounter with a police officer. If our hypothetical son of an African-American Beverly Hills doctor had been pulled over and harassed for no better reason than that he was black and driving a BMW in Beverly Hills, odds are he would also have a hostile view of the police. But it is important to understand why he would share that view. The incident occurred because of his race, but his attitude toward the police was formed by the incident: it's a result of the incident, not of his skin color. So when I am helping to select the jury in a police brutality case, the relevant issue is not whether a prospective juror is white or African-American, but whether he has had good or bad experiences with police officers. Anyone, regardless of race, who has been unnecessarily roughed up by a cop would likely have a negative attitude.

It's almost always easy to tell someone's race, gender, and age, but don't draw any conclusions based upon these isolated facts. Instead, as you explore the many chambers of someone's personality, keep an eye out for anything that answers these questions: Is he compassionate? How was he raised? Does he believe he's had a fair shake in life? Throughout this book, whether discussing appearance, body language, environment, voice, or actions, we will emphasize these essential questions. The answers will provide a solid foundation for understanding almost anyone.

Compassion

After even a brief encounter, most of us walk away from a person thinking to ourselves either "He seems like a really nice guy," "What a jerk," or something in between. We'll usually have some initial impression, based on the kindness of his face, the warmth in his eyes, his smile lines, his openness or friendly words, or his sincere handshake. Scientists have developed a "hardness scale" for categorizing minerals. I have my own personal hardness scale for people. On one end is the cold, unemotional, uncaring person; on the other is the warm and compassionate soul. When I'm evaluating someone, one of the first things I do is try to place them somewhere on this scale. Where someone lies on it often tells me more about how they are likely to think and behave than any other single fact.

I'm not alone in my belief that an individual's level of compassion is a very good predictor of how he will think and act. Time and again, when I've asked attorneys what type of juror they're looking for, they'll say: "We need nice people, the type who will understand that no one's perfect and we all make mistakes. People who won't judge our client too harshly." Or they'll tell me, "We want real taskmasters. Judgmental people who won't believe the other side's witnesses and will make them pay dearly for any mistakes."

The closer people are to the compassionate end of my personal hardness scale, the more they tend to be generous, fair, sincere, affectionate, gentle, family-oriented, forgiving, and understanding of human frailty. They are inclined to give other people the benefit of the doubt and are more inquisitive and patient than people who lack compassion. They may have a harder time coming to a decision than those who are less compassionate, but only because of their desire to do the right thing. They don't want to hurt anyone, so they are unlikely to be dishonest. They tend to believe that what goes around, comes around.

People who fall on the uncaring end of the scale tend to be more critical, intolerant, unforgiving, harsh, punitive, and self-centered. They are also frequently more analytical, more likely to scan the facts and make a quick decision. By the same token, they tend to be more judgmental, impetuous, and inclined to act before all the information is in. Their motto frequently seems to be "What's in it for me?"

If I peg someone as either very compassionate or unusually cold and harsh, I already know more about them and how they are likely to behave than their age, educational background, employment, physical appearance, and sex combined could ever tell me. Because of that, when the following chapters describe traits that reflect whether someone is compassionate, take special note. You will be well on your way to an excellent understanding of a person whenever you've added this piece to the picture puzzle you're assembling.

Socioeconomic Background

A person born with a silver spoon in her mouth will almost always view life very differently from someone born and raised in poverty, regardless of what other characteristics they may share. But socioeconomic background is not measured only by family income. It consists of a combination of social and economic factors. The love and support we receive as children, our exposure to learning and other worldly experiences, the environment in which we are raised, and a thousand other factors come into play. Our attitude toward life is greatly influenced by whether our emotional and physical needs have been fulfilled. Often, financially secure parents are able to meet more of their children's needs than parents who are struggling to make ends meet, but there are frequent exceptions.

I know a man who was raised on a farm in Idaho with thirteen brothers and sisters. It was all his parents could do to put shoes on their feet and food on the table, but the family was very supportive and their actions were grounded in strong religious convictions. All my friend's emotional and physical needs were met. As a result, he does not view the world from the perspective of someone who has lived a life of denial, even though his family had only a little more money than a family on public assistance. Money isn't the only measure of need fulfillment.

Generally, a person's socioeconomic background will have a significant impact on his outlook and behavior. People who have had to scratch and claw for everything they have, whether financial or emotional, may develop a siege mentality and retain it all their life, no matter how much money or success they eventually achieve. They may become hardened and lack confidence; they may be insecure, unkind, inconsiderate, stingy, intolerant, defensive, and unwilling to reveal much of themselves. Because they had to fight so hard to survive, they tend to be more watchful and to believe the ends justify the means. On the positive side, those who have pulled themselves up by the bootstraps also tend to be focused, hardworking, and dedicated to achieving their objectives.

People who have always had their needs fulfilled, on the other hand, tend to be more confident, secure, kind, generous, tolerant, forgiving, and open. But if everything has been handed to them, they also may lack drive and intensity and be rather materialistic and egocentric.

If we experience prejudice as children, we may become suspicious and defensive. If we live with constant criticism, we are more likely to become judgmental and intolerant. If we are treated with kindness and compassion, we will probably become caring. If we had to struggle to make ends meet, we may become less giving. And it doesn't matter whether we're tall or short, black or white, male or female, young or old. That is why socioeconomic background is always a key predictive trait.

Satisfaction with Life

It may seem logical that a person's degree of compassion and her socioeconomic background would be among the three key predictive traits. The importance of the third key characteristic—satisfaction with life— might not seem so obvious. But it almost always has a wide-ranging effect on how people think and how they treat others.

Personal or professional success can't be measured on an absolute scale. One person always dreamed of becoming a doctor, but never made it through medical school. She became a nurse instead. Another has struggled to overcome huge obstacles and has achieved her lifelong goal of becoming a nurse. The second will see life through the eyes of a successful person, while her colleague feels like a loser.

Financial success, too, must be measured in light of the individual's expectations. Someone who dreams of wealth and has set his sights on earning a million dollars a year will be horribly disappointed with a $50,000-a-year salary. Another, who never dreamed of making half that much, might view that same $50,000 job as an achievement beyond his wildest imagination. He will think, "Life is great," and act accordingly.

Over the years, after paying particularly close attention to this characteristic, I have found that people who have achieved their goals tend to believe in personal accountability and responsibility. They tend to be more compassionate, supportive, at peace with themselves and others, and optimistic. They also tend to be more forgiving, hardworking, and industrious.

Those who have not achieved their goals often have a victim mentality. They can be quick to place blame on others and may be bitter, angry, negative, pessimistic, and vengeful. Usually, they are less industrious and more critical and cynical than achievers.

Like the other key predictive traits—compassion and socioeconomic background—the degree of someone's satisfaction with life tells me more than I could learn from any number of other traits. And it's usually not difficult to find out how satisfied someone is. A few simple questions, such as "What did you want to be when you were in high school?" or "How do you like your job?" or "If you could change your life, what would you do?" will usually prompt responses that make it clear whether someone has achieved personal success. That information will be another key piece in the puzzle you are assembling.

PUTTING IT ALL TOGETHER

Chapter 1, "Reading Readiness," described how anyone can prepare for the challenge of reading others. This chapter has emphasized the importance of discovering the patterns within the hundreds of clues you will uncover with patience, attentiveness, and practice. The chapters that follow will describe what many of those individual clues might—and I emphasize the word "might"—suggest about a person's beliefs, attitudes, and probable behavior. But always bear in mind that every individual is a complex and unique mosaic. Nothing you read will apply to every person or every situation.

Undoubtedly, you will disagree with some of my observations. You will have known men with scruffy long beards who were very conservative; women with loud, strident voices who were soft and gentle; and men with nervous twitches who were confident and secure. So have I. There are always exceptions, which is precisely why we've stressed the importance of developing patterns. The conservative man with a long, scruffy beard will reveal his conservatism in many ways. The soft, compassionate woman with the strident voice will show her sensitivity if you stay alert. And the confident man with the nervous twitch will demonstrate his confidence if you watch him long enough.

If this book could deliver but one message, it would be that to read people effectively you must gather enough information about them to establish a consistent pattern. Without that pattern, your conclusions will be about as reliable as a tarot card reading. The pattern, not the individual pieces, is what reveals the person.

Some people, called "phrenologists," actually claim to be able to predict people's personality traits based solely on their facial features. They say people with down-turned noses are shrewd, and those whose noses point upward are spendthrifts. Wide-set eyes indicate tolerance and patience, low-set ears idealism, a broad face confidence, angular chins point to stubbornness, and thick, full lips reflect generosity. Others rely on the "science" of reading body language known as "kinesics." They may tell you that whenever a woman crosses her legs she's defensive, if a man hooks his thumbs in his belt he is making a sexually suggestive statement, and someone who looks away while talking to you is being dishonest and evasive.

All I can say is, "It's not that easy." I've seen every technique imaginable attempted in the courtroom by those who want to read jurors and witnesses. But I've never seen any form of rigid or simplistic analysis work consistently and reliably. And no short cut to understanding people or predicting their behavior will work any better for you outside the courtroom.

As you read on, you'll find we typically identify many *possible* meanings that can be attributed to particular characteristics, not just one. Don't get frustrated by your natural desire to want to be told that a particular trait has a specific meaning. Instead, recognize that throughout the balance of this book, as in life, there will seldom be one clear sign pointing to the ultimate answer to someone's personality. Instead, each clue may point in ten directions, and therefore be of limited value in isolation.

As a result *Reading People* isn't written like a foreign language dictionary in which you can look up a particular trait and instantly find its meaning. Anyone who says they can consistently peg people's personalities based on isolated traits is peddling psychological snake oil. Unfortunately, people are rarely that easy to read, and the individual clues they give off seldom point to just one possible meaning. But even though each clue may point in several directions, as you look at *all* of the available clues and their possible meanings, you can and will see an overlap develop—and in most cases ultimately there will be only one direction in which *all* the clues point.

As a result, the only reliable way to read people is to learn to see the patterns that develop from the many different aspects of everyone's appearance and behavior. This approach, which is the cornerstone of *Reading People,* may take more time and effort than simply making inflexible associations between individual characteristics and particular emotions, beliefs, or values; but it is the only approach that will lead to reliable conclusions. Try it, and I'm confident you'll find it as effective as I have.

KEY POINTS

Look for patterns: Single traits or characteristics seldom hold the key to someone's character or emotions. True understanding comes from identifying recurring themes.

You have to start somewhere: Begin by forming a first impression based on a person's most striking traits. Then keep testing, and if appropriate modifying, that impression as you acquire more information.

Remember, anything unusual is usually important: Watch for extremes and any deviations from a person's norm.

Don't confuse a temporary state of mind for a permanent state of being: Whatever someone's typical character may be, everyone has good and bad days. Reserve judgement until you spot a trend.

Ask yourself, "Is this trait the result of free choice or fate?": Elective or voluntary traits (like choice of clothing) reveal who we would like to be, or how we would like to be viewed *at the moment*. They can change like the wind. Nonelective or involuntary traits (like permanent physical characteristics) cut deeper into our psychological makeup, and have a more pervasive and permanent effect on our beliefs and emotions.

All traits are not created equal: Someone's level of compassion, socioeconomic background, and satisfaction with life almost always reveal more about him or her than any other traits. Give special attention to information that sheds light on these three key predictive traits.

First Impressions:
Reading Physical Appearance
and Body Language

Most of us notice another person's physical appearance and body language before we notice anything else. It's tempting to note a wild hairdo or weak handshake and assume you've pegged someone's personality. That's rarely possible. If reading people were simply a matter of matching a few traits to standardized meanings, you could carry this book around like a foreign language dictionary and "interpret" anybody you meet, within minutes. Appearance and body language can reveal a lot, but they are seldom reliable predictors of human behavior unless they're viewed together with the other traits discussed in this book. But they're a good place to start.

It would be impossible to list every physical trait and body movement people can display. Even absorbing the most common ones, many of which we've included in Appendices A and B, is a daunting task. It's best tackled after you've read the rest of this book, when you can review the appendices at your leisure, armed with a fuller understanding of the people-reading process. The information there will be even more valuable then. Since almost all aspects of physical appearance and body language can mean many different things, at this early stage, the important thing is to recognize that most features of a person's appearance and body language can have a wide range of meanings, and to learn what to watch for as you gather more clues about his personality or emotions from other sources.

THE THIN LINE BETWEEN
APPEARANCE AND BODY LANGUAGE

There isn't always a clear distinction between appearance and body language. You might look at a woman and notice the shape of her eyes, their color, the type of makeup she's wearing, her crow's-feet, and whether or not her eyes have a kindly expression or maintain contact with yours. Makeup can clearly be put in the "appearance" column, but what about shifty eyes or kind ones? Eye contact certainly belongs in the "body language" category. But the expression of the eyes might be classified as either appearance or body language.

Although the categories of appearance and body language may overlap, they often reveal very different aspects of a person's character. We can consciously choose our attire, and to some degree we can determine the way our bodies look. Most of our body language, however, is beyond our control.

All elective physical traits, such as the way someone combs his hair, reflect conscious choices, so they tend to reveal how he wants to be seen by the outside world. Even nonelective physical traits can often be altered. A short man may wear stack-heeled boots and a hat. A particularly tall woman may stoop a bit. A woman who must use a cane may choose either a stylish walking stick with a carved head or a hospital-issue version.

Someone's jewelry and accessories can supply clues about her religion, alma mater, hobbies, degree of economic success, taste, and much more. Clothing may point to a certain value system or lifestyle choice—for instance, does this person prefer the practical or the extravagant? And personal grooming habits can reflect on many aspects of someone's personality. But even when read together, attire, accessories, and grooming sometimes reflect only the beliefs, values, and image the person *consciously wants to project* on a particular occasion.

Body language, on the other hand, provides more basic information. Few people are aware of all their physical reactions to the world around them, and fewer still can always control those actions even if they want to. Manners and poise may be consciously learned, but facial expressions, eye blinking, leg crossing, and nervous tapping are difficult to consistently repress. I've seen enough people on the witness stand to know that it's nearly impossible to control body language, even if one's fate depends on it.

Body language, then, tends to reveal inner character and emotions— fear, honesty, nervousness, joy, indecisiveness, frustration, and much more—that aren't necessarily obvious from grooming or attire. Although appearance and body language usually provide different types of information, the knowledge that can be obtained from each of them is equally important. Sometimes appearance and body language point in the same direction, sometimes in opposite directions. The important thing is to keep your eyes and your mind open.

APPROPRIATENESS FOR THE OCCASION

As discussed in the previous chapter, any trait that is extreme or that deviates from the norm is worth special attention. The same is true of any trait—either appearance or action—that is inappropriate for a particular occasion.

A tank top may be fine at the company picnic, but not at the company Christmas party or in the office. A conservative suit says one thing about a person when worn to church, quite another if worn to a child's Saturday morning soccer game. And a big smile and a slap on the back may be called for at a retirement party, but would raise questions at a funeral.

Be careful to stay objective. An unusually short skirt worn to a conservative job interview would raise eyebrows. The woman's good sense, her understanding of appropriate office behavior, and the reasons why she would choose attire that might sexualize the interview all deserve your attention. But the same skirt worn out to dinner with her boyfriend would not deserve the same scrutiny unless it was so revealing that it was remarkable even for that occasion. The difference doesn't lie in whether you personally approve of short skirts, but in whether they are appropriate attire for a certain situation. If you evaluate her attire solely on the basis of your own tastes or moral standards, you won't learn much about her character, except that the two of you don't share the same attitude toward short dresses.

The same can be said about behavior. You may be very reserved personally and uncomfortable with loud, outgoing types; and there are certainly times when familiar behavior or boisterous conduct would be inappropriate by most people's standards. But if you measure others' behavior by yours alone, you won't learn much about who they are, only that they aren't just like you. So measure people's behavior by what is normally considered appropriate conduct. If, by that standard, someone's behavior is still extraordinary, you should wonder why.

Inappropriate clothing, makeup, and hairstyles, as well as inappropriate gestures or other body motions, can reflect many things. Most commonly, the person may

- be seeking attention
- lack common sense
- be self-centered and insensitive to others
- be trying to show he is spontaneous, rebellious, or a nonconformist and doesn't care what other people think
- not have been taught how to dress and act appropriately
- be trying to imitate someone he admires
- value comfort and convenience over all else (in the case of attire)
- not have the right attire for the occasion

I can make that last point from experience. I recently traveled to the East Coast for a very important meeting with the general counsel and senior officers of a large corporate client. Unfortunately, my luggage was lost en route, and I didn't have time to buy new clothes before the meeting. I had no choice but to show up dressed in the jeans and boots I'd worn on the plane. Believe me, I was quick to explain the circumstances.

I wanted to be absolutely certain that the people I met that day knew the reason for my casual appearance. So I told them. But even if I didn't, by watching and listening for clues in how I talked, what I said, and how I acted, they would have been able to eliminate most of the possible explanations. If I listened carefully to them, spoke confidently, and showed conservative good judgment and intelligence by my comments, they could have concluded I wasn't seeking attention, didn't lack common sense, wasn't self-centered and insensitive to others, and wasn't a rebel. So much for the first four selections on the menu. If I otherwise conducted myself professionally and appropriately during the meeting, they could also strike the possibility that I had never learned how to dress and act appropriately from the list. Finally, if my comments and behavior indicated I was confident and independent, they could have concluded I wasn't just imitating some casual dresser I might have admired.

This still would have left the last two possible explanations for my conduct: I valued comfort above professional appearance; or I didn't have the right attire for the meeting for some reason. Because it was important to me that they knew that I believed a professional image was important for someone in my role and that I had the good judgment to know casual dress at a formal business meeting did not further that objective, I volunteered the explanation.

A lesson to be learned is that if someone's appearance or behavior seems inappropriate on occasion, take note of it, but don't jump to conclusions. Try to identify probable reasons, by asking the person (diplomatically, of course), asking a third party, or waiting to see whether a pattern appears in how the person dresses and acts on other occasions.

Even more important, this example illustrates the process of recognizing all the possible meanings of a particular trait or characteristic and gathering additional information from other clues until the one true meaning emerges. Keep this in mind as you read on. Don't be frustrated when we say "This trait could mean X, but it could also mean Y or Z, or for that matter, A, B, or C." That's reality. But if you are patient and attentive, you'll discover, for example, that choices X, Y, A, B, and C don't match many of a person's traits, but choice Z keeps popping up on the menu of possible explanations. It's only then that you can safely assume that choice Z is the correct one.

HOW IMPORTANT ARE LOOKS?

Physical appearance is just one of the many pieces you'll use to fit together the puzzle of someone's character. But it's a large piece, and like most, it should come with a warning: things are not always what they seem. For instance, it might be natural to assume that an obese woman who sports a brightly colored dress and a large hat adorned with ostrich feathers has a flamboyant personality. Why else would she wear such flashy clothes?

In fact, there might be several reasons. She may simply like bright colors. Or her motivation could be more complicated. People whose appearance is outside the norm tend to make other people uneasy, so they are often ignored. This woman may have chosen her outfit out of insecurity and to attract attention and comment, thus breaking through the discomfort barrier. On the other hand, some people with an unusual appearance feel self-conscious and want to be ignored. Perhaps this woman thinks loud colors will actually distract observers from her body. To her, the outfit may feel like camouflage. Or maybe the woman doesn't even like these clothes, but wears them because they're a gift from her husband. Then again, maybe she really is just flamboyant.

Not only can physical traits have more than one possible meaning, but people can also change their appearance from day to day and situation to situation. To further complicate matters, almost any physical trait can have virtually opposite meanings, as in the example above.

Of course, there are times when you can draw a very accurate conclusion from a strong and consistent set of physical features. I remember a case in which two men were charged with throwing a third man out of an airplane. When I met the defendants, I noticed immediately that one had tattoos on virtually every visible portion of his body. I presume he had more on those portions that weren't visible. His partner wore ostrich cowboy boots, gold chains, and a gaudy gold-and-diamond pinkie ring.

His shirt was open and he carried an exotic men's leather handbag. I assumed the jury would have little trouble reading this pair.

The message sent by a person's outward appearance is normally a bit more subtle. Almost every aspect of a person's appearance will point in several directions—and then you need to add body language, environment, voice, and behavior to the mix. *The key is to identify enough traits pointing in the same direction that you can safely conclude you're on the right track.*

If you're so sure about the reliability of a single trait that you think you don't need to trouble yourself to look for a pattern, you'll usually be off target. I've heard every off-the-cuff conclusion you can imagine:

> "The two-inch fingernails tipped me off to her: gold-digger, right?"
> "Any guy who wears a tiny bikini bottom to the beach has to be gay, doesn't he?"
> "If he's wearing sunglasses indoors, doesn't that mean he's dishonest?"
> "Anyone with dirt under his fingernails must be a slob at home. Doesn't sloppy always mean lazy?"

Wrong!

Two-inch fingernails could also reveal rebelliousness, nonconformity, or trendiness (depending upon the person's peer group), artistic leanings, or a need for attention. Or maybe this is someone just having some fun. A tiny bathing suit on a man could mean he is foreign (usually my first guess), is a bodybuilder or swimmer, has a huge ego, is an exhibitionist, or is wearing the suit to please his girlfriend even though it makes him feel uncomfortable, which would reveal a thoughtful and caring nature. A person may wear sunglasses indoors not because he's hiding shifty eyes but because he thinks they're stylish. He could be covering up a black eye or other evidence of violence. He may be sensitive to light because of physical trauma, a recent eye examination, or allergies. He could be covering up bloodshot eyes or dilated pupils that might reveal drug or alcohol abuse. He may be rebellious or simply forgetful. And as for a little dirt under the fingernails on occasion, what of it? It may just mean the fellow is human. You won't know whether it might mean more unless you look elsewhere for clues.

Even when several physical clues seem to point in the same direction, you may be misled if you don't gather more information. A friend of mine tells a story about his father, who worked for RKO Theaters many years ago. The company's offices were in a plush suite atop Rockefeller Center in New York City. One morning, as my friend's father crossed the office lobby, he noticed a scraggly-looking man with dirty, uncombed hair. The man was dressed in rumpled clothes and sneakers. My friend's father wondered why the man was there and how he'd gotten past building security into RKO's private offices.

A few minutes later, as he sat at his desk sorting through the day's work, his boss buzzed him and asked him to come down to his office immediately. When he arrived, his boss turned and gestured toward the same man he had seen in the lobby. "Mr. Wexo," he said, "I'd like you to meet the new owner of our company, Howard Hughes."

Every aspect of a person's appearance can offer clues to his emotions, beliefs, and values. If you were to stop and catalog all of them, the list would be overwhelming. In Appendix A we've listed over a hundred different aspects of physical appearance. They are classified generally under these headings:

- Physical characteristics (body, face, extremities, skin, and physical irregularities/disabilities)
- Ornamentation/jewelry
- Makeup
- Accessories
- Clothing
- "Bodifications" (elective alterations of the body)
- Hygiene

And these are just the most common features.

In Appendix A there is also a discussion in some detail of what twelve of the most common physical traits or characteristics may mean under different circumstances. They are

Complexion
Hygiene
Fastidiousness
Writing, logos, and pictures on apparel
Tattoos and other "bodifications"
Tastefulness
Regional style
Cultivated images
Flamboyance vs. conservativeness
Practicality vs. extravagance
Sexual suggestiveness
Dowdiness

As mentioned at the beginning of this chapter, we don't recommend that you read the appendices until you've finished the rest of the book. Perhaps more than any other traits, isolated physical characteristics cannot be interpreted accurately without also taking into account other physical traits as well as body language, environment, voice, and actions. For that reason, this chapter, more than any other, is replete with lists of many possible explanations for given traits. But take heart, for throughout the remaining chapters, along with the discussion of clues that can be obtained from other sources will come constant references to physical traits that tend to reinforce that information. You must put everything into the mix and stir for the recipe to turn out right. To illustrate the point, we'll consider some of the possible clues provided by someone's hair. Hair was chosen as our example for two reasons. First, the people you meet won't always wear hats, belts, or shoes. But everyone has something to look at on the top of his or her head, even if it's just skin. Second, a person can elect to change almost all of his or her hair's natural features—color, curliness, and even amount. So it's a common means of personal expression.

Even though hair is an important feature to notice, don't assume that it's more relevant than other traits just because it's highlighted here. In many respects, hair says the same about someone as any number of other traits might. For example, a person generally makes the same statement with flawlessly groomed hair as with immaculate clothing or manicured nails. A flashy or radical hairstyle or color usually means the same thing as gaudy and flamboyant clothing or jewelry. Once you realize what can be learned from someone's hair, and why, you can easily apply that knowledge to other physical features.

THE SECRETS REVEALED BY HAIR

Hair is often an excellent predictor of someone's self-image and lifestyle. Your hairstyle can reveal how you feel about aging, how extravagant or practical you are, how much importance you attach to impressing others, your socioeconomic background, your overall emotional maturity, and sometimes even the part of the country where you were raised or now live.

Keep current fashions in mind when using someone's hair to predict beliefs and behavior. For example, in the 1960s and 1970s long hair on a man indicated rebellion. In the 1990s, a redneck trucker might wear his hair as long as a teenage rock star. Also, bear in mind the person's age. Waist-length hair on a fifteen-year-old girl says something quite different than it does on a woman of fifty, just as a ponytail on an eighteen-year-old man reveals much less about him than it would if he were fifty-five. And, as with all other traits, consider how hair fits into the entire package.

Men's Hair

Long or short   The conventional wisdom is that short hair indicates a conservative bent, while longer hair indicates a radical or artistic nature. This is true sometimes, but not always. Very short hair on a man may indicate that he

- is in the military, or was at one point in his life
- works for an organization that requires short hair, such as a police force or fire department
- is trendy, artistic, or rebellious (if his hair is dyed an unusual color or cut particularly short)
- is conservative
- is undergoing or recovering from medical treatment
- thinks he looks better with short hair
- plays sports
- keeps his hair short for practical reasons

   The last category is the one most people overlook. Many men have closely cropped hair simply because it's convenient. Hair length is no longer a reliable indication of a man's political views. Short hair may indicate nothing more than a practical temperament. So be careful not to jump to conclusions about someone's politics.

Coiffed hair   When a man wears highly styled hair—precisely cut, blow-dried, and sprayed—it's usually part of a "power" image that includes expensive clothes, shoes, and accessories. The package, designed to reflect financial success, usually indicates vanity, a big ego, and a concern with impressing others. Relatively few men have the time, money, or inclination to have their hair regularly styled at a salon. In our culture, it's unusual for a man to pay this much attention to personal grooming. All other things—the suit, the shoes—being equal, the man with the coiffed hair is almost guaranteed to be more concerned with status, power, and image than the man whose hair is neatly cut but not styled or sprayed. Much the same can be said of any similar extraordinary grooming habit, such as manicured fingernails.

Hair loss   Telling information can often be gained from the ways men deal with hair loss:

- *Extreme comb-overs or obvious hairpieces* always suggest vanity, but to me a more important fact is that they usually reveal poor judgment and unawareness of others' perception. When I see a man with his few remaining hairs carefully combed from his left ear, over the top of his head, and down to his right ear, the first thought that comes to mind is "Does he really think we don't notice?"
- *Hair plugs and other hair-replacement surgery* also can indicate vanity or a lack of self-acceptance. Men have hair transplants in an effort to look younger and more attractive. If that's worth the time, energy, and money to them, it's a safe bet they're feeling insecure and uncomfortable because of the loss of their hair and the youthfulness it represents. These remedies may also point to a healthy income, although some people save every penny to pay for the surgery. That would indicate an obsession with appearance.
- *Baseball caps, hats, and ponytails* on a balding man can also indicate resistance to growing older (or growing up). But bear in mind that many balding men have to wear a hat outdoors to avoid sunburn on their scalp or for warmth in cold weather. If the hat stays on indoors, that's another story. The wearer may be self-conscious and insecure because of his hair loss.

Dyed hair   It has become more commonplace for men to dye their hair when it starts turning gray. If they do a good job, you may not notice and therefore won't be able to use this as a means to evaluate them. Dyeing indicates a certain amount of vanity, although not as much as coiffed hair does. Most revealing is a poor dye job or one inappropriate for the man's age. Jet-black hair looks very strange on a balding seventy-five-year-old man. I question his judgment and his ability to correctly assess how others view him. It takes a certain level of self-centeredness, along with a detachment from reality, and a desperate and overpowering drive to return a youthful appearance to adopt such an obviously unnatural style.

Men's Facial Hair

Beards and mustaches   Some people believe that any facial hair indicates a secretive nature. This is rarely true—hiding a weak chin with a beard doesn't indicate secretiveness. More often, it's just a cosmetic choice.

Beards and mustaches can indicate that the man wearing them

- believes he looks better that way
- is young and trying to look older
- is trying to hide his age by growing a beard to cover the wrinkles
- is trying to conceal a facial flaw
- has a rebellious or artistic nature
- works in a job where there is no restriction on facial hair

Carefully consider the length, style, and maintenance of beards and mustaches. Long beards and mustaches may reveal liberal political leanings. Unkempt or dirty mustaches or beards, like unkempt or dirty hair, can be a sign of laziness, lack of concern for appearance, physical or mental illness, poor judgment, and the other traits poor hygiene generally reflects.

Other facial hair Big, bushy, unkempt eyebrows, like excessive nose hair or ear hair, often indicate that grooming and personal appearance are not among a man's priorities, or that he's oblivious to how odd these features appear. Many men with these features also believe that plucking or trimming such hair is not masculine, which reflects a rather traditional view of a mans' role.

Radical cuts, colors, or styles Whether on a man or a woman, a radical, outrageous, unique, or striking haircut, color, or style is worth noticing. No one just wakes up that way. And they didn't go to a salon or barber bent on the usual trim, only to be held at gunpoint while the stylist gave them a purple Mohawk!

A radical cut, color, or style may suggest

- nonconformity
- rebelliousness
- an adventurous nature
- an expressive, artistic nature
- an unconventional job and lifestyle
- a desire to appeal to a particular peer group
- trendiness
- disregard of personal appearance
- a need to be different and noticed
- cultural influence (age, race, social group)

Don't simply conclude that someone with a wild hairdo is a flake, though that option deserves serious consideration. Particularly among the young, an expressive hairdo may be a short-lived feature, and one which says little about the person's essence. However, a bizarre hairdo on an older person, or one worn for an extended period of time by a younger person is a very significant feature.

Women's Hair

Because so many hairstyles are acceptable on women, most stylistic deviations don't indicate much about a woman's personality. Extremes of length, volume, style, and color are the most telling aspects of a woman's hair.

Long or short   In our culture, women's youth and sexiness are often associated with long hair. For that reason, women's and men's decisions to wear hair long or short have very different implications.

When a woman has very short hair, keep in mind the following:

- *Short, chic, carefully cut hair* can signify an artistic, creative and expressive nature. Like any high-maintenance hair, it may also reveal financial well-being. But keep in mind that many women with average paychecks spend a small fortune on their hair. Spending a significant percentage of one's income on hair—or any other aspect of personal appearance—suggests vanity, a need for acceptance, concern about others' perceptions, and possibly insecurity.
- *Less styled short hair* may indicate a practical nature. Long, curly hair is particularly hard to maintain. If other physical clues point to practicality, short hair is probably not otherwise significant.
- *Dramatically short hair attracts attention.* If the woman's clothing is flamboyant, this hairstyle fits right into the pattern.
- *She may be recovering from or undergoing medical treatment,* such as chemotherapy.

If a woman has very long hair, bear in mind the following:

- Since long hair is associated with youth in this society, a woman who is past forty and has waist-length hair may be resistant to growing older. Sometimes women with this trait are caught in a time warp and still think of themselves as teenagers or college students rather than as grown-ups. Such women may be fairly unrealistic in their outlook on life as well as in their perception of themselves.
- A woman may wear her hair long, even though it's not particularly at-

tractive that way, because she believes it makes her more sexually appealing.

- Long hair sometimes indicates a bohemian spirit. To many women, long hair means freedom from conventional style. If that's the case, the woman's clothing usually reflects this attitude, and typically her hair will not be dyed or styled.
- Long, unkempt hair may indicate a lack of judgment, a rebellious nature, illness, laziness, or an unwillingness or inability to put time and energy into good grooming. A woman with long, stringy hair either doesn't realize how it looks, or doesn't care. When the hair is downright dirty, you should wonder if some of the other "poor hygiene" traits we discuss in Appendix A might apply to her as well.

Big hair   Big hair is usually an indication of age or regional background. Women in the South and other areas with a strong "country" influence frequently like their hair more teased and styled than do women elsewhere. This preference cuts across the socioeconomic spectrum, from the wealthiest Dallas society lady to the farmer's daughter.

Older women often favor teased, sprayed hair as well, but this is usually because such styles are easy to maintain between visits to the salon. Also, older ladies may experience hair loss, in which case teasing is sometimes necessary to get any volume at all. Finally, they were raised in an era when poufy hair was stylish, and they may simply have retained that cultural influence. A younger woman who sports big hair is much more likely to do so because she believes it makes her appear more sexy.

Color   Many women color their hair. Unless the color is extraordinary, it is not significant. But a woman who chooses to let her hair go gray may be making a strong statement. Chances are she is comfortable with herself and her age. She doesn't rely on the opinion of others, but decides for herself what looks good on her. Women who go gray may also be doing so for practical reasons, in which case their clothing will be practical too. Some women, allergic to hair dye, have little choice in the matter, so their graying hair says nothing about their personalities.

Body and facial hair   In the United States, the cultural norm is for a woman to shave her legs and armpits, pluck very shaggy eyebrows, and remove other facial hair. Many other cultures are not as hair-phobic. A woman who doesn't shave her armpits or legs may be from another country. Unshaven body hair on a woman who was raised in this country usually signifies rebelliousness, feminist ties, or a bohemian nature. If a woman has long stubble on her legs or under her arms, indicating she hasn't shaved recently, she may be ill, depressed, or lazy, or she may lack interest in her appearance and how others perceive her.

I've found that extremely noticeable facial hair, such as a light mustache or very unkempt eyebrows, is usually a conscious choice, not an oversight. The woman who chooses not to change that aspect of her facial features is often saying: "Here I am, like it or not. This is me." This may indicate a very strong will and a defiant attitude toward societal expectations. It may also signal that she is not appearance conscious, either because she is comfortable with herself and not seeking others' approval, or because she grew up in a family or culture in which facial hair wasn't a big issue. She also may opt to leave things as they are rather than endure the pain, inconvenience, or expense of waxing or plucking her hair.

INTERPRETING OTHER PHYSICAL CHARACTERISTICS

As you can see, various aspects of people's hair can have many meanings, sometimes conflicting ones. The same is true of all physical traits. Usually, you can decode their significance only after you gather and interpret other clues. To make the point, I'll tell you more about the heavyset woman we mentioned at the beginning of this chapter.

I met Clara years ago through a charity with which we were both involved. She was not only fond of wearing very expensive, brightly colored dresses and plumed hats, she also preferred four-inch spiked heels (she was only five feet tall) and very heavy makeup. From her dress alone, I guessed that she was insecure and trying to get attention, but I couldn't be sure.

As I got to know Clara better, I learned that she was married to a wealthy doctor who worked very long hours. She spent most of her free time volunteering for a number of charities and entertaining "the ladies" at her beautiful home, which she loved to show off. She had to be the center of attention at social events. She would bounce from group to group, speaking rapidly in a slightly high-pitched and always excited tone—that is, until it came time to volunteer for a project that involved something other than entertaining. Just the mention of forming a committee to write a proposal to the city, or meeting to discuss building plans with the architect who was working on the center's new building, and she was off to the powder room.

Taken together, Clara's appearance, body language, environment, voice, and actions left no doubt in my mind about what made her tick. She was seriously overweight. Her husband worked all the time. She didn't have enough confidence in her own abilities to become involved in a project that would have required her to venture into uncharted waters. Given all this, her brightly colored clothes and gaudy hats made sense. As I'd suspected, she was insecure and her dress was one way she could make people notice her. But I couldn't be sure of that "diagnosis" without many more clues than those provided by her physical appearance alone, striking though it was.

A BAD ATTITUDE OR A BAD HAIR DAY?

Kinesics, the study of body language, is one of the most widely misunderstood "sciences" ever to have ridden the wave of popular culture. With the publication of Julius Fast's *Body Language* in 1970, people everywhere began to study the crossed legs, facial tics, and pants-hitching habits of their friends and acquaintances. Like kids with secret decoder rings, they hoped that a few behavioral quirks would reveal a person's deepest feelings and motivations.

It doesn't always work that way. Fast himself cautioned that mastering body language is a formidable proposition: "A study of body language is a study of the mixture of all body movements from the very deliberate to the completely unconscious, from those that apply only in one culture to those that cut across all cultural barriers." Any system so complex isn't exactly user-friendly. But despite Fast's own warnings, reading body language became all the rage. A generation later, plenty of people still think twice before crossing their arms at a meeting.

Toward the end of *Body Language,* Fast pinpoints one of the most troubling problems with kinesics. He discusses that always intriguing posture, crossed legs: "Can crossed legs . . . express character? Do we, in the way we hold our legs when we sit, give a clue to our inner nature? As with all body language signals, there is no simple yes-or-no answer. Crossed legs or parallel legs can be a clue to what the person is feeling, to the emotional state *at the moment,* but they may also mean nothing at all."

Body language often reflects just a physical condition (such as a bad back) or a temporary state of mind (like frustration), not a more permanent character trait. A person's body language may shift from moment to moment and setting to setting. So if you've only met somebody once it's risky to judge her personality by her body language. Everyone gets tense at times; that doesn't mean we're all a bunch of nervous Nellies. But if someone seems tightly wound every time you meet her, you've probably spotted a character trait—or, at the very least, a recurring theme in her life—not just a bad hair day.

Consistency, then, is one key to interpreting body language. If you don't know the person and haven't watched her closely in different situations, you won't know what her normal behavior is like, so you won't have any point of comparison. The insight you gain from body language is most useful as you begin to see more of a person's character. And to know someone's character—this point bears repeating—you must identify the patterns not just in her body language but in all the areas described in this book.

USER-FRIENDLY BODY LANGUAGE

Somewhere between the serious study of body language and parlor-trick analysis lies a workable method for day-to-day interpretation of people's movements. Appendix B lists scores of body movements that may help you interpret a person's emotional state or personality. But, like physical characteristics, most body movements can have many meanings or no meaning at all, depending on the circumstances.

The best way to sort the meaningful information from the unimportant details is to learn how various emotions are usually revealed in an assortment of movements that typically occur simultaneously, rather than to memorize separate body movements and their possible meanings. For example, poor eye contact can be a "symptom" of dishonesty, anger, nervousness, defensiveness, embarrassment, fear, arrogance, boredom, and other emotions. You can tell which only if you identify other clues that point in the same direction. For that reason this book describes the *combinations* of movements that typically reflect various states of mind. At the end of this chapter, nine of those basic emotional states are discussed. Thirteen more are discussed in Appendix B. The nine included here will demonstrate how seemingly similar emotions can be revealed through very different body language, and how very different emotions can be expressed with many of the same body movements.

Although you shouldn't rely too heavily on body language alone, there is no denying that it can provide valuable information. For example, if you have a hunch that someone's lying to you, you can try to force the person to tell you the truth, find evidence such as a paper trail, or perhaps confirm your suspicions with information from a third party. But unless you know the physical tip-offs to dishonesty, you may never think to question someone's truthfulness in the first place. Most people are very uncomfortable lying, so it's not too difficult to spot a lie if you know what to look for. You might not be able to prove your conclusions in a court of law—but then again, you probably won't need to. Once a person's body language has signaled to you that he might be lying, you can confirm your hunch through these other sources if the situation warrants it.

EMOTIONAL HIDE-AND-SEEK

Many of our basic mind-sets, such as dishonesty or anger, are generally thought of in negative terms. Others, such as surprise and attentiveness, are neither always positive nor always negative. You may welcome them in one situation and avoid them in another. Some feelings, like happiness, are almost always perceived positively.

It's safe to make a generalization: emotions that are viewed in negative terms are harder to read than those that are seen in a positive light. With the exception of the person who's secretly gleeful at another's misfortune, is playing hard-to-get with a potential sweetheart, or is negotiating a deal, most individuals gladly express their positive feelings. It's not hard to read such an emotion since there's usually no attempt to conceal it.

But the less desirable shades of the human psyche aren't so well received. We are uncomfortable around complainers, people who are indecisive, people who are anxious. We expect all but our closest friends and family to keep their depression, anger, and frustration to themselves, or to deal with it somewhere else. So people often hide these emotions from others. If you need proof that they're unwelcome, the next time an acquaintance asks, "How are you?" when you're having a really bad day, tell him. Then watch his reaction!

People also hide their negative emotions because they fear a confrontation. "What's wrong?" "Nothing." is no doubt one of the most often repeated exchanges in the English language. If you judge from someone's body language that he's upset or anxious, don't just ignore your conclusion. Give some thought to whether it would be best to resolve the issue then and there, wait for a better time, or watch further to see if it blows over. Even if you decide not to pursue the issue on the spot, once you recognize that there is a problem you'll be better equipped to deal with it when and if it does erupt.

There's nothing wrong with these unspoken rules of emotional hide-and-seek—they help keep life civil. But just because people don't feel comfortable showing their negative emotions doesn't mean they're not feeling them. And if you don't know how to identify them, you can't respond appropriately. But if you can learn to recognize, for example, when someone feels frustrated with you, you can try to meet the problem head-on rather than leave it to simmer and turn from frustration to dislike to hostility.

The beauty of knowing how to read body language is that, try as people might to cover up their "unacceptable" feelings, it's nearly impossible if you know what to look for. We mentioned earlier that even those whose lives depend on appearing cool, calm, and honest on the witness stand often fail at their task. The truth shows through in their body language, usually in conjunction with other traits. Unless someone is an accomplished actor, he just isn't going to be able to mask his emotional state.

If you learn which clues point to which basic emotion, you can do much more than just sniff out discontent in those around you. By studying the following pages, you'll be able to tell the customer who's paying attention to you from the one you're boring silly; the nervous employee from the indecisive one; and the frustrated friend from the angry one. By the same token, you'll become more aware of your own body language and what it may be signaling to other people, even if they're only picking up the clues subconsciously. If you are aware of body language you can help fine-tune the way you present yourself to the world. Once you realize the power of body language and what it reveals about you, you might even choose to avoid particularly sensitive situations where you don't care to share your feelings. This might even be one time when you decide to make a phone call rather than have a face-to-face meeting in which you're likely to reveal too much. Any way you use it, the knowledge is a very valuable tool.

READING BODY LANGUAGE

On the pages that follow, nine characteristics are discussed. Each is preceded by a simple visual image designed to help you remember which movements indicate which emotion or trait. The nine states of mind discussed are

Honesty and dishonesty
Attentiveness/pensiveness
Boredom
Anger/hostility
Frustration
Depression
Grief/sorrow
Indecision
Nervousness

   Discussed in Appendix B are

Arrogance/humility
Confidence/leadership
Confusion

Defensiveness
Drug and alcohol use
Embarrassment
Fear
Resentment
Secretiveness/openness
Sexual or romantic interest
Surprise
Suspicion/disbelief
Worry

These lists are not all-inclusive. Human beings possess an inexhaustible repertoire of emotions. But if you learn to identify these, the others won't be too difficult to interpret. As we mentioned earlier, you will find it more helpful if you review the additional detailed discussion you'll find in Appendix B after you've learned more about how environment, voice and behavior can help you better incorporate particular body movements into overall patterns.

Honesty and Dishonesty

Imagine a young boy insisting to his mother that he wasn't the one who took the cookies out of the cookie jar. He can't bring himself to look her in the eye for more than an instant. He's shifting from foot to foot, and stuttering to beat the band.

Honest people are generally relaxed and open. Dishonest people aren't. *Any trait that shows tension, nervousness, or secretiveness indicates possible dishonesty.* In chapter 9, "Exceptions to the Rules," we'll discuss the characteristics of four different types of liars: occasional, frequent, habitual, and professional. Two of those types, habitual and professional liars, are difficult to spot by body language alone. The habitual liar is so accustomed to lying that he may not care or fully realize he's lying, so he usually won't show it. The professional liar has rehearsed his lies so well that his behavior will give little away.

Like drug and alcohol abusers, people who lie won't usually admit it. But lying is often easy to detect when you know what to look for. The symptoms listed here are reliable tip-offs to the occasional liar and frequent liar. These physical clues generally appear only when someone knows he's lying and is at least somewhat troubled when he does. Luckily, most people are at worst occasional liars and reveal their discomfort in many ways.

Symptoms of dishonesty include

shifty or wandering eyes
any type of fidgeting
rapid speech
change in voice
shifting back and forth on one's feet or in a chair
any signs of nervousness
an exaggerated version of the "sincere, furrowed-brow look"
sweating
shaking
any activity that obscures the eyes, face, or mouth, such as putting the
    hand over the mouth while talking, rubbing the nose, or blinking the
    eyes
licking lips
running tongue over the teeth
leaning forward
inappropriate familiarity, such as backslapping, other touching, and
    getting too close (invading personal space)

The signs of honesty are just the opposite of those listed above. Honest people are relaxed and calm. They usually meet your gaze. A sincere smile and the warm, kind eyes that most of us know when we see them also indicate honesty.

When things get stressful, it can be difficult to tell the difference between honest nervousness or defensiveness and dishonesty. If your employee has made a horrible mistake and you've asked him in to explain it, chances are he'll look nervous and defensive no matter how truthful he is. I've watched hundreds of nervous witnesses, and I've found the surest way to detect a lie in a stressful situation is to watch for their patterns of behavior, looking for consistencies and deviations.

Several years ago, I worked on a case in which the owner of a real estate development company was being sued by his partner for fraud. One of the key witnesses was an employee who had worked closely with both men. A very nervous woman under the best of circumstances, she shook like a leaf from the moment she was sworn until the moment she left the witness stand. She showed all the classic signs of dishonesty: failing to maintain eye contact, shaking, fidgeting in her chair, and fussing with small paper cups on the witness stand. But I couldn't conclude from this that she was lying, because had she simply been dishonest, she probably would have been more comfortable during at least some portion of her testimony—when describing her professional background, for instance. The fact that this woman's discomfort was constant revealed that she was nervous, not necessarily dishonest.

You have to pay close attention to someone's normal pattern in order to notice a deviation from it when he or she lies. Sometimes the variation is as subtle as a pause. Other times it's obvious and abrupt. I recently saw a news interview with an acquaintance who I was certain was going to lie about a few particularly sensitive issues, and lie she did. During most of her interview she was calm and direct, but when she started lying, her manner changed dramatically: she threw her head back, laughed in "disbelief," and shook her head back and forth. It's true the questions dealt with very personal issues, but I've found that *in general, if a person is telling the truth her manner will not change significantly or abruptly.* But you won't see those changes if you're not watching carefully.

Attentiveness/Pensiveness

Think of a lioness stalking her prey: body still, eyes fixed, she's motionless except for a slight twitch of her tail.

Attentiveness and pensiveness are both generally characterized by an absence of movement. The stillness, like that of a stalking lioness, indicates concentration either on what another person is saying (attentiveness) or on some private train of thought (pensiveness).

The classic representation of someone deep in thought is Rodin's *Thinker,* who sits with his elbow on his knee and his chin resting on his hand, gaze fixed. *Stillness, a fixed or set gaze, and the chin on the hand are all signs of pensiveness or attentiveness.* Sometimes the person will engage in a simple, repetitive movement, rather as a lioness's tail might twitch as she prepares to pounce. But there's a distinct difference between these small motions and the body language of boredom (discussed next). The thinker's motions are usually unconscious, and they remain constant for long stretches of time. For example, if the person is twirling a pencil, she won't suddenly stop twirling and start tapping her feet, then stop tapping her feet and start shifting in her chair.

Other symptoms of attentiveness or pensiveness are

maintaining strong eye contact
gazing steadily at an object
general stillness
tilting or cocking one's head
chewing one's lip or pencil

furrowing one's brow
folding one's arms and staring into space
leaning back in one's chair
looking upward
scratching one's head
holding one's head in one's hands
resting one's chin on the hands/fingers

It may be tempting to assume that someone who doesn't exhibit the signs of attentiveness must be bored, but someone can be inattentive for many reasons. She may be preoccupied, depressed, ill, drunk, sleepy, or confused, to cite but a few possibilities.

Boredom

It's the last class period on a warm day, twenty minutes before school lets out. Most of the students are gazing off into the distance. A few are whispering, some yawn, others are passing notes, and they're all wiggling like earthworms on hot pavement.

People who are bored want to be somewhere else, doing something else. The less you care about what's going on around you, the more you itch to get up and leave. When someone is bored and longs to be elsewhere, it's almost as if his body wants to move to that fantasy place or person. That tension between mind and body is uncomfortable, so *people who are bored usually distract themselves with physical activity.* They may literally twitch in their seats.

Symptoms of boredom include

letting one's eyes wander
gazing into the distance
glancing at one's watch or other objects
sighing heavily
yawning
crossing and uncrossing legs and arms
tapping fingers, twiddling thumbs
tapping feet
fiddling with pens, eyeglasses, paper, etc.
doodling
pointing one's body away from the other person
shifting weight
leaning forward and backward in one's chair

moving one's head from side to side
rolling the eyes
stretching
cradling one's chin in hand while glancing around the room
picking at fingernails or clothing
attempting to do another task

Boredom is one of the more difficult states to conceal. Many of the signs just listed are really efforts to stay awake or alert—the bored person sometimes simply must wiggle, tap, yawn or stretch, or he'll nod off. This frequent body movement is what most clearly distinguishes boredom from attentiveness, even though some other signs are common to both mindsets. It takes considerable concentration to appear attentive and interested when you're actually bored. Watch for one or more of these telltale twitches if you fear you might be boring someone. And if you're bored and don't want to show it, try to stay still.

Anger/Hostility

Imagine a fuming baseball manager and a defensive umpire, chests thrust out, jaws set, faces red. The manager's arms are flailing and the umpire's arms are crossed resolutely in front of him.

Anger usually manifests itself in one of three ways: aggression, defensiveness, or withdrawal. Aggressive anger like that demonstrated by the baseball manager is usually hard to miss. But most people are not comfortable expressing anger, so it's crucial that you also watch carefully for defensiveness and withdrawal, otherwise you may miss or misinterpret it.

The following are signs that most of us would quickly recognize as indicative of all types of anger:

redness in the face
arms, legs, or ankles crossed
hands on the hips
short or rapid breath
frequent repetition of certain phrases
pointing of fingers
rapid speech
rapid body motions
tenseness
locked jaw

tightly closed lips
frozen expression or scowl
stiff, rigid posture
shaking
fists clenched
frustrated, almost uncontrollable arm movements
false or sarcastic laughter

Someone who is extremely angry may also express his anger by invading another's personal space, literally "getting in his face"; sticking out his face, jaw, or chest like the angry manager above; or glaring intently, as if trying to stare someone down. These signs are usually easy to spot. But sometimes, you need to look for different clues to see when someone is expressing his anger through defensiveness or withdrawal.

A person who has become defensive may set her jaw, cross her arms, scowl, or close her lips tightly. But you probably won't see rapid body motions, redness in the face, and changes in her breathing patterns. Nor will she display the more aggressive behaviors cited in the preceding paragraph. Instead, you'll see a stiffening, as if she has hardened to protect herself. Her limbs will draw closer to her body and will be positioned between you and her. Her face will set. Often she will avert her gaze to avoid direct eye contact.

If her anger is expressed by withdrawal, you will often see more exaggerated versions of the symptoms of defensive anger. She may try to avoid contact by turning her body and eyes away. She'll become quiet, and might even sulk. In extreme cases, if these behaviors don't relieve her stress, she may get up and leave the room.

Be alert to all the possible signs of anger. Relying on just one could mislead you. Redness in the face, for instance, can be caused by recent exercise, a medical condition, embarrassment, sunburn, bad makeup, or even a face peel. If you relied on that clue alone to decide whether someone is angry, the odds are you'd be wrong.

Frustration

Think of a teenager aggressively pitching the notion to his dad that he should have his own car. His arms are flailing. He's staring intently and frequently pointing. Unsuccessful, he tosses his hands in the air, shrugs, sighs, turns, and walks out of the room, shaking his head as he leaves.

Frustration comes in two flavors: confrontation and surrender. If someone believes she can correct whatever is frustrating her, she may show signs of confrontational frustration by attacking the problem head-on. Many of the signs of confrontational frustration resemble the signs of anger. But once a person thinks a situation has become a lost cause, she'll exhibit signs of surrender frustration—an irritated passivity—not signs of anger.

Symptoms of confrontational frustration include

frequent direct eye contact
uttering repetitive phrases
closeness to the other person, frequently within his or her personal
 space
gesturing with the hands
pointing
shrugging

Surrender frustration may begin with

sighs
rapid exhaling
grimacing
hands on the hip
hands on the head (in exasperation)
exaggerated or melodramatic movements

Once the point of total surrender has been reached, the signs are

rolling the eyes or closing them
shaking one's head
throwing one's hands in the air
shrugging
turning and walking away

It's important not to mistake confrontational frustration for anger, although sometimes it turns into anger, as it appeared to do in the tense exchange between Laura Hart McKinny and prosecutor Christopher Darden in the O. J. Simpson trial (as described in the "Reading Readiness" chapter). Ms. McKinny began her testimony about Detective Fuhrman in rather neutral tones. However, after being aggressively questioned by Mr. Darden, she became frustrated and demanded, "Why are we having this adversarial conversation?" Ms. McKinny clearly wasn't about to surrender to Mr. Darden's badgering, so she confronted him.

When he didn't back off, she appeared to get angry, and her testimony became more critical and more damaging to the prosecution.

Likewise, be careful not to misinterpret boredom as surrender frustration. Many signs of boredom resemble those of surrender frustration, but bored people aren't necessarily frustrated. Perhaps the most common way to distinguish between boredom and surrender frustration is by the tempo of a person's body motions. The bored person will tend to move more slowly and repetitively. The frustrated person's movements will be rapid and more random.

Depression

Visualize an ice statue in the noonday sun, slowly melting into a formless puddle.

Severe or "clinical" depression is a very serious illness. People suffering from clinical depression can become virtually nonfunctional. They may suffer from severe eating disorders, completely neglect personal hygiene, be unable to concentrate on anything, even their work, and ultimately require medical intervention to recover. This discussion isn't concerned with clinical depression, but rather with the type of gloom each of us experiences for short periods of time as we cope with the stresses and disappointments of everyday life.

That kind of depression is usually revealed not only by physical appearance and body language, but also by voice and actions. However, it's usually possible to identify depression simply by watching someone. People who are depressed move differently. There is no spring in their step, no twinkle in their eyes. They will seem tired and listless. The depression has taken the wind out of their sails.

Symptoms of everyday depression include

isolation and avoidance of social contact
poor concentration
inability to focus or plan ahead
low and quiet speech
relaxed, slackened body
downcast eyes
slow and deliberate movements
change in appetite (some people quit eating, others overeat)
inattention to hygiene and dress
forgetfulness

Grief/Sorrow

A young boy is holding a small, lifeless bird that has fallen from its nest. His head is bowed. His eyes are filling with tears and his shoulders are slumped.

You might expect depression and grief to "look" alike, but sometimes they don't. Nor are they always related. Sometimes depression is not the result of grief, and occasionally someone who is grieving does not act depressed. If you focus on just the body language common to both, you may misunderstand someone's emotional state.

Grief can lead to somewhat contradictory types of behavior. Most frequently, those who are grieving have lost their positive energy, and their appearance and body language reflect that. Their loss tends to dominate their mind and override most other emotion. In these cases, grief and sorrow are usually accompanied by some degree of depression, so you may see signs of that as well.

The typical signs of grief or sorrow include

tears
listlessness
inability to complete normal daily tasks
isolation
apathy
downcast eyes
signs of depression and confusion
relaxed facial muscles
slumped or slackened body
motionlessness, or slow and deliberate motion

It's easy to tell when someone is suffering grief when it is accompanied by depression. In the early stages of the grieving process, however, people often experience denial, anger, and searching. Their body motions may actually appear exaggerated and animated. They may seem "hyperactive," talk quickly, or ramble from subject to subject just to keep conversation moving and their mind off their sorrow. If you carefully watch someone you suspect is compensating in this fashion, you will usually notice brief moments when she allows her grief to creep through the barricades she has erected. Her face will slacken, she'll stare off into the distance, and then she'll quickly recenter herself and be off again.

Indecision

A baseball player is stuck between first and second base. The pitcher has the ball. Which way to go? The base runner glances right, glances left; he leans one way, then the other.

People who are trying to decide between two options—to agree to the deal or reject it, to say yes or no, to leave or stay—usually will reveal that indecision in their body language. They will literally "go back and forth."

Symptoms of indecision include

shifting back and forth in one's chair
looking back and forth between two fixed objects
tilting head from side to side
opening and shutting hands, or moving one hand, then the other
opening and closing one's mouth without saying anything

My friend David is a serious poker player and tells a story that describes the back-and-forth of indecision. In poker, body language that reveals a person's hand is called a "tell." David was playing seven-card stud with a woman he suspected had a full house. She had two queens and two sevens faceup on the table before her. He noticed that she quickly glanced back and forth several times between the three cards she held and the four that were faceup on the table. David knew that if she wasn't holding a seven or a queen in her hand she would realize it immediately, and would not need to double-check. But if she *was* holding a queen or a seven, before she increased her bet she might glance back and forth between the cards she was holding and those on the table to double-check. He had seen this many times before. Because of this "tell," David folded, even though his hand would have beat hers if she did not have a full house. He was right.

Interestingly, David tells me many high-stakes poker players wear sunglasses even in dimly lit rooms so their opponents can't see even the slightest involuntary flicker of their eyes. They even motion for their cards in silence, so their voice doesn't betray them. Their counterpart in business is someone who chooses to communicate by phone or in writing to avoid revealing emotional "tells."

Nervousness

Stare at a dog. Watch his eyes dart back and forth to avoid yours. His head will start turning left to right as he glances back at you. He'll shift his weight from foot to foot. Maybe his tail will twitch or he'll turn his body away.

Like boredom, nervousness is uncomfortable. To ease the discomfort, the nervous person requires distractions, and he creates them with body motion. Although it's fairly easy to spot *severe* nervousness, sometimes the signs are not so obvious. I recall, for instance, a witness who at first glance appeared to be absolutely calm. No shaking, no tapping, no shifting in her chair. But during her testimony, she repeatedly reached for the water pitcher, carefully poured, and thoughtfully drank. It seemed she went through a gallon of water. Maybe she was just thirsty, but I doubt it. I concluded that she was nervous, and that she channeled her nervousness into the water-pouring-and-drinking ritual so that it wouldn't be revealed in more obvious ways.

Someone who is nervous will need an outlet for his nervous energy. In the world of high-stakes poker, where reading and disguising emotions is a prerequisite to success, smoking is common. It provides a physical release for players' nervousness and prevents other, more obvious signs from creeping out. As smoking is banned in more and more casinos and card rooms, many players are revealing "tells" they used to be able to hide. The nervous energy that had gone into smoking is spilling out in other ways.

Common symptoms of nervousness include

eyes darting back and forth
tensing of the body
contraction of the body (curling up)
shifting one's weight from side to side
rocking in one's chair
crossing and uncrossing the arms or legs
tapping hands, fingers, feet
adjusting or fiddling with pens, cups, eyeglasses, jewelry, clothing,
    fingernails, hair, hands, etc.
wringing the hands
clearing the throat
coughing nervously
smiling nervously (nervous people often smile, then resume a normal
    expression, over and over, very quickly)
biting the lip
looking down
chattering nervously
shaking or quaking (in extreme situations)

sweating (in extreme situations)
chewing nails or picking cuticles
putting one's hands in one's pockets
rotating side to side with the upper body
becoming silent

Because there are so many symptoms of nervousness, many of which can indicate other states of mind, you must not rely on isolated clues. For example, although sweating can signify extreme nervousness, it also can mean that someone feels hot, has just exercised, is ill, or is even having a menopausal hot flash. Most nervous people show more than one symptom. If you see only an isolated symptom keep in mind that the person may just have a habit that makes him appear nervous even when he's not.

A FINAL WORD OF CAUTION

If life were a silent movie we would have to rely on appearance and body language as we struggled to read and understand people. And if people overplayed their emotions in real life the way actors did on the silent screen, we might be fairly successful. But life is not silent, and most of us rarely exaggerate our dress or mannerisms enough to broadcast our emotions unambiguously. The villains among us don't have long handlebar mustaches to finger gleefully as they commit their dastardly deeds, and heroes don't all wear white hats. In real life, distinctions in physical appearance and body language are often very subtle and may convey many different and often contradictory meanings. After all, a woman may cross her arms because she's angry, defensive, or nervous, or she may also just feel cold.

Physical characteristics and body language are what you'll often notice first, but file those observations away for a while. Unless you absolutely must, never evaluate another person solely on the basis of his attire or the way he walks across a room. You need much more information to make a sound judgment. These are just the first steps along the path to understanding others. Don't stop here—continue the journey.

KEY POINTS

Scan from head to toe: You'll never know where you'll find that critical clue—hairstyle, watch, shoes, chewed finger nails—unless you look everywhere.

But don't judge a book—or a person—by its cover: Our physical appearance, dress, and body language always provide clues, but seldom definitive answers, about our personalities and character.

Remember, it's easy to dress the part: Characteristics which can be consciously adopted—like hairstyle, dress, and even a distinctive walk—generally have less meaning when viewed in isolation than involuntary actions—like a nervous laugh or furtive eyes.

Look for consistent combinations of clues: If you're on the right track, the signs should point in the same direction.

Remember, involuntary body language may be the only sign of "negative" emotions or traits: We've all learned to disguise dishonesty, resentment, and other socially undesirable traits. Keep alert; their signs will often leak out only through someone's body language.

Actions that are inappropriate under the circumstances deserve special attention: An isolated lapse of propriety may simply mean someone was caught off guard. But if someone consistently dresses or behaves inappropriately—skirts too short, dress or behavior too casual or too formal—find out why, and you'll find a critical key to his or her character.

Watch for anything which is uniquely peculiar or peculiarly unique: Whether grooming, clothing, or mannerisms, if something stands out, it's usually significant.

Scanning the Environment: Seeing People in Context

Imagine you're a contestant on *The Sherlock Holmes Show*. You and your fellow contestants are left alone in someone's office and given ten minutes to spot as many clues about him as you can. The object of the game is to test your powers of observation and deductive reasoning. When your time is up, you will be asked to tell the audience as much as possible about the man who works there.

From the photographs on the desk you learn that he's married to a young woman and has two children, a boy about ten years old and a girl about six. You also notice that some of the photographs were professionally taken at a pricey studio. This suggests the man is a touch extravagant and is very proud of his family. In one of the other photographs you see the family skiing. In another they're at the beach. He must be active and athletic.

You also see a diploma showing a degree in psychology from a local university. A small paperweight bearing the logo of the local chamber of commerce—this suggests that he is civic-minded—sits atop a tidy stack of papers. The rest of the environment is equally orderly. He is organized and neat. In one corner are several college social science textbooks. Maybe he's a college professor. Brightly colored modern artwork adorns the walls and tastefully complements the polished Danish modern furnishings. He is stylish, trendy, and cares about the impression he makes on others. By the time you have examined these and the dozens of additional clues available in the room—from the color of the walls to the type of pen he uses—you almost feel you know the man.

By the time you return to the studio, you have gathered so much information you're confident the audience will gasp with amazement at your incredible powers of observation and deduction. Surprisingly, each of the other contestants has performed at least as well. What is even more remarkable, all of you have reached very similar conclusions about the man. In this artificial situation, motivated by competition, you all paid careful attention. The results speak for themselves.

Now back to reality. How much information did you gather from the environment the last time you visited someone's home or office for the first time? Did you notice the photographs, their subject matter and quality, their frames? Did you note any distinctive characteristics of the knickknacks or furnishings? Did you give any thought to how the decor, the arrangement of the furniture, or other features of the environment reflected the person's personality, values, or life experiences? If you are like most people, you probably paid little attention. It's just as likely that you haven't given much thought to the image your own home or office projects to those who walk through your doors. But to people who know what to look for, your environment is a rich source of information about your personality, values, and lifestyle.

A person's environment can reveal clues about her job, education, hobbies, religion, culture, marital and family status, political affiliation, friends, priorities, and wealth. Perhaps more important, environment can confirm, cast doubt upon, or deepen what you've already learned about someone from her personal appearance and body language—whether she is flamboyant or conservative, practical or extravagant, egotistical or humble, neat or messy, trendy or traditional, and much more.

Environmental clues are easy to see—they're just sitting there. And most of us enjoy exploring other people's habitats anyway. As children we may have been taught not to be snoopy, but curiosity is just part of human nature. Besides, you don't have to poke around in somebody's sock drawer to learn about him.

Because so much can be learned from someone's environment, try to stay focused when you enter it, particularly when you're first getting to know the person. Above all, you're looking for the patterns that will reveal his or her true nature. As always, pay special attention to deviations, extremes, and appropriateness.

We spend most of our time either at home or at work. It's not surprising that both environments can be extremely revealing. You will get the most complete picture of an individual only if you have some exposure to both and can compare them. Our workstation, office, company vehicle, or locker tells a story. But our home may say something very different, since most of us have more control over it than over our workplace. A book on modern art would probably be a less revealing clue in your insurance agent's waiting room than it would be in his den at home.

Any disparity between the image someone projects in public and what is revealed in a more private environment can be an eye-opener. For example, you can learn a lot about a man if his car and the clothing he wears to work are expensive, stylish, and immaculately maintained. But you'll have a very different picture if you also know that his house is modest, messy, and not at all stylish. If you discover that he seldom invites people over, you might assume he places a high priority on impressing others: he has chosen to devote his money and attention to aspects of himself that other people will see regularly. The fact that he's perfectly comfortable spending his private time in a modest, disorderly home underscores the likelihood that he's concerned with appearances rather than just fond of the finer things in life.

You would learn even more about him if you met his wife and two children and found that their wardrobes weren't as snazzy as his. This would suggest that he prefers to spend his money on himself, not his family. You might conclude that he's self-centered and even selfish.

This chapter will describe how to learn more about someone from his workplace, his home, and even his car. It'll reveal which aspects of these environments are most meaningful. You'll also learn the potential significance of where someone chooses to meet with you. And you'll find out why the human environment—the company we keep—is so telling.

READING THE WORKPLACE ENVIRONMENT

Knowing how to read your colleagues' work spaces can clearly help nurture your on-the-job relationships. From environmental clues, you can learn who has tastes and values like your own, determine which co-workers are most likely to be well-organized and reliable, and perhaps even conclude who is committed to the job and who is merely marking time there. But reading the workplace environment of those who are *not* your co-workers comes in handy, too. Many of your first encounters with people—your pharmacist, your mechanic, the principal of your child's school—occur in their place of business. What a person has chosen to do for a living, and what her environment is like, provide many clues about her personality, which you can evaluate along with her appearance and behavior.

The Workplace Neighborhood

If you hold a job, you don't usually have a say in where your company's offices are, but you do have a choice about where you live. Someone who buys a condominium downtown to be close to work may reveal a lot about himself, particularly if he has children and living in the suburbs is an option. In the suburbs, the children might have more opportunity to play outdoors and participate in other activities. But with a short commute, Dad can spend more time at work. If I knew nothing about a person except that he'd moved his family downtown so he could be close to work, I would wonder whether he is a workaholic; derives personal satisfaction more from his work than from his family; and is self-centered and ambitious. This is a very harsh judgment, and I wouldn't act on it in any way unless I was able to gather enough information from other sources to validate it. After all, it could be that he and his wife agree that the city's cultural opportunities are more important for their children, and that a shorter commute actually leaves more time for Dad to spend with his family.

If someone is self-employed, the location of her workplace can be much more telling. For example, most successful lawyers in large cities have offices on the top floors in downtown buildings. When I encounter one who has chosen an alternative, such as an old Victorian house in the suburbs close to home, my people-reading antennae begin to wiggle. I can't help but consider all the possible reasons she might have chosen this office location:

- The location is closer to home and family: family is important to her.
- She likes to renovate old buildings: she's active and creative.
- She likes the relaxed atmosphere of a smaller building in a less congested area: she's informal and unpretentious.
- She likes having an unconventional office: she's a freethinker who wants others to know it.
- Owning this small building is less expensive than renting space in a skyscraper: she's frugal and practical.
- She's looking for an investment, not just rental space: she plans ahead.

Before I spent too much time speculating, though, I would simply ask her about her choice of office location. Let's say she responded as follows:

I'm shifting my focus. I've decided to cut back on my general trial practice and devote a good portion of my time to representing parents and

children in divorce and custody cases. This house is a lot more appealing to that type of client. There's a backyard where the kids can play,
and a spare room with toys and videos. There's also plenty of street
parking, so parents don't need to hassle with a big parking garage and
elevators while they've got their kids in tow. It's casual; my clients feel
comfortable here.

This would tell me a tremendous amount about her. It would reveal
compassion and sensitivity to her clients. Moreover, it indicates a major
shift in her life goals. What inspired this shift? Was she, or someone close
to her, involved in a custody battle? Or had she reached some milestone
that resulted in a reevaluation of her priorities? These issues are extremely significant when sizing someone up.

The neighborhood a person chooses for his or her work can be trendy,
practical, inexpensive, functional, or showy. Often, the neighborhood reflects the business or clientele: a fledgling apparel designer would probably set up shop near the garment district, and a marine carpenter near
the marina. In those instances, the person's choice of locale is primarily
a practical one, but you can still make note of whether the establishment
is strictly no-frills, or fancy and upscale, or somewhere in between. The
person who has chosen the more luxurious route, particularly when he
doesn't need fancy digs to attract business, is making a statement. Scenic
views, spaciousness, or comfort may be important to him, but it's more
likely that he's motivated by a desire to obtain the public image this more
prestigious location projects. The choice indicates a certain level of success, but it also can reveal a person's need for approval, arrogance, self-
centeredness, extravagance, or impracticality. On the other hand, the
person who chooses a modest location, particularly if he could afford a
more luxurious one, may be revealing confidence, practicality, frugality,
and self-esteem that doesn't depend on outward appearances.

Office Props

Movie set designers add props to the background of every scene to provide context and emphasis to the actors' words and gestures. In real life,
most of us select the props that surround us. And these objects are often
much easier to read than nuances of body language or the cut and color
of someone's hair.

Workplace props offer wonderful browsing for the attentive people-
reader. Space is usually limited, so you're less likely to be overwhelmed
with visual information than you would be at his home, and what you

do see is more likely to be there for a reason. The workplace is sometimes a mini-replica of home, with many of the same elements squeezed into a few revealing items. But someone's shop or office may also contain clues a home lacks. Away from the influence of spouse or family, some people more freely express themselves. This is especially true if the person's mate makes most of the decorating decisions at home.

The following list includes items most frequently found in someone's workplace. (It's not as long as it may seem—you'll need only a few minutes to visually register these items.) How often have you really thought about what such props might tell you about someone? If you make note of them the next time you visit someone's workplace, you will be amazed at how much information you'll accumulate.

Workplace Props

artwork
blotter/desk set
books, magazines, and other
  reading material
bookshelves
business cards/holders
calendars
clocks
coffee/tea service
collectibles
computer
corkboards and the items they
  display
diplomas
display case and contents
exercise equipment/sports gear
fax machine
flowers
furniture
gym bag
hat stand

knickknacks
lamps
liquor bottles or flasks
mirrors
mugs (especially with logos or
  quotes printed on them)
musical instruments
paperweights
pen sets
phone
photographs
plants
plaques
posters
radio
refrigerator
Rolodex
television
tools
trophies
umbrellas

The Most Revealing Items in the Workplace

Although every item on the list can provide important information, certain objects consistently reveal more than others. Those described below can be found in most workplaces. You'll notice that they are all easily replaceable and relatively inexpensive. For this reason, they are usually a better indication of a person's current state of mind than permanent fixtures such as a desk, computer, chairs, and carpeting. Many people have no choice when it comes to those more expensive and permanent items anyway, and those who do frequently opt for the style associated with their job. For instance, an attorney may favor costly traditional furnishings at the office, and a hairdresser may select clean, functional, comfortable decor at the salon—even though both prefer Danish Modern furniture for their homes. Office furnishings, then, usually won't reflect an individual's personal taste or priorities as well as photos, calendars, and the other items listed below.

These items have one other thing in common: they are all available in a nearly endless assortment of styles. Consequently, a person's choice is going to make a fairly specific statement. There's always the chance a particular item was a gift, but even so, people generally don't display gifts unless they like them.

Calendars   Does a workplace boast a Sierra Club calendar, or one that features show cars, pinups, Norman Rockwell paintings, or *Far Side* cartoons? Calendars not only broadcast an individual's hobby or passion, they're great conversation pieces. Just ask the person about the calendar, and you're off and running.

Photographs and frames   The people or places in the photos, the number of photos, the type of frame (expensive or inexpensive, country craft style or black lacquer), and the type of photograph (snapshot, amateur photograph, professional portrait, or art photo) are all very telling. For example, photos of the person with celebrities, community leaders, or other famous types are a form of (often harmless) braggadocio. These, and all photos, are great conversation starters.

Books and other reading material   The subject matter is important, naturally—a person with a stack of dog-eared science fiction paperbacks is probably a fan—but there are other factors to consider as well. Someone whose shelf is filled with unread leather-bound volumes by the "great masters" might just be pretentious. Are the shelves loaded with well-thumbed professional journals, or with magazines unconnected to the job? Is there a Bible or other religious book? What sort of reference works does the person have? Are there plenty of computer manuals, but little else?

The variety of reading material in someone's workplace may reflect more than the person's taste in books. It can also reveal his or her attitude toward the job. A pile of romance novels or a stack of parenting magazines on a desk suggests that this person's attention might often be elsewhere. Too many of them also point to a lack of judgment: the boss is sure to notice all the extracurricular reading material and wonder when the work is getting done.

Artwork   Art—paintings, posters, even figurines—in someone's workplace, like art at home, reveals a person's tastes and often his or her sense of humor, hobbies, and interests, all of which indicate personality. But keep in mind that much of the art displayed in a workplace may have been chosen with a view to the nature of the business rather than according to the individual's personal preference. Your mechanic may like oil paintings of waterfront scenes but hang posters of cars in the garage where he works. An oil painting might get dirty or be stolen or he may want to show his customers that he doesn't just work on cars, he loves them.

Desktop items   At least some of a person's limited desk space has to be reserved for getting work done. What someone chooses to occupy the remaining area will often tell you what is most important to him. Is it a picture of his wife and kids? A golf trophy? A pen and pencil holder his son made in wood shop, or a marble and gold desk set he received when he retired from the Navy? Is everything functional—computer, telephone, Rolodex—or is there space on his desk (and in his workday) for family and hobbies? Does he opt for an expensive designer pen or the company-issue Bic? And is the desktop cluttered or neat?

Someone's desk can be a small collage of his personality. A messy, disorganized desk usually points to a messy, disorganized person, and never mind the standard assurances to the contrary. The person's home and car will probably look the same way. And someone who tries to impress office visitors with expensive pens and crystal paperweights will likely find the need to do so in all aspects of his life.

Plants and flowers   The person who goes to the trouble of keeping fresh flowers or growing plants at work often cares a lot about beauty and nature in his environment. He's also likely to be somewhat artistic and health conscious. In addition, flowers and greenery are inviting, so they're a sign of a hospitable and caring nature.

I recently visited a courtroom before the trial of one of my cases began, as is my practice. I discovered that the judge routinely kept cut flowers in the courtroom. He had also made cushions for all the spectators' chairs. These special touches were very significant, particularly since they'd been provided by a male judge. Indeed, the judge's personality emerged during the trial as caring, considerate, open, unpretentious, and humane.

The Layout Tells a Tale

The way a person arranges the props in his workplace, as in his home, can also provide insight into his personality. Before you start tallying up sofas and chairs, however, find out whether the individual had a choice. If so, consider these points:

- Is the desk facing the door, a window, or a wall?
- Are there chairs for a guest to sit on, and if so, are they comfortable? (Remember that the office's occupant may not have chosen the chairs.)
- Is the space arranged so that guests and co-workers can talk comfortably?
- Is there a table with a coffeepot or coffee mugs?

Both at work and at home, the bottom line is that *any layout that removes barriers is significant.* If I walk into an office and see that its occupant has set up a conversation nook in one corner, I infer that he probably likes to speak with guests more casually and comfortably than he can when sitting behind his desk. He probably wants to put people at ease. He's informal and probably confident and not egotistical. On the other hand, the person who chooses to sit on one side of a large desk with his guests in smaller (and almost invariably more uncomfortable) chairs across from him is assuming a position of control and superiority.

Of course, most work spaces simply don't have room for such a setup. So look for items such as a coffeepot and mugs, bottled water, or other personal touches, which point to a person who cares about his guests. I can make some tentative judgments from these details about where the office's occupant might fit on my personal hardness scale.

READING A PERSON'S HOME

Our home is our castle. It is usually the most private, personal, and permanent environment we enjoy. At work, others almost always control appearances to some degree; and even when they don't, we may not reveal much of ourselves in such a public place. But home—that's different. Once you enter the space someone has created for her own comfort, you are in a position to find out some very pertinent information about her. If she shares her home with someone else, it may be more challenging to identify who is responsible for what features, but with close observation, a little time, and a few tactful questions, you can almost always find out.

Reading someone's home means looking around the "public" areas, not digging through the medicine cabinet. I mention this only because some people are terrible snoops, and I draw the line there. Privacy is sacred. Besides, if you're a good observer you don't need to delve into others' intimate territory. I consider "public" territory to be the neighborhood, the outdoor areas, the living room, the family room, the kitchen, and the guest bathroom. When you first visit and are taken on a "tour" you might get a peek at the bedrooms, too, but generally I'd consider them off limits.

Secret Lives

I've occasionally been surprised at how different someone's house is from the image he or she presents to the outside world. Sometimes the discrepancy is quite startling, though a dramatic direct conflict between someone's outer demeanor and home is unusual. Still, we all lead double lives to a certain extent. A stack of *People* magazines on the end table in the living room of a seemingly no-nonsense businesswoman, or a collection of classical music CDs in the home of the rough, tough guy from work doesn't mean these people have split personalities—just that they may be more complicated than you assumed.

The point of this type of observation isn't to identify "deceivers" but to get a sense of the real person and compare that with his or her more public persona. If there are obvious and astonishing differences, something is off-kilter and you should proceed with caution. More often, by comparing the public persona with the person's home, you can learn how contented they are, whether they feel insecure or confident, what they spend most of their time doing, and in general what matters most to them.

The House Reflects the Person

Whenever you enter someone's home, be alert to public-private inconsistencies like those just described. If someone's home is entirely consistent with her public persona, you can usually presume that she is fairly comfortable with who she is and where she is. She has accepted herself and is not a "wanna-be."

If someone's home differs dramatically from the way he presents himself publicly, a red flag should go up. The first question you should ask is "Which is the more authentic presentation?" Time and again I've found that when there is a disparity between the person's public appearance and his home, the home offers more reliable clues. Home is where we literally and figuratively let our hair down.

Before passing judgment, however, make sure you're not seeing an inconsistency where none really exists. Take, for example, the issue of financial success. Our homes, like our wardrobes, may reflect not only our taste but our financial well-being. But what may at first seem an inconsistency between how a man's home and his attire reflect his financial circumstances might make perfect sense once you get to know him a little better. I have a wealthy client who wears jeans and a casual shirt to work every day (he owns the company). If you saw him on the street, you'd never think he was rich. But enter his house—an architectural gem perched high on a cliff overlooking the ocean—and you are instantly aware of his financial success. He doesn't feel like dressing the part, and he doesn't have to. He doesn't care what anyone thinks of his level of success; he's happy and secure with who he is. His home clearly presents a more accurate picture of his socioeconomic standing than his attire, but the two images aren't really inconsistent. The fact is, he loves his beautiful home, and can afford it. He also loves comfortable, casual clothing, even though he could afford to dress any way he chose.

More often, though, blatant differences between the way a person dresses and the house in which he lives do signal that a choice has been made about where to spend money. When someone dresses elegantly but lives in a modest apartment with few trappings of wealth, the apartment probably represents where he actually is financially, while the clothes reflect where he would like to be. The bigger the gap, the more intense the drive to appear financially successful. The emphasis on appearance over creature comforts may indicate he's ambitious, driven, farsighted, and willing to delay gratification in order to achieve a long-term goal. But be on the lookout for other possibilities: materialism, insecurity, and vanity.

On the other side of the coin, the person who puts most of his income into his home and spends little on wardrobe and physical appearance is more likely to be comfortable with himself and less concerned about others' perceptions of him. He is probably more oriented toward family and friends than toward career.

Sometimes people will even pretend to have interests, hobbies, or talents that aren't supported when you visit their home. This unsettling information should always be considered carefully. Why, for instance, would a woman claim to be an avid chef if her kitchen looks as if it's poorly stocked and rarely used? If she has boasted of her cooking abilities to the whole office, it's probably because she believes others would admire that skill. The bare-bones kitchen has to make you wonder how insecure she is and question her truthfulness.

A person's home will rarely reveal "the key" to her personality all by itself. But sometimes a consistent, strong pattern will emerge from the clues you find there and will enable you to draw some fairly reliable conclusions. A friend of mine recently described her experience in searching for after-school day care for her youngest son. Ultimately, her choice was driven almost entirely by her evaluation of the environment.

In the first day-care provider's home, she noticed immediately that almost all the children were toddlers. Her son was in elementary school, and she wanted a person who would offer him activities he'd find challenging. Notwithstanding the care provider's assurances, the environment told her that wouldn't happen there. It was the middle of the afternoon, and the children sat clustered in front of a TV set in the family room. It was bad enough that they were staring at the TV like zombies; even worse, they were watching a talk show. My friend might have felt differently had the set been tuned to a Disney movie or a nature program, but a talk show for toddlers? She didn't need to see more.

Not long afterward, she found a woman who appeared to fit the bill perfectly. Again, the environment provided many critical clues. A tarp was spread under a tree in the backyard. There was a kiddie-size picnic table on the tarp, where children her son's age were painting. The day-care provider's assistant was actively involved with the children, who in turn were socializing with one another.

In the house were several items that indicated a strong Christian influence. This may have been a bad sign for someone with a different (or no) religious background, but given my friend's Christian beliefs and her interest in seeing her children grow up in such an environment, she found this even more comforting. The house was immaculate. There were safety plugs in all the sockets, rubber covers attached to the corners of the coffee table, and double sets of latches on every door, one at a height where none of the children could possibly reach it. Everything spoke of a very dedicated, careful, and caring woman—exactly who my friend was looking for.

Usually it takes this sort of pattern building and attention to details to draw a reliable conclusion from a person's environment. So don't stop looking as soon as you've found what you believe to be one notable discovery. Keep searching.

The Neighborhood

The neighborhood in which a person chooses to live says much the same as her choice of work environment—but louder, because there are so many more options. Our choices can reveal our financial status, our marital and family situation, our image-consciousness, and in some cases, traits that might not be expected. For instance, the black families who chose to move into all-white neighborhoods in the 1960s and 1970s showed courage, drive, and strength of character. And, like most people who choose improbable neighborhoods, they were strong-willed and independent thinkers. Our choice of neighborhood doesn't often reflect such resolve or commitment to our ideals, but it's often an important indicator of lifestyle and priorities.

The husband and wife who opt for a tiny apartment in an expensive area because it has topflight public schools have made a statement about the value they place on their children's education. The couple who give up vacations, piano lessons, and most other day-to-day luxuries to move into a more prestigious neighborhood show how much they value status and other people's impressions of them. Whenever someone chooses where to live he must make trade-offs. If it isn't obvious, ask why he decided to live where he did. The answer may tell you a lot about him.

Indoors and Out

Frequently the outside of a house looks very different from the inside. That disparity will often suggest what is more important to the inhabitants: outside appearances or their own comfort and aesthetic pleasure. When people move into a new place, that's a particularly good time to look for signs of their priorities. Most people have a limited budget for repairs and interior decoration, so they'll make a choice: fix up the inside or spruce up the outside. Their decision may offer some insight into what matters more to them.

The difference between inside and outside also underscores how crucial it is to wait until you see the whole picture before drawing any conclusions. A house that presents a very plain face to the street may look stunning on the inside. By the same token, a person who has put every last dime into buying the most expensive house he can possibly afford may be "house poor" and have only the most basic furniture. Both these people have made choices that may speak to their values. One may be more concerned with his own comfort and the other with outward appearances. But never forget, there are a host of possible motivations for most decisions. Perhaps the one who spends all his time and energy on landscaping just loves to garden and couldn't care less about what his neighbors think.

Usually, the first thing you'll notice when you enter someone's home is the decor. Style often gives clues about personality, although, as usual, there are exceptions. But by and large, traditional furnishings reflect traditional views on life, whereas more modern or unusual decor reflects more open, experimental views. Choices in furnishings may also reflect a person's background. If you were raised in the country, you may prefer country-style furnishings. Most of us associate our childhood home with feelings of security and love. It's rare that a person will divorce himself entirely from those feelings.

If someone has left home decoration to another, whether a spouse or professional designer, the decor is much less helpful in predicting character. While it's true that a designer's client usually has to approve his plans, often the client is either too busy to put much thought into the decisions or is willing to defer to someone with stronger feelings about the matter.

Using Your Senses

When you enter someone's home, your first inclination is to look around. After you've had a few minutes to absorb some of the visual information, concentrate on three other senses: hearing, smell, and touch.

Listen to the room   Is quiet, soothing music playing, which might indicate the person who lives there is calm and serene—or wants to be? Or is the TV blaring? If so, what channel is on? Listen for wind chimes, dogs barking, children playing. If you hear rock and roll coming from a back room, are there teenagers in the home, or is the fifty-five-year-old occupant possibly stuck in the sixties? If you're not listening, you won't hear a lot of great clues that might provide you with valuable information—and point you in directions where you'll find even more.

Smell the room   Notice any good or unpleasant odors, and try to identify them. Good smells may come from the kitchen or from an open win-

dow that lets fresh air flow through, or someone may have gone out of
her way to make her home smell wonderful, or to mask the scent of medication, illness, or smoke. Sniff the air and try to identify smells associated with

flowers
food
fireplace/wood smoke
animals
children/babies
medication
alcohol
cigarettes, pipes, cigars
cleaning products

Smells may tip you off to a person's interests (such as cooking or gardening), their use of tobacco and alcohol, whether they have a pet or
young children, and even their health.

The odors someone introduces into his environment, or fails to remove, can tell you more than you might imagine. People with unclean
homes tend to have the same traits as those whose personal hygiene
leaves something to be desired. And those who create beautiful-smelling,
inviting homes tend to be more socially adept, considerate, and sensitive
to others and how others perceive them. They also tend to be more sensual and emotional.

Touch the room   Don't put on white gloves and start feeling for dust on
the fireplace mantel, but pay attention to items within your reach. Notice whether the furniture is cozy or stiff and inhospitable. Sofas uphol-
stered in soft cotton might indicate a sensualist, while slick Naugahyde
would point to a more practical nature. Are the floors slippery and
highly polished, or carpeted and warm? Is the place comfortable or cold?
Is it clean? All of this information will add detail to the pattern you are
beginning to see develop.

House Props

A home contains thousands of items. When you visit, focus on those that
may be most revealing. The list that follows includes many items worth
noting, but there is no end to the list of potentially telling items that may
be found in a home. You'd be amazed at how much can be revealed by
even the most seemingly mundane objects.

One example of something to which you've probably never given a second thought is the type of facial tissue you find in someone's home. We all know people who splurge on the extra-soft, scented, flowery variety. And then there are those who buy whatever brand is on sale, even if it feels like newspaper. Almost everyone can afford the luxurious variety if they want to. Those who do are more likely to be sensual, extravagant, willing to pamper themselves, concerned about the comfort of others, and eager to be a good host. If they choose tissue decorated with flowers or pretty designs, they may also show their desire to surround themselves with beautiful things. Those who opt for the cheap, harsh, plain white variety are more likely to be frugal, practical, unconcerned about appearances, and unwilling to spend money on their own creature comforts or on the comfort of others.

Should you make a blanket assessment about someone based solely on the brand of facial tissue she prefers? Of course not. But you should consider it a useful clue in combination with others. Keep that in mind as you review this list of common house props.

House Props

alcohol
animal toys or bowls
artwork
ashtrays
books and other reading
   material
candles
children's toys and furniture
clocks
collections
entertainment center
flowers and green plants
food
garden equipment
guns or gun racks
holiday decorations
items on the refrigerator
   (magnets, cards, drawings)
items reflecting a physical
   disability (cane, wheelchair,
   oxygen tank)
knickknacks

mailbox
mirrors
musical instruments
pharmaceuticals
photographs
religious pictures, books, or
   other paraphernalia
rugs
signs
special features (such as a wine
   cellar, a darkroom, a fireplace,
   a pool)
sports paraphernalia: equipment,
   clothing, trophies, posters,
   and so forth
stereo system and record/CD
   collection
television (size and location)
tools
vitamins
welcome mats

The significance of many of these items is obvious if you take the time to notice them. A large-screen television located in the middle of the living room broadcasts a straightforward message about the person's priorities, as does a small TV tucked away in the corner. Records and CDs reflect someone's taste in music, candles a romantic or sensitive side, and vitamins an interest in health. Sports equipment, guns, musical instruments, and the like reveal the person's interests and hobbies.

As with everything else, individual features take on special significance if they create a pattern when combined with other features. If a home has security lights, bars on the windows, an alarm system, gates, a "Beware of Dog" sign, and several deadbolts or locks on the doors, it's a good bet that the person who lives there is very concerned about his security, perhaps even paranoid. Likewise, holiday decorations, swing sets, and children's toys suggest the person has a family-oriented lifestyle and values.

Most of these props are great starting points for a conversation about their owner's pastimes or interests. A few of the items listed deserve particularly close examination. Like those highlighted in the discussion of workplace props, these objects are chosen not because the person needs them but because he desires them.

Books and other reading material   What someone reads can be one of the most revealing items a home has to offer, particularly if it is unique. You won't learn much from the presence of the local newspaper, but you would from a copy of *Soldier of Fortune* magazine. However, not everyone displays her reading material in the living room, and not every avid reader reads magazines and owns a lot of books. Some people go to the library. Others like to keep their homes uncluttered and keep their book collection in a back room or in boxes in the garage. If the house does have bookcases and tables that display books or magazines, take a close look at them. Look for patterns—mystery novels, cooking magazines, science journals. You'll be surprised at what you can learn. For example, someone who owns many books on health might only be a bit obsessed with the subject. But the presence of even one book on a specific serious illness may mean that the person or someone he knows suffers from the disease.

Items on the refrigerator   Imagine a list of what is most important to someone tacked on a wall for you to review. That's what many refrigerators are like—they practically vibrate with life. Appointments, cartoons, magnets, photos, children's drawings, favorite sayings, poems, tickets, business cards . . . the list of what people put on their fridges is endless. And every item has been taken from a more obscure location and placed where it will be seen. Not everyone decorates her refrigerator, and I wouldn't draw any conclusions from a naked Amana. But when someone treats her refrigerator like a bulletin board, pay attention to what she posts on it.

Collections   Collections are often passed from generation to generation. My mother collects beautiful porcelain teacups, and over the years my sisters and I have added to them. We know someday the teacups will be divided among us, and that we in turn will pass them along to our children. Collections can indicate stability, the importance of family, and a love of tradition. What someone collects is meaningful as well: rare and valuable coins say something different than an array of spoons acquired over years of family vacations. Someone's collections may reflect his or her socioeconomic level, trendiness, investment interest, hobbies, and life experiences. From baseball cards to Elvis paraphernalia, collections provide a wealth of information.

Photographs   Photographs in the home can be more—or less—revealing than photographs in the workplace. There's usually more room for photographs at home, so you'll find a wider range of subject matter from which to gather clues. On the other hand, because space is less limited, the person doesn't need to be as selective, so the choice of photographs may not be as revealing. Still, look closely. There's almost always a lot to learn about—family activities, hobbies, travel interests, involvement in sports, cultural and religious background, and much more.

Artwork   Since we usually have complete freedom to choose the art in our home, it's a more reliable indicator of our taste than artwork in the office. If you are instantly attracted to something hanging on a person's walls, or if it reflects your sense of humor or interests, you may have encountered someone with whom you have a lot in common. If their paintings, posters, or photographs strike you as tacky or offensive, your worldviews are probably very different. Most people don't spend a lot of money on art, even if they could afford to. But whether someone buys poster art or original oil paintings, he will reveal his sense of humor, interests, traditional or untraditional values, and much more in his choices.

Children's toys and furniture   If there are children in a house, I always look to see how far their influence extends. Some families willingly turn over the living room to the kids, stocking it with toy barrels and indoor climbing equipment. These people probably also like family-oriented leisure activities. They're also more apt than some others to enjoy having your children around.

In other homes the kids' toys stay in the kids' rooms, and the parents reserve the rest of the house for adult-oriented activities. You may want to take that into consideration when you visit with your own children. Families fortunate enough to have separate family and living rooms can have it both ways.

Alcohol   In the 1950s, 1960s, and 1970s, many new houses were built with wet bars, which were probably meant to supply a Frank Sinatra–Rat Pack look. These days, hard liquor has lost much of its glamour. When I find a fully stocked wet bar or any open display of liquor, I take notice, particularly if the resident is under fifty. Don't label someone an alcoholic simply because he has a well-stocked liquor cabinet, but nowadays it's unusual to find a lot of bottles prominently displayed. Their owner may be fond of drinking or of entertaining those who are.

Flowers and green plants   Flowers and plants require time and care. They make a house more comfortable, beautiful, and inviting. A person who is willing to devote time, energy, and money to their upkeep is likely to be sensuous, sensitive to beauty, and hospitable. (But because it's common, and easier, to keep plants at home, they're less significant here than they are in an office—unless, of course, the person has a *lot* of them.) On the other hand, unhealthy or dying flowers and plants may suggest their owner is unobservant, sloppy, or very busy. Usually the rest of the house will be in the same state of disarray.

Signs   Whether indoors or out, signs offer plenty of information. "Beware of Cat" indicates not only that someone is probably fond of cats but also that she has a sense of humor and wants to display it. "Beware of Dog," on the other hand, tells you the person has a dog and is concerned with security. Signs announcing security systems or organizational memberships are all useful clues to a person's background, beliefs, and priorities, as are symbols of religious affiliation.

Any object in a person's home may provide extra material for your mental file. Each detail contributes to the overall pattern. If you notice anything that's unusual or that sticks out like a sore thumb, ask about it if you can do so tactfully.

MY WHEELS, MYSELF:
READING A PERSON'S AUTOMOBILE

"It Also Functions Like a Résumé," boasts the Lexus ad. Indeed, many people think of their automobile as a way to telegraph their financial success, masculinity, class, or style. Our cars do say a lot about us—not only our money, but also our priorities, interests, work, and personality. Cars are easy to read, although what they say may differ from region to region. However, if you spend more than a week in a town you'll quickly learn the regional "rules." Someone who drives a pickup truck in downtown Chicago probably uses it in his work. The same truck in Austin, Texas, may never be used for anything but show. A convertible in southern California is not nearly as extravagant or impractical as the same car in Seattle, where the top can come down only rarely. And don't fall victim to the stereotype that wealthy, successful, status-conscious people all drive expensive European sedans. In Detroit, they may drive Cadillacs and Lincolns, and in Tulsa, the wheels of choice may be big extended-cab pickup trucks.

When you're evaluating a car, keep in mind its practicality with respect to the region and the owner's work, family, and hobbies. Is it a sports car, a convertible, a "muscle car," a family car, a minivan, a truck? What did it cost? Does it get good mileage, and is it easy and cheap to repair? Is it practical, given the owner's family status, income, and line of work? Every car says something about the person who picked it out. An expensive three-hundred-horsepower sports car tells me its driver is probably status conscious, aggressive, and a touch egotistical. The six-cylinder minivan speaks of practicality, frugality, and conformity.

Add-ons

Like the props in a home or office, the extras people add to their vehicles offer another glimpse of their interests, priorities, and values. Here we've listed only the more common items you might notice on someone's car.

alarm
antenna ornaments
bumper stickers
car phone (watch out if you also see a car fax)
Club or other steering wheel lock
customized license plates
decorative painting

floor mats
hubcaps
license-plate holders
lights (ornamental/spot)
mirror ornaments (dice, crosses, etc.)
mud flaps (the silhouette of the Playboy Bunny may say a lot about the
   man driving)
music system
racks (bikes, ski, luggage, gun)
raised or lowered height
roll bars
seat covers or cushions
signs
tires and wheels
trailer hitches

Just how much can be learned from a car's accessories was brought home to me recently as I was driving down the freeway. I passed a small car driven by an elderly, white-haired lady. The license-plate holder read, "Timmy's and Julie's Nana," and the customized license plate "Nana N." From this I could tell not only that the woman had grandchildren named Timmy and Julie (obvious), but also that those grandchildren were extremely important to her, and probably a huge part of her life.

Car Maintenance

How a person takes care of her car is often a clear sign of her priorities. I have an acquaintance whose mother, after interviewing prospective tenants for her rental house, always walked them out to their car. As she put it: "I may not be able to see how they take care of their house, but I can see how they take care of their car, and that'll tell me just as much." This isn't always true, but it's a sound notion to keep in mind.

The owner of a consistently filthy car is probably: unconcerned about the impression he makes; not meticulous or detail oriented; very busy; disorganized; or lazy. Someone whose car is always immaculate probably exhibits the same fastidiousness in her dress and grooming. She's likely to be organized, orderly, concerned with how she appears to others, and attentive to detail. Children (and dogs) do weaken the equation, as it's very difficult to maintain a spanking-clean automobile when you're ferrying kids (or canines) around in it every day. If you meet someone who manages to accomplish this feat, you can probably assume that he or she runs a very tight ship.

SOCIAL ENVIRONMENTS:
WHERE DO WE CHOOSE TO PLAY?

How many times have you heard someone complain about a spouse who drinks too much, only to learn the two lovebirds met in a bar? Where we choose to spend our free time is extremely revealing, yet we often overlook these environmental signposts. If abstinence from alcohol is important, why not try meeting people at alcohol-free functions? If you want to meet a religious person, your chances are best at church or synagogue. If you are looking for intellectual stimulation, check out a university or a library. Athletes can be found in the gym, and nature lovers at Sierra Club meetings. You find polar bears in the frozen north, not the tropics. Common sense, right?

It *is* common sense, but for some reason we frequently overlook how much the environments people choose tell about them. The more the choice is within their control, the more it reveals. If I meet someone playing softball with the kids at the park on a Saturday afternoon, I'd guess that she enjoys the outdoors, spending time with her family, and playing sports. But if she were doing the same at a company picnic, I wouldn't automatically draw this conclusion. Even if she's enjoying herself, I can't be sure that this is what she'd freely choose to do—only that she's adaptable enough to enjoy it when it has been chosen for her.

Before you place too much weight on a single encounter at the park, or anywhere else, you need to know how much time the person spends there. Most of us don't spend a significant amount of leisure time anyplace unless it fulfills our needs in some way. Church is probably important to someone who attends church most Sunday mornings, but religion may still not be a big factor in his life. However, it's a safe bet that his religious beliefs are central to his worldview and may even dominate how he thinks and behaves if he not only attends church on Sunday mornings but also goes to Wednesday night Bible study classes and Saturday church socials. The same is true of any environment, from health club to shopping mall to Little League. The more time a person freely chooses to spend there, the more that environment will reflect his beliefs and foretell his behavior.

Sometimes the choice of environment on even an isolated occasion can tell much about a person. If an old college friend is in town and calls to get together and catch up, her choice of locale for our chat can be a clue worth noting. Even the restaurant she selects can reflect her character, values, and lifestyle. Does she suggest we grab a bite at a fast-food restaurant, a family coffee shop, or a chic French bistro? Someone who opts for a very expensive restaurant for a casual lunch with an old friend may have moderate wealth—or an out-of-control credit account. Either way, she may be concerned with appearances and trying to impress. She apparently enjoys indulgences, and she may not be particularly practical. All that could reflect insecurity. I wouldn't necessarily draw the same conclusions if a businessman chose the same high-priced restaurant to meet his most important client. Perhaps he knows the client expects to be wined and dined.

On the other hand, someone who chooses a coffee shop is more likely to be frugal, practical, and either unable or unwilling to sacrifice financially for the sake of gourmet food or the image it presents. If my friend made that choice, I would assume that she just wants to talk, not to impress me with her success or status. If the successful businessman took his best client to a coffee shop for lunch, I would be inclined to believe he was very comfortable with their relationship and that neither he nor his client was concerned with showing off.

The person who suggests you meet at a bar also says something very different than the one who offers to meet you at an outdoor café or at your place for a cup of coffee. Even the type of bar sends a message— after all, bars run the gamut from topless joints to swank lobby bars at four-star hotels. The drinking habits of Americans have changed drastically over the past ten or fifteen years. To an extent, coffeehouses, restaurants, and clubs have replaced bars as popular places to get to know someone. Therefore, the person who suggests a first meeting at a bar may reveal that, to him, alcohol is an important social lubricant. If this is what you're looking for, fine. If not, keep an eye out for a pattern to develop.

I would never draw any final conclusions about someone on the sole basis of his choice of restaurant or bar, but I would notice and consider it. If he chose the same type of meeting place consistently, that would be even more significant.

BIRDS OF A FEATHER: EVALUATING
THE HUMAN ENVIRONMENT

"Birds of a feather flock together," goes the old saying, and it's a priceless piece of wisdom. The people we befriend, marry, hire, work for, and socialize with make up our human environment. They often reflect either who we are or who we'd like to be, since to a large degree we have a choice about them. Most parents are acutely aware of this, which is why they monitor their children's friends so closely. Given enough time and contact, youngsters will begin to adopt the values and behaviors of their peers. An adult's crowd is very revealing as well.

The lawyer who has represented your sleazy brother-in-law for years is probably just as sleazy. He would have been fired long ago if he weren't willing to do your brother-in-law's dirty work. And that new boyfriend whose best buddy's favorite pastime is a ball game and a few beers must have something in common with him. Similarly, a woman tells you where her priorities are if her best friends are all mothers of children in her young son's play group.

Whenever you're reading someone, take note of their friends, confidants, business associates, and mates—especially if a person's acquaintances all seem to fall into the same category. Many people are skilled at disguising their personality and value system. If you can visit their home and workplace, you'll probably be able to discover more of their true nature. But if you have access to nothing else, *sizing up someone's friends and associates will give you a pretty reliable indication of his or her character.* While I hesitate to either damn or praise on this basis alone, association makes a very powerful statement.

GEOGRAPHIC LOCATION AS PART OF THE ENVIRONMENT

The conclusions I draw about someone's personal appearance may depend on geography. People with very similar personalities and values will look, dress, and act differently if they are from different locales. Expectations, norms, and cultural influences vary from town to town, region to region, and country to country. You can't hold everyone to the same standard. Before you draw any firm conclusions, make sure you've allowed for any unique geographical factors. If I see a young woman in Manhattan wearing heavy makeup, a severe hairstyle, and a trendy designer suit, I won't give her appearance much thought. She's probably style-conscious and conforming to what others in her environment deem appropriate. On the other hand, if I saw the same woman walking down the street in a small town in Middle America, I'd find that curious. Perhaps she's flamboyant, expressive, looking for attention by standing out. Maybe she's even bored and discontented with her life. Or maybe she's just visiting from New York.

TIME OF DAY, DAY OF WEEK, AND SEASON OF THE YEAR AS PART OF THE ENVIRONMENT

If I stopped by someone's house at five in the morning to pick her up for an early meeting, and she met me at the door bleary-eyed, moving slowly, and complaining of fatigue, I'd probably attribute that to the hour. But if she showed up at work at ten looking and acting the same way, I'd wonder why.

The day of the week also can be significant. A person says a lot about himself if he chooses to drink and dance until the wee hours on a Wednesday night. On the positive side, he is energetic and fun-loving. But—assuming he is due at work early the next morning—his behavior also suggests he is willing to sacrifice peak performance there. I wouldn't consider this an issue if I ran into him in the same club late on a Friday or Saturday night.

Even the time of year can be important. A man whose face is very red the day after a sunny Fourth of July weekend is probably sunburned. In December, after weeks of overcast and rain, I would look for other causes: fatigue, alcohol, medical treatment, or even embarrassment. If I met a man with a flawless tan in Seattle in December, and I knew he had not been on vacation in the tropics, I would assume he regularly visits a tanning salon. That would demonstrate vanity and concern for the way others perceive him. During the summer in San Diego, I wouldn't draw the same conclusion from a man's tan.

IS THE ENVIRONMENT FRIENDLY OR HOSTILE?

A person's behavior can change dramatically when he is in an unfamiliar or hostile environment. You can't expect a lamb to act the same way when thrown into the lion's den as it would when grazing in a pasture, and the same is true of people. We typically show signs of anxiety, antisocial behavior, and lack of confidence when we are in a hostile environment. That doesn't mean we're all nervous, reclusive, and insecure by nature.

There are few environments in which people feel less comfortable than a courtroom. I've seen hundreds of people testify, ranging from professional experts to those who are on the witness stand for the first time. Often, someone I know to be completely truthful will come across as nervous and dishonest. His voice may crack. His eyes may be downcast or flicker from side to side. He may lick his lips, fiddle with objects in front of him, stutter, and even fail to recall recent events. It would be a grave error to conclude that he must be lying. By the same token, many expert witnesses have testified literally hundreds of times in court and are totally at ease. They know what they are doing and perform effortlessly and confidently. Many of them are in essense accomplished performers, and able to appear completely candid even if they're stretching the truth to its limits.

Outside the courtroom, people are no different. If I go to a party where I know everyone, I may be very outgoing, confident, sociable, and relaxed—I'll move freely from person to person. At a function where I've never met a soul, I may be more tentative, quiet, shy, or reserved. I may break the ice with one person, then spend a substantial amount of time in conversation with him rather than mingle freely with a crowd of strangers.

When you meet people for the first time and try to size them up, take into account how they may be feeling in that environment. Try to determine whether they are on familiar territory or feel like strangers in a strange land. If someone is on well-known turf and yet seems skittish and ill at ease, you might conclude that she's unusually shy or insecure; or perhaps she's suffering through some temporary personal difficulty. But if she behaves that way in a foreign or hostile environment, these conclusions would be unfounded—unless they were supported by further independent evidence.

ALWAYS REMEMBER HOW ENVIRONMENT MIGHT BE INFLUENCING BEHAVIOR

From the first chapter of this book you've been reading about characteristics that can have virtually opposite meanings depending upon the circumstances. Someone who is loud may be confident—or insecure. Someone who wears mismatched clothes may be socially inept—or at the height of style within her peer group. As you attempt to determine which, never lose sight of how a person's environment may be influencing her appearance or behavior.

I can offer a remarkable example of this from the federal prosecution of the four police officers accused of beating Rodney King. The day after the jury was selected, one of the jurors, a middle-aged African-American woman, appeared in court wearing black gloves. She wore the same black gloves every day for the rest of the trial. It was driving me crazy. Was she making a racial statement? Were the gloves a political commentary? Did they have some other unknown significance? After the trial was over, I learned from her fellow jurors that she wore the black gloves simply because she found the courtroom to be uncomfortably cold.

The importance of viewing every trait in the context of the environment in which it is found can't be overstressed. Like the animated characters in a Disney movie, our actions have little meaning absent their backdrop. Observe that carefully, and the rest of the details will come into sharper focus.

KEY POINTS

Read the environment with all your senses: Listen, smell, feel—don't just look.

See the big picture: Someone's work or home environment includes everything from the interior decor, to the lobby or yard, type of building, and even the neighborhood. Take it all in.

There are clues everywhere, but some tend to stand out: Calendars, photographs, reading material, artwork, plants or flowers, and desktop or refrigerator door "props" are often the best place to start.

There's more to "reading" someone's home, workplace, or automobile, than just identifying the "props": Notice how everything is maintained and where it is positioned; and always ask how much choice the person had about the matter.

Watch for distinctions between someone's private and public environments: Our work environments, to the extent we have a say in them, often speak most loudly about what we want others to think of us. The environment we create in the privacy of our homes usually tells more about who we really are.

Ask "where they choose to play": Where people enjoy spending free time—the ball park, a jazz bar, the mall, expensive restaurants, the library—provides insight into both their interests and values.

Birds of a feather flock together: Our human environment—who we choose to work, play, and live with—is an excellent measure of our true values and character.

Remember, our appearance, speech, and behavior are affected by our environment: Hostile or unfamiliar environments; the time of day, week, or year; the weather; and many other factors all have an impact on us.

It's Not What You Say, It's How You Say It: Learning to Hear More Than Just Words

When I was a child, my mother used to tell me, "It's not what you say, it's how you say it." Years later, I find myself saying the same thing to my own kids. Their behavior reminds me daily how much of our attitude is revealed not by words but by the way they are spoken.

Two dialogues really take place in every conversation—one uses words, the other tone of voice. Sometimes the two match, but often they do not. When you ask someone, "How are you?" and get the reply "Fine," you're not usually relying on the word "fine" to tell you how she feels. Instead, you let her tone tell you whether she really is fine, or whether she is depressed, anxious, excited, or feeling any of a dozen other emotions. When you listen to tone, volume, cadence, and other vocal characteristics, you tune in to the nonverbal conversation, where the true substance is often found.

Anyone with normal hearing can detect the signals people convey with their tone of voice, but few of us understand all of them. This is partly because when we're interacting with someone, there's a lot of competition for our attention. We size up their appearance and body language, listen to the content of their words, and watch their actions. We may even struggle to identify some intuitive reaction we're having to the person or situation. Vocal subtleties can get lost in all this. It's easy to notice the message someone sends with a pouty, sad, or frustrated tone of voice, but a fleeting note of anxiety, fear, or embarrassment may slip right past you if you don't pay close attention.

I've trained myself to listen for these vocal clues and recognize their nuances, since such a momentary glimmer may be the only tip I get about a prospective juror's doubts or true feelings toward a client. This chapter will explore the ways people communicate intentionally and unintentionally through tone of voice, explain how you can tune in to these often elusive vocal clues, and decode the messages contained in the most common vocal traits.

HEARING BETWEEN THE LINES

Outside the therapist's office, few of us are willing to announce, "You hurt my feelings," or "I'm sad and I want to talk about it," or "I'm frustrated with my work and would like to complain to you about it for an hour." Instead, we signal these feelings with vocal clues. *We play emotional hide-and-seek.* Someone who is sad may be longing for sympathy but feel she needs your "permission" to broach the subject. She'll sigh, speak softly, answer questions briefly, and couple these vocal clues with body language such as downcast eyes and limp, lifeless gestures. Eventually you'll get the message and ask what's wrong, thus giving her the permission she seeks.

Such behavior might seem manipulative, but it's a product of our socialization. We're taught not to ask openly for sympathy, express resentment or jealousy, or show anger, hurt, or other unpleasant emotions. But sometimes we badly need to express ourselves and, not wanting to come out and say so, we use tone to convey the message. This nonverbal communication is nearly universal. You can test it yourself: tune in a TV channel in a language other than your own. Find a soap opera, turn your back to the set, and listen to the dialogue. You may not be able to follow the plot, but you'll surely be able to pick up on the actors' emotions.

Two recent trials in which I was involved illustrate just how important it is to pay attention to the way words are spoken. The first case involved the family of a young man who was in a car accident and died because a paramedic misread the label on some medication he administered. The family argued that the bottle wasn't labeled clearly enough, and sued the pharmaceutical manufacturer, which hired me to help pick the jury. The jury had to decide who was at fault and how much money, if any, should be awarded to the man's family.

During jury selection, the family's attorney asked a middle-aged, conservative white man whether he would put any cap on the amount of money he would be willing to award to compensate the family for the death of a loved one. The man responded, "There is no amount of money that could compensate someone for the death of a loved one." The plaintiff's lawyer thought he had a great juror, who would award virtually unlimited damages. The man had "said" the right thing.

But the plaintiff's lawyer missed the vocal clues that revealed the juror's true meaning. The man had spoken almost critically, even sarcastically. That tone suggested to me he resented the attorney's asking him to put a price tag on the young man's life. The juror's response was also crisp and to the point, which indicated a certain emotional distance from the case. Given all this, I understood him to mean not that unlimited damages were warranted, but rather that he felt it inappropriate to attach a dollar figure to a human life. We left him on the jury, and as it turned out, we were right. He voted with the others, who after only thirty minutes of deliberation found the pharmaceutical company wasn't responsible for the young man's death.

The second example comes from the criminal trial—the one in Simi Valley—of the four police officers accused of beating Rodney King. During jury selection, a young Hispanic woman said that one of her sons wanted to become a police officer. She also said, with apparent sincerity, that she had no personal belief the four police officers were guilty. Officers Larry Powell and Stacey Koon recommended that we keep her on the jury. Because of her son's ambitions and because she seemed open-minded, they believed she would make a sympathetic juror.

I was wary, however, of how she responded to a number of other questions. When asked whether she had spoken with anyone about the case, she said that she had discussed it with her husband. She also acknowledged that he believed the officers were guilty and should be punished. While she promised not to allow her husband's views to influence her and not to talk to him about the case during the trial, I had my doubts. As she spoke of her husband, it was clear from her very deferential tone that she had a traditional marriage, in which she took care of the house and children and he wore the pants in the family. There was no reservation or qualification in her voice when she relayed her husband's strong feelings about the officers' guilt. His opinions were spoken as if they were gospel. When she promised to try to keep an open mind despite his beliefs her voice grew softer and much more tentative and uneven. That suggested she was nervous and not confident of what she was saying. I believed she would have to overcome a significant psychological barrier to vote "not guilty," since to do so would incur her husband's wrath and disrespect. As it turned out, she was one of three jurors who voted to convict Officer Powell.

You will be able to respond to the potentially critical messages embedded in a person's tone of voice if you understand what various vocal clues mean and teach yourself to listen for them. You can do so by following these steps:

- Focus on the voice—not the words—from time to time during the conversation.
- Ask yourself whether the voice reflects elective (voluntary) or nonelective (involuntary) characteristics.
- Look for patterns. Ask yourself whether the voice is different now from its usual tone or is in any way exaggerated. (That is, listen for deviations and extremes.)
- Compare the voice to the person's body language and words.
- Consider the environment.
- Decode the vocal clues.

FOCUS ON THE VOICE

You can absorb only so much information in a given moment. It's difficult to concentrate on someone's words while simultaneously cataloging her jewelry and noticing whether she's crossing and uncrossing her legs. With so much competing for our attention, it's easy to pass over tone of voice unless it's extreme. We tend to pay more attention to words than to tone for the simple reason that words require a reply. Sometimes if we take our attention off the content of the conversation we'll lose track of it altogether.

Even so, in every conversation there are moments when you can briefly turn down the content and turn up the tone. It takes only a second, and with practice you'll be able to listen to words and tone simultaneously. The trick is to do this in short spurts rather than minute-long segments. There are bound to be moments when you can mentally step back and attend to nonverbal clues even in a fairly complex conversation. And almost always, if you really listen to someone's voice you will enrich the meaning of their words.

DISTINGUISH BETWEEN ELECTIVE
AND NONELECTIVE VOCAL CHARACTERISTICS

The significance of characteristics both elective (intentional and voluntary) and nonelective (involuntary, resulting from genetic or socioeconomic background or an uncontrollable response to other circumstances) was discussed in chapter 2, "Discovery Patterns." What's tricky about vocal patterns is that many typically involuntary vocal characteristics, such as a high-pitched or raspy voice, can be due to some temporary medical or emotional condition over which a person has no real control, or can even be entirely intentional. When someone is purposely altering his or her voice, he is often trying to manipulate the listener. Sometimes you have to listen carefully to the content and consider the circumstances to determine whether a vocal trait is intentional or not.

I recently had a chance to witness a master of voice manipulation during a meeting with two new clients, whom I'll call Steve and Sarah. Both were intelligent, well-educated, and articulate. Steve was a successful businessman, while Sarah had been a homemaker and mother to their now adult children for most of her life. Outwardly, Steve was aggressive and domineering. Sarah was passive and submissive, with a high pitch, little-girlish voice and a gentle manner.

I concluded that Sarah had learned to manipulate situations with her voice rather than communicate her feelings and ideas with words. When she had something negative to say about someone, she'd adopt a victim tone, complete with slightly lowered voice, hesitant speech, and a whine, to accentuate her main points. The message she sent was "This bad, mean person is hurting me by his behavior. Help me." She used a different vocal technique when she had an idea to contribute. In their household, Steve was apparently the one who officially had all the worthwhile ideas, so when Sarah had a serious thought she'd switch to a singsong. Translation: "I have an idea to express but I know that isn't my role, so I'm going to pretend I don't feel strongly about it and am just tossing it out for someone smarter to evaluate." All her vocal traits were emphasized by a high, breathy, Marilyn Monroe–style delivery.

Sarah must have learned that Steve would be more responsive to her needs if she played the helpless little girl and let him come to her rescue. The high-pitched tone was probably elective, but she had been using it for so long that it was second nature. I couldn't help but wonder what she sounded like when she became really angry.

Nonelective, involuntary traits also should be evaluated carefully. How a person exploits them—or compensates for them—may be very telling. For instance, a man with an unusually high or "feminine" voice may adopt a coarse manner of speaking to come across as more masculine. Someone who stutters may speak very slowly to overcome that trait and ease his self-consciousness. A woman with an exceptionally beautiful speaking voice may be more outgoing than a woman whose voice is harsh and unpleasant. Someone with a thick foreign accent may become unusually quiet in a room full of strangers. None of these people is being intentionally manipulative. Rather, they're reacting to an involuntary condition in the way that serves them best.

As you read about the various vocal characteristics described later in this chapter, and as you apply this information to your life, always ask yourself whether the vocal qualities you hear are elective or nonelective. If they're elective (intentional), there is purposeful communication—and maybe even manipulation—going on. But nonelective (involuntary) traits that are purely physical in nature—a raspy or breathy voice, for example—may not have any relationship to the emotions of the moment.

LOOKING FOR VOCAL PATTERNS, DEVIATIONS, AND EXTREMES

This book has repeatedly emphasized the importance of identifying patterns. Only when a certain characteristic—for example, extravagance—crops up consistently in a number of different areas can you be confident that the person really is extravagant, and from that draw conclusions about how he will probably think or behave. In considering vocal traits, just as in considering any other characteristics, remember that deviations and exaggerations in someone's normal patterns are especially significant.

Deviations in Vocal Traits

We've all seen a normally calm person explode in anger. After he leaves the room, the rest of us glance at one another, grimace, and say something like, "Boy, he must really be mad. I've never seen him like that before." On the other hand, we all know a hothead who flies off the handle at the slightest provocation. When he leaves the room, people glance around, shrug, and say, "There he goes again." Because we're familiar with his normal behavior, we know not to take the outburst too seriously.

You may not be able to familiarize yourself with a person's vocal style in one meeting, but during your first encounter, try to notice her general tone, cadence, and other basic vocal traits. Once you've identified her fundamental vocal pattern, stay alert to any deviations from it. Somebody who is naturally even-tempered, with a calm vocal delivery to match, may express anger by becoming uncharacteristically quiet or breathing heavily, not by raising her voice and speaking more quickly, as many others might. *Everything is relative to the person's normal behavior.*

It's equally important to keep in mind that someone who may seem unusually emotional the first time you meet him may appear very different the following day or week. Don't make snap judgments unless you absolutely have to. Let a pattern develop over at least three or four meetings, longer if possible. That way you'll be able to accurately assess whether the vocal clues you notice reflect a temporary state of mind or a permanent character trait.

In assessing someone's character, determine whether you're seeing an isolated deviation or part of someone's normal pattern. For example, if I was asked to select a jury in a case in which it was very important that the jurors be compassionate and forgiving, I might not give too much weight to a single comment delivered in a somewhat harsh or sarcastic tone by a juror who otherwise appeared compassionate. However, if the same juror consistently maintained that tone, even if it was not extreme on any particular occasion, I'd assume she was sarcastic and critical—not compassionate—and I'd reject her.

Extremes in Vocal Traits

Pay special attention to any exaggerated characteristic. A slight tremor in a person's voice does not indicate nervousness as strongly as a bad stammer. There is a difference between someone who has a rather loud voice and another who sounds as if he's warning ships away from a rocky point. *The significance of a vocal trait is often a matter of degree.*

As I just mentioned, I don't usually give much weight to an isolated comment spiced with a particularly expressive tone—unless the tone and content are extreme. Recently, I was helping pick a jury in a case involving alleged insurance fraud. Jury selection went slowly, and many of the jurors had to wait in the hallway for what must have seemed like ages before they were called in to court to be questioned. A bland-looking middle-aged woman was among the last to be called. As she sat down in the jury box, she slammed her book onto her lap and announced *to the judge* in an angry, frustrated tone, "It's about time. I was falling asleep out there." Her level of irritation, coupled with the disrespectful tone of voice, and the fact that she spoke that way to the judge, left an indelible impression. Even though she quickly composed herself and did not take that tone again during her lengthy examination, that one comment, coupled with her body language, was all it took. I thought she would be quick to judge and uncompassionate. Confident that I'd seen her *real* personality slip out during that instant, I suggested that she be excused.

Extreme vocal characteristics such as these are easy to notice but can be rather difficult to interpret, especially when the speaker isn't someone you know well. The exaggeration may indicate the intensity of his emotions: Is he happy or ecstatic? Is he sad or in the throes of a serious depression? If you notice the extreme trait over several encounters, there's a pattern that may point to a permanent condition. You'll have to evaluate it accordingly.

Extreme vocal characteristics are also meaningful because their "owner" is usually aware of them. Many vocal clues sneak in and out of conversations without the speaker noticing. But when someone's voice is cracking with excitement or sobbing with despair, she usually knows it. This, of course, doesn't mean the tone has been adopted intentionally. Expressions of extreme happiness, sorrow, fear, and anger often can't be repressed. In fact, if the person would prefer not to reveal an emotion, she might well be sorry it has crept out through her voice. Recognizing when an emotion is being expressed against the speaker's will provides the astute people-reader an opportunity to respond appropriately. For instance, if a woman is trying to appear confident in front of her boss but her voice begins to quiver, she'll probably be embarrassed. Recognizing that, her boss may want to make a special effort to put her at ease. Or, if she's usually upbeat but on this occasion her voice is entirely flat and lifeless, she may be sad or depressed. Alert to that, her boss may decide that this isn't a good time to place additional burdens on her.

Regardless of the actual words exchanged, any vocal characteristic that is extreme compared with the speaker's usual manner should give you pause. Often people consciously choose to broadcast their feelings through their tone of voice, like the woman mentioned earlier in this chapter who sought permission to ask for sympathy. And often people who are crying out for help do so not with words but with tone of voice. This is particularly true when someone is depressed, hurt, or angry. She may insist that she is "just fine," but her tone will reveal that all is not well. By being sensitive to these subtle vocal clues, you will not only be able to understand people in a way that will help you achieve your goals, you will also be in a better position to offer your support to those in need.

COMPARE THE VOICE WITH THE PERSON'S BODY LANGUAGE AND WORDS

Feelings are seldom revealed by tone of voice alone. However, by comparing someone's tone of voice with both body language and words, you can usually determine his or her true emotions.

When a person's tone of voice, words, and body language are in sync—when they all fit a consistent pattern—it's fairly easy to interpret how he's feeling and predict how he'll react to various situations. When the tone of voice and body language are at odds with each other or with the person's words, that's another matter. Then you must consider which elements form a more consistent pattern, and draw your conclusions appropriately.

How body language, tone, and words can be interpreted together was important in a case I worked on recently. During jury selection, the lead attorney's wife had a miscarriage. The attorney asked the judge for a one-day continuance so he could be by his wife's side. The judge refused because the delay would have inconvenienced the many prospective jurors who were still under consideration. The lawyer had to leave jury selection in the hands of his associate and me while he tended to his family's personal crisis. In his absence, the judge asked us to pass on his condolences to the attorney and his wife.

If all I had to go by was the printed transcript, the words would have suggested the judge's compassionate concern. However, they were spoken in a perfunctory and unemotional way, with neither warmth nor compassion. As he spoke, his face did not change its expression. He continued to look down and shuffle papers on his bench, as if more concerned about the next motion to be heard than the loss of the attorney's unborn child. His tone of voice alone was certainly a powerful clue, and in conjunction with his body language it created the impression that his words were not heartfelt.

Later in the same trial, the judge revealed more of himself through a slightly different combination of words, tone, and body language. A juror asked to be excused from what was sure to be an eight- or ten-week trial, claiming it would be a hardship for him to attend. "I want to know what your hardship is," the judge barked in a sarcastic, aggressive, and almost mean-spirited tone. Again, his words taken alone would not have suggested any particular emotion or state of mind. This time, the judge's tone could best be characterized as angry or hostile. His body language, however, provided the most telling clue to how he was really feeling. His facial expression wasn't angry. On the contrary, it was impassive. Nor did other aspects of his body language reflect anger—he didn't lean forward, gesture, or flush, for example. Here, an analysis of the entire picture—words, tone of voice, and body language—suggested to me that the judge was simply using an angry tone as an intimidation technique to get the juror to confess that there really was no compelling reason to excuse him.

These two exchanges revealed a pattern. The judge was concerned about moving the trial along. He was determined to keep his courtroom efficient and to make sure everyone, attorney and juror alike, participated to his satisfaction. Personal issues took second place. In both instances, the judge's apparent motivations were revealed only when I compared his words, tone of voice, and body language. Once we recognized his characteristics and priorities, we had a basis for predicting how he would respond to various events through the balance of the trial.

The same process can be used by the boss whose employee complains of the flu in a low, halting, pained tone of voice yet walks to his car with the usual spring in his step; by a customer talking with a salesman who speaks confidently, loudly, and unhesitatingly about his product yet immediately stops making eye contact when asked questions about its warranty record; and by a woman whose boyfriend professes his undying and committed love in the most sincere tone while glancing over her shoulder as a good-looking woman walks by.

Unless tone, body language, and words all match, something may be amiss. Take a second look to find out what.

CONSIDER THE ENVIRONMENT

If I notice that someone seems nervous on the witness stand, I take into consideration that the courtroom is a very stressful environment. Of course, *any* environment has some impact on the way a person sounds. A loud voice, for example, may be a meaningful clue to a person's character and state of mind, but only if it is consistently or inappropriately loud. In fact, the significance of almost any vocal trait may be diminished or eliminated entirely in certain environments.

I wouldn't draw the same conclusions about someone who speaks in a loud, booming voice in a library as I would if he were at a crowded party. Nor would I draw the same conclusions from someone's rapid speech if she were warning me about an oncoming car as I would if she were trying to sell me a vacuum cleaner. A person may talk rapidly because she is happy, nervous, excited, or afraid. Knowing which often requires some assessment of the environment. This is particularly true if you're encountering someone for the first time. When people feel comfortable in a given setting, their tone of voice is a fairly good indicator of their mood or personality. If they don't feel comfortable, their tone may reflect little more than their uneasiness.

DECODING VOCAL CLUES

Understanding the messages encoded in vocal traits takes some practice and requires that you pay close attention. More than other traits, tone of voice shifts from second to second, depending on environment and circumstances. If you're not alert, you can miss something critical. While permanent traits such as a loud, booming voice may be fairly straightforward and easy to interpret, other, more transitory characteristics such as pitch, pace of speech, and stammering can be harder to peg. A given tone can sometimes have opposite meanings, like many other traits. Look for patterns, as always, and pay special attention to whether the tone matches or conflicts with the person's body language and words.

There are far too many different vocal traits to discuss them all; these are the most common and most telling:

Loud voice
Soft voice
Rapid speech
Slow speech
Halting speech
Pitch
Intonation and emphasis
Flat, unemotional voice
Pretension/snobbery
Whining
Breathiness
Raspy voice
Mumbling
Accents

Loud Voice

From time to time we all encounter someone with an exceptionally loud voice—a big, booming baritone or a loud, shrill soprano that you just can't miss. That's the idea. People with loud voices usually have acquired them for a reason. The key to evaluating the significance of a loud voice, therefore, is to assess when and how the person uses it and what he is attempting to accomplish by it.

Control A loud voice is often used to control the environment and those in it. Loudness is authoritative and intimidating, so those who are seeking to dominate or control others often cultivate high-decibel voices. In some instances, loudness is coupled with the practice of "speaking over" others, another probable attempt to control, and one that suggests insensitivity and rudeness as well. Excessive domination of the conversation may also reflect egotism and impatience. Most people assume those with loud, booming voices are displaying confidence. That may be the case—but some people shout because they're afraid no one will hear them if they whisper.

Persuasion   Some people have discovered that a loud voice is a terrific tool for persuading others, or at least forcing them into submission. They have learned that if they speak loudly and stridently enough, many people will interpret their tone as confident and fall in line. Even if they think the speaker is dead wrong, they may not want to argue with him. In my profession, I have seen more than my share of blowhards who use volume to intimidate the weak, fool the feeble-minded, or control the insecure or lazy who would just as soon have someone do their thinking for them anyway.

Compensation for a perceived flaw   I have also seen many instances in which volume compensates for other perceived deficiencies, such as small stature or a physical disability.

I was involved in a case where we examined a prospective juror who was a very small, rail-thin middle-aged man. He sat, as rigid as if he were wearing a back brace, throughout the examination of the other jurors, his hands carefully folded and perfectly still on his lap. He looked like a heavily sedated Don Knotts. The first time he answered a question, his response nearly knocked us all over backward. I have seldom heard a louder, more booming voice. It had to have been purposely acquired. I concluded that he compensated for his diminutive stature and rather bookish bearing by developing a voice like a foghorn.

Reaction to hearing loss   This usually occurs among the elderly, in which case the problem is usually obvious. But be alert to hearing loss among younger people as well.

Inebriation   Drunk people sometimes get loud, but their volume won't be the only sign of intoxication. If you're meeting someone for the first time at a hard-drinking Christmas bash, withhold judgment about his or her loud voice until you meet again under calmer circumstances.

When you're evaluating into which category the loud-voiced person falls, keep these questions in mind:

- Is the voice appropriate for the occasion?

- Is the loudness constant, or does it vary according to the number of people in the group?
- Is the voice used aggressively, to control, intimidate, or speak over others?

Generally speaking, I have found that people who have a loud, dominant voice but use it courteously and appropriately are confident. Those who abuse others with their loud voice, like a bully with a big stick, are often insecure.

Soft Voice

A soft voice can be used to manipulate others, or it can indicate a person who himself is easily swayed. While a low tone may initially suggest that the speaker lacks confidence and assertiveness, don't be fooled. A soft voice may well reflect calm self-assurance: the speaker feels no need to dominate a conversation. There also may be an element of arrogance: "If you want to hear what I have to say, you'll just have to listen more closely."

When evaluating the significance of someone's muted tone, you'll first need to determine whether he or she always has a soft voice or whether it has dropped on this particular occasion. If the latter is the case, ask what has occurred that may explain the decrease in volume.

- Has there been a confrontation, from which the person is withdrawing?
- Is the person in an uncomfortable situation in which he feels nervous or intimidated?
- Do you see indications of grief or sorrow?
- Is there some sign that the speaker is lying, and acting on the natural preference for lying quietly if she must lie at all?
- Is the speaker attempting to force someone else to come within earshot? This is a power play.
- Is the speaker intentionally lowering her voice to limit who can hear it?
- Does the speaker seem tired?
- Could the soft tone be the result of illness?

You will almost always find an explanation if you look for one when low volume is not characteristic of the speaker's normal tone. The speaker's demeanor will probably provide confirmation if you look carefully for the signs of grief, nervousness, embarrassment, and other emotional states discussed in chapter 3 and Appendix B.

When you evaluate somebody with a consistently soft voice, focus on the appropriateness of whatever modulations do exist. Does the person make an effort to speak louder when it is clear some of those present may not be able to hear him? If not, he may be unobservant, inconsiderate, or arrogant. If the volume is low but he makes good eye contact and his body language is relaxed, the soft voice has little significance. If, on the other hand, the consistently low volume is combined with body language that reflects discomfort, such as lack of eye contact, turning the body or face away, or fidgeting, I would "read" the voice as a symptom of discomfort and lack of confidence.

Two attorneys with whom I've worked illustrate how differently a soft voice can be perceived. The women are about the same age and have the same number of years' experience. Both are bright and articulate. Both are also extremely soft-spoken. One, however, exudes confidence and control, while the other does not.

The confident one sits very still in her chair as she speaks with me. Her hands are usually relaxed on the desk in front of her unless she is writing notes, which she does only when appropriate. We always have excellent eye contact. Her voice, while quiet, has no hesitation and incorporates appropriate emphasis, although subtly.

The other attorney, while equally intelligent and insightful, often speaks haltingly and uneasily. There appears to be no pattern to the emphasis she places on various words, which gives me the impression that she stresses one word or concept over another because of anxiety rather than as a conscious choice. The low volume and other vocal traits are mirrored by her body language, which includes frequently downcast eyes, nervous fiddling with her pen or paper, and a hunched-over body posture. All of these point to a lack of confidence, the opposite of the impression given by the other soft-spoken attorney.

Rapid Speech

We've all heard the phrase "fast-talking salesman." It usually refers to somebody who is not only speaking quickly but lying quickly. Rapid speech does sometimes indicate untruthfulness, but that's only one of several possibilities.

There's a difference between fast-talking all the time and fast-talking in reaction to specific situations. People who always speak quickly may have grown up in households where they had to talk fast to get a word in edgewise. Other fast-talkers are type A personalities, tightly wound from the get-go. Regardless of the cause, I have found that consistently fast-talkers are often as quick to assess and judge a situation as they are to express themselves. As a result, they are often not cautious, but impulsive and judgmental. I usually don't like them to sit as jurors when I'm working with the defense in a criminal case because they tend to jump to conclusions quickly rather than carefully evaluate the evidence.

I've also found that many fast-talkers are compensating for a basic insecurity. These fast-talkers will show signs of poor self-esteem, such as a generally nervous personality and inappropriate efforts to gain attention.

The occasional trip into the verbal fast lane by someone who usually speaks at a normal pace is typically caused by one of the following:

Nervousness
Impatience
Anxiety
Insecurity
Excitement
Fear
Drugs or alcohol
Anger
Desire to persuade
Being caught in a lie

Most people have observed someone suffer the unpleasantness of being caught in a lie. Someone's chatting along at normal speed, then realizes there's an inconsistency in her tale. Suddenly she switches to fast-forward as she tries to explain herself. The more she lies, the faster the words spring from her lips. I saw a prime example of this a few years ago, in the form of a reluctant juror.

This man desperately wanted to be excused from jury duty, so he told the judge his wife was sick and he had to take her to the doctor. When the judge suggested scheduling a late-afternoon appointment, the juror, talking faster and faster, explained that he actually had to take his wife to the doctor *a lot,* and he didn't think he'd be able to get late-afternoon appointments. When the judge suggested he call the doctor, find out, and report back to the court that afternoon, the juror added that he also had to take his dog to the vet (I'm not kidding). Finally, he told the judge his roof needed to be repaired. Half of us in the courtroom could not restrain at least a chuckle, if not outright laughter, as the excuses mounted and his voice and body movements sped up.

I'm always alert to the possibility that a fast-talker is trying to obscure the truth in a barrage of words—but it's much more likely that he's just nervous and insecure, and speaks quickly out of anxiety, or a desire to mask his lack of confidence or to make his point. We recognize this in our kids: childhood excitement often gets translated into fast speech. Usually, it's not much different with adults.

Slow Speech

People who speak slowly tend to fall into one of two categories: those who sound and appear comfortable and relaxed; and those whose slow speech is accompanied by other physical and vocal clues suggesting discomfort such as poor eye contact and frequent shifting of their body. By determining which camp the person belongs in, I can make an educated guess about the causes of the slow speech.

Some people who consistently speak slowly have a physical or mental disability. In the latter case, the slow speech will be coupled with an inability to express ideas. Physical ailments are also fairly obvious once you've spoken with someone for a few minutes. People who are unfamiliar with the language may also speak slowly, as might those who are self-conscious about their level of education. And there are common regional variations in the speed of speech—for example, Southerners typically speak more slowly than people from New York City.

Teachers, the clergy, and others who frequently speak to large groups sometimes adopt slow speech to be sure their audience gets their drift. The technique then sometimes bleeds into everyday conversation. Occasionally, slow speakers are being condescending, in which case they'll usually adopt a noticeably sarcastic tone.

If someone usually speaks at a normal pace, slow speech on a given occasion may mean he is

trying to make a point that is very important to him
anxious
confused
lying
sad or grieving
fatigued
deep in thought
ill
under the influence of drugs or alcohol
not very intelligent

To decide which, consider the speaker's body language and the content of his speech.

Halting Speech

Halting, hesitant, or broken speech is different from slow speech. A stop-and-start pattern is usually caused by insecurity, nervousness, or confusion. On occasion, it may reflect untruthfulness, as when someone struggles to come up with an excuse. But it can also point in the opposite direction: the speaker wants to be very accurate and is searching for just the right words. Or she may pause to give you an opportunity to interject something.

To determine whether someone's halting speech signifies insecurity, nervousness, confusion, untruthfulness, or an attempt at precision, look at the entire pattern of his speech, words, and body language. People have to be pretty uptight about what they're saying for the tension to cause broken and halting speech. Other signs will nearly always appear, too. Someone who's fibbing will lose eye contact, inadvertently cover his mouth or other parts of his face, or fall prey to one of the other body-language tip-offs we discussed in chapter 3. A nervous person won't just speak haltingly. She'll also shift in her chair, tap her fingers, and so forth.

Assuming the speaker isn't lying or nervous, you can often chalk up halting or broken speech to an honest struggle to articulate thoughts. A woman I've worked with is an excellent example. She's an extremely bright and very precise attorney, but has a sometimes disconcerting habit—she'll stop mid-sentence, pause, and then continue again, sometimes in a slightly different direction. She shows no signs of nervousness, dishonesty, evasiveness, or insecurity. Rather, her body language reflects thoughtfulness and focus. Her gaze is fixed, and the volume of her speech doesn't vary significantly. She is clearly concentrating on what she's saying, and is trying to be precise.

You should distinguish such an attempt at precision from scatter-brained chatter—when someone appears to lose his train of thought, heads off in another direction, seems to bounce off an invisible wall, and careens back and forth, with his mouth obviously preceding his brain by several seconds. Halting, hesitant, broken speech coupled with disjointed content indicates confusion or a lack of concentration and focus. It can also mean the person wants attention even if he has to ramble on to get it.

When halting speech dissolves into actual stuttering or stammering, it's usually because of nervousness. Of course, there are also people who stutter because of a physical condition. Notice whether the stuttering is consistent over several conversations, or whether the speaker stutters or stammers only when he or she seems nervous or tongue-tied. The chronic stutterer is not necessarily chronically nervous. Severe stuttering is a vocal condition that's not yet fully understood.

Pitch

People's voices range from the calm and soothing to the shrill and irritating. Vocal pitch is largely nonelective: if you were born with Fran Drescher's fingernails-on-a-chalkboard voice, you pretty much have to live with it—or develop a routine and head for Hollywood. But within the range that is normal for each of us, we raise and lower our pitch for a few standard reasons.

Most people's voices will rise in pitch when they're especially scared, joyful, agitated, excited, and so on. If the feeling is intense enough, their voice will crack. In these cases, the cause is usually clear from accompanying body language, words, and actions.

Some people noticeably lower their voice from its normal range when they're trying to seduce someone. They tend to come across like the late-night deejay on a local jazz station or the sultry temptress in a 1940s detective flick. Pitch may also drop when someone is sad, depressed, or fatigued. Once again, the meaning is hard to miss if you pay attention to all the available clues.

Intonation and Emphasis

In many languages, words take on completely different meanings depending on which syllable or word is stressed. While English doesn't rely as heavily on intonation and emphasis as some languages, we all communicate different emotions and meanings by altering our speech pattern. Pay attention to this, and you'll catch important clues.

We've all asked someone whether he or she would like to go somewhere with us, and been told in response, "I'd really love to go." Sometimes as we heard the words we knew immediately that our invitation had been accepted. On other occasions, as the person completed the phrase "I'd really love to go," we knew the next word out of his or her mouth would be "but."

If you listen carefully to intonation, pauses, and emphasis, you can recognize "incomplete" sentences. Even if you can't make an educated guess about what words might complete the thought, at least you'll be able to detect ambiguities and follow up with appropriate questions.

Not surprisingly, vocal emphasis is usually also accompanied by physical emphasis. While stressing a word, the speaker may lean forward, nod, or gesture. As a result, even subtle changes in intonation or emphasis can be easier to recognize if you listen for them while watching for changes in body language.

Flat, Unemotional Voice

Remember the judge who offered condolences to the attorney whose wife had just suffered a miscarriage? The judge's apparent insincerity was revealed not by his words but by his flat, unemotional tone of voice. A flat voice can also tip you off to boredom, anger, resentment, frustration, depression, and some physical ailments.

If you tell a friend you just received a big promotion, you expect her response to reflect some level of excitement and happiness for you. There should be some bounce in her voice. Perhaps she'll offer a warm and sincere "Congratulations." You don't expect a flat, quick "That's nice." When you get an unexpectedly unemotional response, you should go on the alert. Look first to body language to help you determine whether the person is distracted, bored, or depressed. Or is the flat voice an attempt to camouflage more intense feelings, such as jealousy or resentment? Those, too, will probably leak out in her body language. Depending on what you learn, you can proceed accordingly, either pursue the matter then and there or file away the response for later reflection.

Pretension/Snobbery

As a kid, I watched *Gilligan's Island*. The "millionaire and his wife" spoke in an overstated, pretentious way, which my sisters and I loved to mimic. Thirty years later, I hear my young son ask, "Pardon me, do you have any Grey Poupon?" in that same tone. Pretension and snobbery aren't usually revealed so dramatically in someone's voice, though to my amazement I do occasionally meet someone who has a bit of Mr. Howell in his vocal delivery.

If I admit that I am unfamiliar with a particular current event, my comment may be met with the response "Oh, really," said in a tone suggesting surprise that anyone could be so ill-informed. Or someone may describe their new house or car in a voice more suited to the narrator of *Lifestyles of the Rich and Famous*. It's difficult to capture a snobbish tone in writing, but (to paraphrase what U.S. Supreme Court Justice Potter Stewart said of pornography) "You know it when you see it." The question is, what does it signify?

Many people adopt a snobbish tone or other pretentious mannerisms to present an image of success, sophistication, intelligence, wealth, or upper-class values. Those characteristics may not be at the core of their personalities. Instead, the apparent snob may just be insecure and seeking approval and recognition.

Many other snobs really, truly believe they *are* better, more intelligent, and more worth listening to than the rest of us. They're not at all insecure. They're confident. And try as you might, you will not be able to persuade the snob to respect "lesser" folk or their ideas or lifestyles. Such a hard-core snob usually comes from a family that's upper-class or thinks it is. Since socioeconomic background is a key predictor of how people think and behave, don't assume you'll ever change the way a true snob sees the world. That view usually has been set in concrete.

Whining

Whining is not always a singsong lament coupled with a screwed-up face and hand-wringing. It can be much more subtle. But whether it's underplayed or obvious, whining is a technique used to manipulate others without forceful words. It's often an effort by someone to get what he wants without asking for it outright. A sentence whined is a sentence that says, "I really feel strongly about this, and I am going to moan and complain until you do what I want."

Over the years I have watched thousands of mock jurors deliberate. I have seen my fair share of whiners among these men and women. They complain there's not enough ice for the Coke, but they don't go get more themselves. They whine that the lawyer's presentations were confusing, but they seldom exert the effort to sort through the evidence. If their views are rejected by the majority, they withdraw and pout.

Whiners are usually followers—on juries as in life outside the courthouse. They don't have the courage or confidence to lead. They want others to take care of them. They feel helpless and out of control. If you want to know whether someone is truly a whiner, try to get a sense of her human environment—in other words, meet a few of her friends. How does she behave with them? How manipulative is she? If she's married, pay particular attention to her interaction with her husband. Whiners whine because it works for them. And whining is a difficult trait to overcome, even if the whiner wants to change. The whiner's behavior toward others will give you a preview of what your relationship with her might be like. It's up to you to decide whether you feel up to the challenge.

Breathiness

"Happy Birthday, Mr. President," Marilyn Monroe cooed in her tribute to JFK, a classic example of breathy seductiveness. Voluntary breathiness can usually be chalked up to seduction. Involuntary breathiness is caused by other equally important emotional states or by illness or fatigue.

Since we normally don't hear significant audible breathing, whenever I do, I wonder why. Is it physical or emotional? People afflicted with emphysema, other lung diseases, or any number of debilitating illnesses may have difficulty breathing, in which case the breathiness is only an indication of the illness.

If I can rule out illness (by looking at body language or asking tactfully about the person's health), I consider the other conditions that commonly cause breathiness:

anger
sexual interest
excitement
frustration
exercise or fatigue
disbelief
nervousness
stress

During trials, I often detect changes in the breathing patterns of jurors, witnesses, and even lawyers. Given the circumstances, it's usually fairly easy to eliminate several possible causes, such as sexual interest or exercise. Most frequently, audible breathing in court is the result of frustration, surprise, disbelief, or nervousness. Even the most experienced trial lawyers will sometimes get nervous and begin inhaling and exhaling in an unusual manner. By the time the trial actually starts I've usually seen and heard them speak many times, so I'll pick up those subtle changes instantly. Normally people reveal such nervousness not just by deeper or less rhythmic breaths, but also by body motions like drinking water or making exaggerated hand movements. I also listen carefully for the quick, audible bursts of air exhaled by jurors (and sometimes the judge, lawyers, or witnesses) as signs of surprise, disbelief, or exasperation. Again, these vocal clues are usually accompanied by shakes of the head or other visual signs. The key is to notice the characteristic, identify its various possible causes, and then see which of these causes matches the person's body language, behavior, and words.

The Raspy Voice

A raspy voice is often a sign that the speaker smokes, but it can also be caused by a cold or bronchitis, or by a permanent physical condition. It also could be that the speaker has recently stressed his voice in some way. Ask about it. If he frequently sings, or gives speeches that leave his voice tired and rough, you have a good starting point for a conversation that could reveal a lot about him. Often people's voices get raspy from yelling at sporting events or elsewhere. Again, ask: Was he cheering on his son at peewee football, or shouting encouragement to the hometown baseball team? If he yelled so much he made himself hoarse, I know he's an avid fan, and I suspect he may be fairly aggressive and controlling. (On some level, he may believe that if he yells loud enough he can influence the outcome of the game.) If nothing else, I'm confident that he's outgoing and excitable. Few quiet, shy, reserved people will yell until their voices give out.

Mumbling

Some mumblers speak so softly they're inaudible. Others habitually cover their mouths with their hands when they talk. Still others avert their heads or look down. Some mumblers will speak more clearly when asked to, but others seem virtually incapable of clear speech, even though there is no physical explanation for the phenomenon.

The mumbler who responds to a request to speak more clearly may have been distracted, tired, chewing, under the influence of drugs or alcohol, or otherwise straying momentarily from a normal pattern of clear speech. The chronic mumbler (one who doesn't respond to the request to speak clearly, at least not for more than a few minutes at a stretch) often reveals

lack of confidence
insecurity
anxiety
an inability to articulate thoughts
self-consciousness
preoccupation
fatigue
illness

Mumblers seldom demonstrate significant leadership ability or even any desire for such control. Often mumblers also appear depressed or sad. I have seen very few animated, upbeat, happy mumblers. And this is usually reflected in their body language: limp, passive motions, a weak handshake, and a tired demeanor.

Accents

We live in an increasingly diverse world. I hear the accents of at least six different nationalities and as many regions of the United States on any given day. A person's accent can provide you with valuable clues about how he might think or act.

If I meet a man who speaks with a heavy foreign accent, I watch to see if he has any language limitations that might affect his speech or behavior. I'm also alert to the possibility that he may have an unusual cultural background, which may have an impact on his vocal mannerisms. For example, some cultures are more verbally expressive and uninhibited than others.

Someone who does not feel comfortable with the language he's speaking may also be self-conscious about his lack of fluency or preoccupied with his search for the right words. He may feel frustrated or nervous because of this difficulty. If I didn't consider his accent, and the possibility that he may communicate very differently in his native tongue, I could misread his personality completely. I might wrongly assume he is passive, shy, or nervous; in fact, he may be very aggressive and confident when language doesn't present a barrier to communication.

To a lesser degree, the same applies to those from different areas within the United States. General attitudes about appropriate manners, social decorum, and self-expression vary from region to region. In large metropolitan areas, such as New York City, people generally learn to speak faster, louder, and more aggressively than they do in small towns in the South or Midwest. There, the New Yorker's speech patterns might be considered rude. Unless you are very familiar with the region or country reflected in someone's accent, you won't know how her particular cultural background may affect her vocal mannerisms. So ask her about where she's from. It's a great way to break the ice and learn more about her.

KEY POINTS

Learn to hear between the lines: Two dialogues take place in every conversation. One uses words, the other relies on conscious or subconscious vocalization techniques. Sometimes the two match; often they don't. When in conflict, vocal variations are usually a more reliable indication of the message someone is really sending than the words he uses.

Listen for emotional hide-and-seek: When we're feeling emotions or thinking thoughts that we don't want to discuss for some reason—embarrassment, insecurity, fear—we often ask others for permission with vocal signals.

To hear the unspoken message:

- Focus on the voice, not the words, in short spurts from time to time during a conversation.
- Consider whether the vocal characteristics are voluntary (often manipulative) or involuntary (usually reflecting true emotion).
- Look for patterns, extremes, and deviations from the person's normal voice.
- Compare voice to body language and words.
- Consider the context and environment in which the words are spoken.

CHAPTER 6

Learning to Ask the Right
Questions—and Listen
to the Answers

I'm sitting in a restaurant, and I see a couple walk in. They ask to be seated in a corner booth, where I watch them as I finish my meal. It's clear they're just getting to know each other, probably on their first date.

They have come to a quiet restaurant, and their attention is focused on each other. I can see mild nods and gestures of understanding and interest, and what seems to be a lively exchange of information. Each listens intently as the other talks, rarely interrupting. While I can't overhear their conversation, their body language reflects enthusiasm, empathy, and curiosity. They sincerely want to learn, to understand, and to be understood.

Fast-forward a year. I'm in the same restaurant and the same couple walks in. This time they don't bother to ask for the quiet corner booth. Instead, they accept a table near the kitchen. As they hunker down with their menus, they barely bother to speak. After the waiter takes their order they sit in silence for a while, as each gazes absently about the restaurant. They are so close to me that when they finally begin speaking I can hear every word. As the woman talks about her day at the office, her boyfriend sighs, stares across the room, then changes the subject to his plans for the weekend. She greets that topic with a sarcastic remark about the amount of time he spends on his mountain bike. He responds with a jealous and accusatory comment about her having lunch with an old boyfriend earlier in the week. They're still pursuing that topic with gusto when I leave the restaurant, glad to have escaped.

What happened? They quit talking. They quit listening. Once they began to feel they knew each other, the lines of communication corroded. They no longer asked meaningful questions and quit listening with an open mind to the answers. Instead they accused, denied, and bickered.

Each of us has the ability to ask meaningful questions and really listen to the answers—when we want to. The problem is, we get busy, or lazy, or too familiar, and we quit trying. Think back to the last time you met someone you were interested in getting to know, either as a friend, an employee, or a lover. Remember how you asked questions and truly listened to the answers during your first few conversations? Do you still listen as intently, now that you know the person better? Chances are, you don't. And while we can't expect to maintain the intense interest we feel when we first get to know someone, many people backslide to an astonishing degree.

You'll never truly understand people unless you know how to ask good questions and listen to the answers. Without understanding them, you won't be able to predict their behavior or know how to meet their needs or whether they'll meet yours. This chapter will explain how to ask questions that matter, and offer some advice about creating the best possible environment for a productive conversation. It'll also show you how to phrase follow-up questions if you don't get the information you need the first time out. Perhaps most important, you'll learn the secrets of becoming a good listener. Unless you learn to hear, *really hear,* a person's replies, all your questioning may be a complete waste of time.

THE DOS AND DON'TS OF GOOD LISTENING

Learning to listen is more difficult than learning to ask good questions. I'm reminded of this constantly in court as I watch inexperienced lawyers question witnesses. Intent on sticking to a carefully constructed line of questioning, many of them will overlook an evasive answer or neglect to pursue important clues that a witness drops. If I taught law, I'd insist that my students learn how to listen long before they started drafting questions. Listening is critical, but because it is seemingly passive, it's frequently overlooked. It may sound like we're putting the cart before the horse, but before we cover the ins and outs of asking good questions, here's a crash course on the listening skills I've developed from years of close observation.

As you read through the following pages, consider how well you listened to another person the last time you were at a party, in the lunchroom, at an employee performance review, or having dinner with friends. If you're like most people, you'll see lots of room for improvement in several of the areas discussed. Don't worry—the wonderful thing about the process of reading people, including learning to listen to them, is that no matter how badly you've botched it in the past, you'll always have a fresh opportunity tomorrow.

First and Foremost, Don't Interrupt

Adults often listen to young children much more carefully than to other adults. We expect children to have trouble expressing themselves, so we give them the time they need; we hear them out. What's more, we really try to understand how they're feeling, not just what they're thinking. When we interrupt, it's usually to help the youngster express himself, not to change the subject or control the direction of the conversation. We tend to show the same courtesy and interest to the elderly and to those who suffer from a disability or language barrier. Why not listen to everyone that way?

The first rule of good listening is, don't interrupt. It's impossible to listen well when you're talking or planning what to say next. Even when someone is venting, keep quiet and let him get it off his chest—you might learn a lot. You can always go back later to correct, challenge, or dispute him—or, who knows, maybe even agree with him. Besides, he's more likely to listen to your point of view after he's let off some steam.

If someone's rambling, stop and listen for a while, unless you have a fire to put out. I know it can be tempting to cut her off, but what somebody rambles on about can tell you what's important to her, or at least what's on her mind at the moment, and may give you insight into her thought process or the associations she makes between one event and another.

When we interrupt someone, we derail him, even if only briefly. By the time he gets back on track and moving forward again, the spontaneity and rhythm of the conversation may be lost for good. At least half of my gray hairs come from watching this process in court. A lawyer has just gotten a prospective juror relaxed and chatting freely. I'm feverishly typing notes into my laptop and can see that the juror is just about to really open up when, out of the blue, the lawyer cuts in to ask a long, convoluted question on a completely different topic. It's like the end of a dream sequence in a bad movie: I'm snapped back to reality. The juror stops in mid-sentence, her mouth hanging open, while the lawyer finishes his question. The mood is broken. I start looking for things to throw.

Such interruptions occur regularly in our everyday conversations. There are many ways to break the flow besides a poorly timed question. The most deadly is what I call "the goldfish gulp." Just as fish come to the surface of a dirty pond as if to inhale large gulps of air, so the would-be interrupter stares at you, mouth opening to take a deep breath, as he prepares to plunge headlong into the middle of your sentence. Completely distracted, you stop talking. Why not? There's no sense talking when the other person has clearly stopped listening.

Then there are those who interrupt with sudden movements or gestures, by looking elsewhere, or even by getting up and moving away. And there are those who start taking notes feverishly. Even if their intentions are good, note-takers always make me want to stop talking until they stop writing and are ready to listen again.

Any distraction is a potential interruption, and interruptions are fatal to meaningful conversation. Learn to pay attention, and wait your turn. Think of yourself as a good referee, whose job is to keep the game moving but not to control it.

Be Empathetic: Don't Condemn, Argue, or Patronize

Don't you hate it when you confess that you don't know who the mayor of Chicago is and your companion bleats out, "You're kidding! I thought everyone knew that." If you want to make someone stop confiding in you, just be judgmental, argumentative, or patronizing. If she doesn't quit talking to you altogether, whatever she does say will be distorted by her desire to avoid your biting response. "Don't be so hard on yourself; we all make mistakes" will do a lot more for good conversation than "I can't believe you did something so stupid." "I'm sorry to hear you were laid off. Are you okay?" is much more likely to lead to meaningful dialogue than "I told you you'd get fired if you didn't quit calling in sick so much."

People who feel compelled to point out every misstatement or mispronounced word are usually insecure themselves. Belittling another may give them a temporary thrill or feeling of superiority, but it sabotages the lines of communication. *To encourage candid conversation, resist the urge to correct, criticize, or gloat.* When you really can't, in good conscience, support someone's behavior, you'll have to honestly (and tactfully) express your feelings, but those cases are relatively rare. The rest of the time, follow Mom's advice: "If you can't say something nice, don't say anything at all." This will make you the type of listener other people feel they can trust and talk to.

Stay Close, but Don't Be a Space Invader

People feel most comfortable talking to someone who is within a few feet of them. Experienced trial lawyers recognize this and, if the judge will allow, try to position themselves as close as possible to the jurors to whom they are speaking. However, they carefully avoid invading the jurors' personal space.

In most cultures personal space generally extends to about the distance of your outstretched arms. As you become closer to someone, the personal space you both want will become more flexible. Under normal circumstances, however, any time you are within arm's length of a stranger you risk making her uncomfortable. If you don't believe me, next time you get into an elevator with a stranger, stand right next to her and watch her reaction. Touching is also a risky proposition. Unless you know a person well, touching her, even in a supportive way, might make her uncomfortable and distract her from what she's saying.

Using the arm's-length distance as a guide, move in or out as seems appropriate depending on your degree of intimacy with someone. To some extent, you'll be able to judge her comfort by her body language. As you get too close she'll withdraw or grow tense. She may cross her arms or turn at an angle away from you. If you withdraw too far out of her contact zone, she may start looking around the room as if she's preparing to leave, or simply stop talking.

Be Involved, Not Intense

When we speak, particularly about something important to us, we want relatively constant affirmation that the person to whom we're speaking is paying attention. A subtle nod or an occasional "I understand" or "Right" is all it takes. We're so accustomed to hearing these subtle acknowledgments that they don't interrupt or distract us. Rather, they encourage the speaker to continue. Total quiet can be very disconcerting.

I used to work with a consultant who believed the best way to get people to talk was to say nothing, taking advantage of the fact that people hate awkward silences and automatically try to fill them. This may work for a while, but at some point the other person will become too uncomfortable or get tired of pulling the laboring oar. He won't want to talk to you anymore, and he'll think you're rude, uncaring, socially inept, or just dull.

Too much intensity, however, can be just as distracting as too little involvement. A fixed, unblinking gaze seems uninviting or even threatening. While eye contact is a wonderful tool for developing intimacy and trust, it can be overdone. The same can be said of the intent look of concern and compassion some people adopt whether you're telling them about a traumatic childhood experience or what you had for dinner last night. Inappropriate, overplayed compassion or intensity seems phony and often turns people off.

Be Aware of Your Body Language

The angle of your body or the look on your face can signal that you're about to interrupt, delivering the death blow to a good conversation. Similarly, if someone sees you grimacing, frowning, or shaking your head in disbelief midway through a story, he's likely to stop, or at least change direction.

But you can also encourage a particular line of conversation with positive body language—nodding slightly, leaning forward attentively, maintaining eye contact, and smiling. This sort of positive reinforcement comes pretty naturally to most people. The next time you're really enjoying a conversation, take note of your body language and expressions. Chances are you will realize that your physical reactions are encouraging the other person to perk up and warm to her story.

Take care, however: even positive reinforcement can be overdone. Because we all crave approval, nonverbal encouragement is a powerful force. If you don't use it prudently, the person with whom you're speaking may get carried away and overstate her true feelings or opinions just to keep getting your approval. I've seen this happen many times during jury selection. For example, in a death penalty case, a juror who is at first ambivalent about capital punishment will, after active reinforcement by the prosecutor, end up practically begging to pull the switch herself. Then the defense lawyer stands up and starts questioning her. Now the juror gets positive "strokes" every time she expresses reservations about capital punishment. In most cases, she ends up back where she started—uncertain. I know from experience that the juror's original statements probably reflected her true beliefs, and she was just trying to please everyone. If you want reliable answers, don't manipulate someone, intentionally or unintentionally, into saying what she doesn't really believe by broadcasting "Good answer!" or "Bad answer!" with your body language.

Talk About Yourself, but Don't Get Too Familiar Too Fast

Good conversation is a two-way street. Even if you ask wonderfully penetrating and thought-provoking questions, you usually won't get far unless you also reveal something of yourself. Previous chapters have stressed how important it is to engage other people and establish a rapport with them. *Disclosing something of yourself is essential if you want to keep other people speaking candidly so you'll have something worthwhile to listen to.*

Johnnie Cochran's jury selection in the O. J. Simpson criminal trial was the best I have ever witnessed. Whatever their opinion of Mr. Cochran or the case, everyone in the courtroom had to appreciate his mastery of the art of self-disclosure. It was as if he were sitting down for a cup of coffee in the living room of each juror. He laughed. He smiled. They laughed and smiled back. He struck a perfect balance, telling the jury something about himself without revealing too much. That balance is key to the art of self-disclosure.

Pick your revelations carefully, and time them just right. If you're uncertain about how much to reveal, it's usually better to err on the side of revealing less—you can always close the gap as the relationship matures. But if you reveal too much too soon, you may scare your new friend away forever.

Consider the Context

Many people are not particularly precise with the words they choose. Lawyers love to hang on every word a witness says, combing through depositions and trial transcripts looking for inconsistencies. "Aha! On page 412 she said it was a 'warm' afternoon, but on page 723, she said it was 'hot.' " Or, "Oh, I've got him. On page 114 he testified that he went straight home from work, but on page 212, he said he stopped off at the gas station." Well, the first witness probably drew no distinction between "warm" and "hot," and the second one probably did go "straight home" from work: the gas station was on the way.

To truly understand someone's words, you have to view them in the broadest context. That includes much more than where the words fall within a sentence. It may also include when, where, why, and to whom they were spoken. Consider, too, what emotions may have been at work. There is nothing more potentially misleading than to take words spoken in one context and transplant them into a different context as if they were simply interchangeable parts.

Almost every married couple will have disagreements. Sometimes, angry and even hateful words are exchanged. A heated argument spawned by anger, frustration, hurt, fear, or other powerful emotions can easily result in overstatements like "I hate you" and "I can't believe I ever married you." To treat such statements as if they had been spoken calmly and after deep thought and reflection may lead you to incorrect conclusions—unless, of course, they are consistent with a pattern of similar statements.

As a good listener, you are wise to be on the alert for inconsistencies that may creep into a conversation, but never forget that in real life people are rarely 100 percent accurate. *Every slip of the tongue is not Freudian, every emotional outburst doesn't reflect a person's true innermost feelings, and every inconsistency is not a willful lie. Don't view them as such.*

Listen with All Your Senses

As chapter 1, "Reading Readiness," mentioned, telephones, e-mail, and answering machines have reduced our opportunities to speak to others in person. And that's a significant loss, since the ideal conversation takes place face to face. To be a good listener, you need to be able to pick up all the available clues, with all of your senses.

In person, you'll hear nuances in someone's voice that may not carry over the telephone line. You'll be able to see the emotion in his face and the tension or relaxation in his body. When you're speaking with a more intimate friend, you can reach out and take his hand or give him a pat on the back, which may encourage him to open up even more. You may even be able to smell clues, such as alcohol, medication, or sweat. Listening may technically refer only to sound, but true understanding requires that you use all your senses. Don't hamstring yourself by using just one.

CREATING THE ENVIRONMENT
FOR GREAT CONVERSATIONS

Now that you've learned the basics of good listening, you're ready to set the stage for a great conversation. All face-to-face conversations have to occur somewhere—and that somewhere shouldn't be left to chance. Certain environments have a hothouse effect on conversations, making them thrive and blossom. Others kill off discourse as thoroughly as an icy blizzard. You wouldn't ask someone a personal question during the middle of a staff meeting, or discuss her family background over the din of a rock concert.

It's rare that we don't have any choice about a conversation's environment. Even at work, there are options—your office, her office, a meeting room, the lunchroom, or even the lawn out front. The door can be closed or open. Waiting for the appropriate time and place may require a little patience, but if what you have to discuss is important, it's worth it.

What that best environment is depends on what you want to discuss, and with whom. We've all seen 1940s detective movies in which a suspect is given the third degree in a stark cell with a bright light boring into his eyes. The theory is, the more frightened and uncomfortable the suspect is, the quicker he'll "spill." In reality, most suspects are treated more humanely, but making them uncomfortable is still part of interrogation technique.

On the opposite end of the spectrum might be the environment a friend of mine chooses when he takes a woman on a first date. He has a favorite Moroccan restaurant where seven-course meals are eaten slowly in private booths over two and a half or three hours. How better to get to know someone?

Whether you have days to plan the setting or only moments to adjust a few details, keep the following in mind.

Your Turf or Their Turf?

People are most comfortable on their own turf. If you want someone to relax and open up to you, meet in her office, at her home, or wherever else she chooses. Or, if you're already together when the conversation starts—at a party, for example—follow the other person's lead. If she suggests you move out to the patio or to a quiet corner, agree willingly. Don't be afraid to ask, "Where would you like to talk?" Or "Do you feel comfortable here, or would you rather go somewhere else?"

But if *you* want to feel more comfortable and in control of the conversation, steer the other person to your turf. Have you ever noticed that when the boss delivers good news, he usually come to the employee's workstation or office, but when he disciplines someone or terminates her, it's usually in his own office? When delivering bad news, he wants to maintain more control and authority, and he can best do so on his own turf.

There's a trade-off: control for information. It may be harder to read people on your turf because they'll be more guarded, more defensive, and less willing to reveal themselves than they would be on their home territory. You, however, will be more in control. I have found that it is seldom worth sacrificing meaningful dialogue for more control.

Avoid an Audience

In the courtroom, issues about which jurors may be sensitive are often discussed in the judge's chambers with only the judge, the lawyers, and the prospective juror present. It's embarrassing to discuss personal issues in public, so jurors don't tend to be very candid if forced to respond to such questions in open court. In daily life, too, you'll be disappointed if you try to draw personal information from someone in front of an audience.

An audience also tends to bring out the worst in people. When confronted with personal questions while others are standing by, many will respond by bragging, becoming confrontational, getting defensive, or clamming up in embarrassment. You'll never know what they might have revealed about themselves or their beliefs if you had asked the more personal questions in a private setting.

Remove Physical Obstacles Between You and a Good Conversation

Any object between you and the person with whom you're talking may interfere with your conversation. That's why many experienced speakers step away from the podium when they lecture: they don't want anything between them and the group. It's also why many businesspeople choose not to speak with clients, customers, or employees from behind a desk, but instead come around their desk and sit next to them.

If you want to have an unconstrained conversation with someone, get rid of any obstacles between the two of you. Move out from behind your desk, unless maintaining control is more important than exchanging information. At a restaurant, ask the waiter to remove tall flower arrangements, extra glasses, or any other objects that clutter the visual space between you and your tablemate. If you're wearing sunglasses, take them off. Even air is an obstacle if there's too much of it: stay close, but not too close.

Get Rid of Distractions

While I was a graduate student I worked as the administrator of a small private school. Frequently I met with parents to discuss problems with their children. Emotions often ran high, and I sometimes felt more like a therapist than an administrator. The last thing I wanted during these tense meetings was to be distracted by phone calls or other interruptions, so I always saw parents in my office with the door closed and instructed my secretary to hold all calls.

When you eliminate distractions, you clear the stage for candid, uninterrupted dialogue. Turn off your cell phone or pager, the TV, the radio.

Choose a quiet booth in the restaurant or a peaceful park bench, away from in-line skaters and shouting schoolchildren. If you're at a party, step away from the action as much as possible so your conversation won't be interrupted by passersby or the temptation to people-watch.

Good conversation flows like a river. It twists and turns, but is never broken. Interruptions are a dam in that river. Once that dam is up, the conversation may never flow freely again. By removing distractions, you'll reduce the likelihood that your conversation will be interrupted. Both you and your companion will be more relaxed and better able to concentrate on the discussion at hand. Good communication is difficult enough. Avoid putting any additional hurdles in its path.

Position Yourself to Receive Information

In both my personal and professional life, I try not to ask a really important question unless I'm close enough to clearly see the other person's eyes. A slight twitch of the eyelid, a quick tightening of the jaw, a grimace, or even a subtle slacking of facial muscles may make a significant difference in how I evaluate his response.

Reading people is all about building patterns from every possible clue you can gather. Facial expressions can be a valuable source for this information. If you choose to have an important conversation with someone while driving in your car or walking down the street, you'll be distracted, and what reactions you do see, you'll see only in profile.

This isn't to say we haven't all had wonderful discussions while taking long car trips or jogging in the park. But ideally, you should be squarely in front of the person you're talking to, where you can see her entire face and body and she can see yours.

TIMING CAN BE EVERYTHING

Why do some newlyweds have so many arguments? Maybe it's because they haven't yet learned what a bad idea it is to bring up important issues at the end of a long hard day. In all relationships, personal or professional, there are good times and bad times to broach any subject. Ignore this fact at your own risk.

Anger, frustration, joy, depression—almost any state of mind—may color someone's reaction to a question. If you don't bother to gauge his mood before bringing up a delicate subject, at least take into consideration how it may be influencing the response. Ask someone a perfectly civil question when he's just found out his son crashed his brand-new car, and you're likely to get a surprisingly short-tempered response. At the other extreme, you might get an unrealistically rosy answer if he just received a big Christmas bonus.

Is it a good idea to ask your friend's opinion of your new boyfriend when she's three sheets to the wind? Perhaps you'll get a more candid answer. On the other hand, maybe you'll hear an alcohol-inflamed tirade against your boyfriend that has only a passing similarity to your friend's real feelings. There are those who believe you'll get more reliable information from people who are drunk or angry because they've lost their inhibitions and will blurt out "the truth." That may be so sometimes, but often people deeply regret their angry or drunken words, not because they revealed some hidden secret but because they didn't really mean what they said.

It's common for someone who is drunk, angry, or otherwise highly emotional to lose his perspective temporarily. He may ignore the big picture—or pattern—in someone's behavior and focus on an isolated event that dominates his thoughts at the moment. Whatever he says in these circumstances may have no resemblance to what he would say upon sober reflection.

To have a successful discussion, pick your time carefully. Make sure it's good for the other party, too. Avoid discussing a sensitive issue with someone who's been drinking or is already agitated and angry. Don't try to force someone to sit down and talk with you when he says he's too busy; he'll be distracted, unfocused, and ultimately unresponsive to your needs.

Go Slow and Easy

The normal progression of communication between two people moves from the general to the specific, the casual to the meaningful, and the impersonal to the personal. The process needn't take weeks or months. I've seen good attorneys develop a bond with prospective jurors or witnesses in minutes. There is nothing like a broad smile and a self-effacing, self-disclosing manner to make jurors relax. They quickly start trusting the lawyer, who can then elicit candid answers to difficult questions about their biases and personal beliefs. But before he begins probing, the great lawyer establishes rapport. He warms the juror up.

If you move too quickly from general, unthreatening questions to penetrating inquiries about someone's faith and marriage (for instance), the conversation may skid to a halt. Many people will simply clam up; others will be offended and think you're rude and insensitive. Some might conclude that you're socially inept. What replies you do get may not be very reliable. People may simply say what they think you want to hear so you'll back off and leave them alone.

I saw an excellent example of this at a recent seminar that featured a mock trial and jury selection. The case involved a schoolteacher who'd been fired for teaching the Christian doctrine of creation in violation of a school board policy—a reversal of the famous Scopes "Monkey Trial" featured in the play and movie *Inherit the Wind*. Naturally, during jury selection the questions quickly turned to the jurors' religious beliefs. The jurors pleasantly answered the lawyers' questions: "Yes, I'm a Christian, but I don't go to church much"; "I never did get into that"; "I'm a devout Catholic." They did not appear to be put off by the questions, and everything went smoothly—until we got to one elderly lady. "Do you consider yourself a religious person?" the lawyer asked her abruptly. She bristled and through clenched teeth replied, "I think that's a matter for me and my creator." *Whoa,* I thought. Never forget that what one person believes is perfectly appropriate, another may find deeply offensive. Most of the jurors were comfortable with the pace at which personal information was elicited. But everyone's threshold for self-disclosure is different. It's always wise to test the waters before you plunge in.

Should I Let Him Think About It?

You have a question you want to ask. The answer is critical to you, and it must be reliable. You don't want it tainted or manipulated in any way. Do you give the person you're asking as much time as he needs to answer, or do you ask for an answer on the spot? It depends.

We face this dilemma all the time in litigation. On the one hand, before trial we can present written questions to opposing parties, who then have weeks to prepare written answers. In theory, this gives them plenty of time to provide the most truthful and complete answers possible. In practice, they generally use the time to carefully massage their answers. Our other option is to wait until the person is seated before us in court before we spring the pivotal question on him. We certainly get a more spontaneous answer this way, but often it's not very complete or well thought out.

Most lawyers believe that you're much more likely to get a truthful answer from somebody if he must respond immediately, particularly if the question raises a sensitive issue. This applies outside the courtroom as well. While there are exceptions (you can't always demand that somebody decide right this minute whether to accept a job, buy a car, or elope to Paris), *in general if you want reliable answers to delicate questions, don't allow somebody too long to ponder his possible replies.* When you crave spontaneity, but also need reflection, ask for a quick response; once you get it, suggest: "Think about it more overnight and we'll talk again tomorrow."

THE DOS AND DON'TS OF GOOD QUESTIONS

The questions you ask, like the time and setting, should take into account all the circumstances, including what sort of information you need. There are times when you must have precise answers, in which case your questions must be equally focused. And in rare cases, you may even need to get tough with your questions. Usually, however, you'll learn more from broader questions that trigger a free flow of information. In any situation, you'll get better results if you plan your inquiries before you actually sit down with the other person.

Preparing Your Questions

A good lawyer wouldn't dream of winging her examination of a witness. But the *best* lawyers don't remain wedded to a particular line of questions, either. They pay close attention to other leads that crop up during the testimony. *Whether you're on a first date, interviewing for a job, or looking for a day-care provider, plot out the questions in advance that will get you the information you really need.* By doing so, you'll achieve several goals. First, you'll save time during the actual conversation. Second, you'll ask more precise and illuminating questions than you would if you winged it. Finally, if you prepare your questions beforehand, then during the conversation you can focus on the other person's answers and body language instead of thinking about your next question. This will make the conversation not only more informative but more spontaneous as well. You'll be able to go with the flow, knowing you can always return to your prepared questions after you address whatever topics might pop up unexpectedly.

Preparation doesn't mean making up a set of flash cards to flip through during the course of a conversation, although sometimes it's not a bad idea to write down questions in advance. I always write down any questions I have before an important meeting. Even if you don't take the list with you, writing down your most pertinent questions before any critical encounter will etch them more firmly in your mind.

What Should You Ask?

Tell me the nature and history of the relationship and what each party wants from the other, and I would be able to fashion some useful questions for them. The truth is, there are as many good questions as there are moments of human interaction. The cardinal rule is to be clear on what is important to *you*. If you're a divorced man with young children looking for a long-term romantic relationship, your potential mate's attitude toward children is obviously something you'll want to explore. If you're a dentist interviewing for an assistant, you'll want to know about the person's schooling and experience.

As you learned in chapter 2, "Discovering Patterns," three general traits tend to shed most light upon all others: compassion, socioeconomic background, and satisfaction with life. In any context, knowing about them will give you a substantial head start on understanding someone and being able to predict his or her behavior. So if you can't think of anything else to ask, focus on these.

Many of the questions we ask prospective jurors before trial are designed to enlighten us about these three key areas. We ask questions like

Where were you born?
Where were you raised?
Where do you live now?
What did your parents do for a living?
What do you do for a living?
How many brothers and sisters do you have?
What do you do in your free time?
What books and magazines do you read?
What TV shows do you watch?
Do you belong to any organizations or clubs?
What are your goals for the next five years?
What did you want to be when you were in high school?

Since people love to talk about themselves, these questions can be just as useful outside the courtroom. Just remember to proceed slowly and tactfully and watch for clues that might indicate you're getting too personal too soon.

I find it especially helpful to know about people's family lives when they were growing up. Did their parents help them with their homework? Did they play Little League, sing in the church choir, take dance lessons? If so, did their parents come and watch? These questions can be asked of almost anyone, and the answers will indicate what kind of socioeconomic background someone has.

Questions that will help you gauge someone's satisfaction with life are also always worth asking. One of my favorites is "What did you want to be when you were in high school?" If the person didn't do what she wanted to, ask why. Even a few questions along this line will quickly provide you with some insight about whether she has achieved her objectives in life and how she feels about missing those goals if that's the case. Again, sensitivity is everything. Don't forge ahead like a reporter with a hot lead if you can tell the other person wants to avoid the subject.

You can learn whether someone is compassionate in any number of ways. Is he close to his family, especially his parents? Does she do any volunteer or charity work? How does he feel about the homeless, about paying taxes to support public schools, about the minimum wage? You can always formulate a few questions that can be tossed casually into a conversation to get a sense of someone's degree of compassion. Also watch for revealing behavior and body language: How does he treat cashiers, waitresses, and others in service positions? What's her reaction if someone bumps her accidentally, or absentmindedly cuts her off on the freeway? People's attitudes and behavior will enable you to determine their place on the hardness scale shortly after meeting them.

By preparing some general questions concerning these three important areas, you'll be able to learn more about people more quickly than you have in the past. In all but the most casual encounters, you'll probably want more specific information as well. To get it, you can use three types of questions: open-ended, leading, and argumentative.

DIFFERENT QUESTIONS FOR
DIFFERENT CIRCUMSTANCES

Say what you will about lawyers, the great ones definitely know how to ask good questions. While a scathing cross-examination may be what comes to mind when you think of a lawyer interrogating a witness, that type of blitzkrieg happens only rarely. Good lawyers devise their line of questioning to coax out truthful answers. Sometimes one approach works best, sometimes another.

All witnesses and jurors are sworn to tell the truth and most do, at least most of the time. But some are, let's say, reluctant. Others are so eager to please they just need to be pointed in the right direction and turned loose. For these reasons, good lawyers have developed a keen sense of which types of questions work best in various circumstances.

When you think of the different types of questions that you can ask, visualize a funnel. The wide-open end represents open-ended questions that call for a "wide-open" narrative explanation and give someone latitude to answer however he wants. The argumentative or "pointed" questions are at the narrow end of the funnel. These are very focused, often confrontational, and may call for just a one-word or two-word response. In between lie leading questions, which focus the person's response but leave some room for explanation, though not as much as open-ended questions do.

Each type of question is more appropriate in some circumstances than others. Knowing when to use which type can be critical to getting reliable information from others.

The Open-ended Question

The open-ended question is an invitation to chat. The key aspect of this type of question is that it doesn't suggest what you might like the answer to be. That is its great advantage: since the other person can't tell what answer might please you, he's much more likely to say what's really on his mind. *For gaining objective, untainted information, open-ended questions are usually your best bet.* In addition, because open-ended questions give the person so much room to wander, the answers will almost always include extra information that may be very revealing.

There are some drawbacks to open-ended questions. One is that because they're so broad, the answer may wander entirely off the track so that you'll never get the information you really need. Another is that open-ended questions take time to answer and so are best used when time isn't a priority. A third disadvantage is that an open-ended question leaves the other person more room to avoid answering altogether.

Even if you need very specific information, however, a good strategy is to start with a few open-ended questions and become more focused as you go. This gives you the opportunity to develop a rapport with the other person while at the same time getting some valuable background data. It just takes a little patience, which is essential anyway if you want to get honest, reliable information.

In most instances, open-ended questions are the best way to find out what you need to know. For example, let's assume a woman has decided she wants to have children, and have them relatively soon. She's been dating a man for several months and thinks he could be Mr. Right. At some point, she'll want to find out whether her new love shares her priorities. If the relationship is developing nicely, she might be inclined to

confide in him, "Becoming a parent and raising kids is extremely important to me. How about you?" If the purpose of this question is to find
out how he really feels, she's botched it.

First, her question clearly broadcasts the "correct" answer. This taints
the response, making it unreliable. Second, suppose the man was to
reply, "I feel the same way"? This tells the woman nothing about when
the man wants to have children, how many he wants to have, how he believes his life will be changed by having children, or much else of substance. They could have completely different ideas about all of these
important issues. However, the woman will probably be delighted to get
such an agreeable response, and will go home blissfully believing that she
has found her future husband, who wants to build exactly the same life
she does. Not necessarily.

Now let's assume that, instead, the woman simply asks: "How do you
see your life five years from now?" This is a truly open-ended question.
If the man responds, "I want to be married, have a couple of kids, a
house with a picket fence, a dog, and a motor home for family vacations," the woman might justifiably conclude that he shares her dreams.
However, if his reply does not specifically include children, perhaps parenthood is not a priority for him in the near future. If he doesn't mention
children at all in his response, she can follow up with a more focused but
still somewhat open-ended question, such as "Where do kids fit in to
your future plans?" By phrasing her questions in a general, nonsuggestive way, she'll receive more reliable information from which she can
read his intentions better.

The same holds true for job interviews. If you want to hire a secretary
who will be satisfied in that position for a long time, ask, "What do you
see yourself doing five years from now?"—not "I'm really looking for
someone who will be happy being my secretary for the next five years.
Would you want to stay in the same position that long?" Similarly, instead of asking, "Are you willing to work overtime?" a better question
would be "What is your preference about working overtime?" Even if
you plan to ask your new employee to work overtime regularly and feel
compelled to warn her of that fact, hold off. First find out what her real
preference is. Maybe she'll volunteer that she needs extra money and
would love the opportunity. Maybe she'll say she has commitments most
evenings and weekends. Whatever her response, you can ask her about
her willingness to meet the job's actual requirements after you've found
out what her preference would be.

During jury selection, I'm able to see the tremendous improvement in
the quality of information lawyers obtain if they're good at phrasing

open-ended questions. In capital punishment cases—particularly high-profile ones—we frequently encounter people who are eager to be on the jury. When they are asked by the prosecutor simply, "Do you believe in the death penalty?" they almost always respond, "Yes." However, this doesn't tell us why they believe in the death penalty, how strongly they feel about it, or whether they think there ought to be exceptions to its application. Even those who generally support the death penalty have some reservations. The key is to find out what they are.

In the Night Stalker case, one of the prospective jurors, an African-American man, was asked how he felt about the death penalty. He said he thought it was appropriate in many instances, but that it had been "disproportionately applied." The prosecutor thought he would be a good juror for the prosecution. As the consultant for the defense, I disagreed. The well-phrased open-ended question allowed the man the freedom to express his feelings. It was extremely significant that in his relatively brief reply he pointed out that the death penalty was disproportionately applied. Obviously the prospective juror was troubled by the fact that African-American defendants in capital cases are sentenced to death more frequently than defendants of other races. From this answer, I believed he would be a hard sell for the prosecution. People don't like to enforce rules they think are unfair.

We decided to leave this man on the jury. Just before the trial began, another juror reported that he had announced to the other jurors that he could never vote for the death penalty. At that point, the judge excused him. I'd been right, but only because the prosecutor's open-ended question allowed the man the freedom to give me the information I needed to read him correctly.

The Leading Question

Whereas open-ended questions don't focus the answer to any great degree, leading questions do. Sometimes it is helpful to restrict the scope of an answer. Because leading questions direct a person's response, they can avoid a lot of wasted time and energy. If you want to know when your employee arrived at work, don't ask, "So, what did you do today?" Instead, ask a leading question: "When did you get to work?"

Leading questions are also essential if you want to get a straight answer from someone who is trying to sidestep you. You can ask some people open-ended questions until the cows come home and never get a straight answer. At some point, the open-ended question has served its purpose: it has demonstrated the person doesn't want to talk about the issue. If you want to find out why, you'll need to ask a leading question.

On some occasions, leading questions can be helpful precisely because they do influence the response. A life insurance salesman effectively used this technique with me shortly after the birth of my first child. "Can you think of anything more important than having your daughter financially secure if something were to happen to you?" he asked. The question wasn't meant to gain information, but to make me focus on the importance of providing for my child in the event of my death.

Another very handy use of the leading question is to let the other person know that you're aware of certain facts. For example, many businesspeople make it a habit to learn everything they can about a prospective new customer before they meet in person. They then prepare a few leading questions, such as "Does this project have anything to do with your acquisition of the ABC Company last year?" A few well-planned leading questions along this line impress the customer, encourage his confidence, and prompt him to share more information.

In your personal life, leading questions often smooth the way to closer relationships. I have a friend who is gay but doesn't reveal her sexual orientation publicly. It was obvious to me from the first time I met her that she was gay, but it was equally obvious that she didn't want me or anyone else to know. As I got to know her better, I wanted our friendship to be more open. So I picked an appropriate time and asked her if she had a "partner"—a term that's often understood as meaning a same-sex spouse or lover. This gave her the choice of either letting the matter pass or dropping her guard, realizing I had guessed her sexual orientation. As it turned out, she *did* have a partner, and she was eager to talk about her. This leading question enabled us to move more quickly to a relaxed, honest friendship.

Sometimes Things Get Ugly: The Argumentative Question

Argumentative questions are just that: argumentative. While they're often handy in the courtroom, they're seldom productive elsewhere. But sometimes it's necessary to get in someone's face if you want to learn crucial information or uncover a lie.

Those who watched the O. J. Simpson trial may recall F. Lee Bailey's confrontational examination of Detective Mark Fuhrman about his use of "the 'N' word." You might have expected Detective Fuhrman to crack under such a barrage. On the contrary, he faced Mr. Bailey's onslaught with little signs of emotion, denying he had used the word at all in the past ten years. When the Laura Hart McKinny tapes were revealed, Detective Fuhrman's staunch denial in the face of such aggressive questioning made his lie even more damaging to the prosecution.

In daily life, the most common use of argumentative questioning is to force someone into a reluctant admission: "Fine. Here's what you want to know—now leave me alone." It's not unusual for people who have revealed information under such interrogation to later claim they said it only to get you off their back. Such reversals should be viewed skeptically. Except in the movies, even under the most aggressive assault, people rarely confess to crimes they didn't commit or admit nonexistent "facts."

The drawback of badgering someone is that although it may get you the facts you need at the moment, it usually exacts a stiff price. In life outside the courtroom, we actually have to maintain relationships with most of the people we question. Argumentative questioning can permanently alter those relationships. So bullying or threatening someone into sharing information with you should be a last resort.

If at First You Don't Succeed—Follow Up!

No matter how carefully you choose your questions and listen to the answers, there will be times when you don't get what you're after. Perhaps the person honestly doesn't know the answer or has trouble sticking to the topic. Maybe she's responding evasively. Or maybe you didn't ask the question clearly or loudly enough and she didn't hear it correctly. In any case, don't give up if the information is important to you.

The first rule of good follow-up questions is to ask them as soon as you realize you need to—ideally, while the original conversation is still taking place. To do this, you have to be a good listener.

Steer the conversation back on course if you realize it's veering away from the topic you want to discuss. There are many ways to do this without being rude or offensive. Before you step in, however, let the person finish speaking. Remember, don't ruin the spontaneity by interrupting. Once there is a natural pause in the conversation, make your move.

One of the most effective approaches is to take full responsibility for the lack of communication. After all, it may well be that your question was unclear. Why not give the other person the benefit of the doubt? You might confess you don't remember whether she gave you the information you needed: "You may have already mentioned this, but I don't remember—what did you do at your last job?" Or acknowledge that you may not have grasped her explanation: "I don't really understand how that happened. Could you explain it again?" Unless the person is being evasive, she'll be glad to comply.

A little self-disclosure before you ask the question again may warm someone up, relaxing him enough to reveal what you need to know. Consider the boy who's reluctant to tell his father about his fear of trying out for the school football team. When his dad asks about it, the youngster may do everything possible to skirt the issue because he doesn't want to admit he's afraid he won't make the cut. If the father perceives this and confides that when he was his son's age, he was afraid to try out for the team, chances are his boy will respond by acknowledging the same fears. Now they're out on the table and can be discussed. But when you use this technique, be alert to the possibility that you're tainting the response. Maybe the boy's real reason for not wanting to try out is he doesn't like sports and doesn't want to admit that to his father. His father's suggestive self-disclosure has given him an acceptable out, which he has pursued gladly. Because of this risk, I don't suggest using this approach unless others have failed.

If the person won't respond to any of these approaches, try another strategy. Go all the way back to some safe ground—something that the person feels comfortable talking about. Reconnect there, and work forward again to the area where the apparent sensitivities were. If that still doesn't work, let the matter go for a while. Wait for a better time or circumstance, or until your relationship with the person matures to a point where he feels comfortable talking with you about even sensitive issues.

Sometimes there is no subtle way to pursue the information being withheld. If the salesman won't give you a straight answer, you have to be very direct: "Can you tell me whether or not this car has ever been in an accident?" Or ask the prospective employee, flat out: "Were you fired from your last job?" The more difficult it is to pry information out of someone, the more significant the information may be. In fact, at some point the entire exercise becomes meaningless—the person's secretive and possibly dishonest behavior itself should steer you away from him.

GETTING INFORMATION FROM OUTSIDERS

After reading this chapter about drawing other people out, you ought to be able to get most of the information you need, most of the time. But there are occasions when you need more than you can tactfully ask for, or more than the person has any intention of giving you. In those situations, you'll find you can learn an extraordinary amount from third parties.

It's not this book's purpose to train private eyes, but those so inclined can learn immense amounts about others from public and private records. It's amazing what personal information is housed in sources like the Internet, Dun & Bradstreet, credit reporting services, court files, school records, professional licensing bureaus, and motor vehicle departments. During a recent American Bar Association program on legal issues raised by the electronic revolution, one of the speakers demonstrated how he could pull his outstanding home mortgage balance out of cyberspace. It's scary, but with a little effort and ingenuity many of our best-kept secrets are accessible for all the world to see.

Closer to home, we can learn much about someone from his friends, family, co-workers, and even acquaintances, such as the clerk who waits on him at the local market. You can usually tell how others feel about someone simply by watching their interaction. Do others treat him with respect, deference, fear, intimidation, love, concern, humor, friendship? How does he treat them? And you don't have to rely on observation alone: ask!

It makes sense to check personal references, just as an employer would check education or job references, yet we seldom do. Partly, this is because of social taboos. You can't casually call up your boyfriend's ex-fiancée and ask her opinion of him. However, there is nothing awkward about remarking to his mother, "It must be nice to have Joe come visit." There's a broad range of potentially revealing responses from "It sure is—he never calls or stops by anymore" to "I never get tired of him stopping by or calling, even though he does it all the time." The first response paints a picture of a neglectful son. The second suggests he is considerate and devoted.

You'll be impressed by what you can learn if you take a little time to pose productive questions to others who already know the person you are just getting to know. And you don't have to pry. Ask your boss's wife at a party, "Do you play golf with your husband?" The question may elicit a number of responses, all of which can tell you a lot about your boss's character and priorities. A quick "You've got to be kidding—he takes that game way too seriously" tells you how competitive he is. "I would love to, and I keep hinting, but he never asks me" reveals a selfish and insensitive side. "We've played every Sunday morning at seven o'clock for the past six years, rain or shine" demonstrates both his commitment to his wife and his obsessive adherence to schedules and routines. This in turn indicates that he expects to see loyalty, organization, and promptness in his employees. Any of this information would help you to better understand what is important to your boss and to predict his behavior accordingly.

Once you're looking for them, you'll discover many opportunities to learn about people from third parties. Each can provide you with a different perspective, and the more perspectives you have, the more reliable your picture will be.

KEY POINTS

Learn to listen: Even great questions won't help you "read" if you don't know how to listen. The cardinal rules of good listening are:

- Don't interrupt
- Be empathetic: don't condemn, argue, or patronize
- Maintain a comfortable physical distance
- Be involved, but not too intense
- Don't let your body language impact the free flow of information
- Self-disclose, but not too much, too soon
- Don't take what someone says out of context
- "Listen" with all your senses

Create an environment for great conversations: Consider where and when your conversations should take place, and who else, if anyone, should be present. If the conversation is important, don't leave the setting to chance.

Be patient: Let others move at the speed with which they are comfortable.

Prepare questions: Productive conversation is stimulated by good questions. Whether preparing for a job interview or a first date, think of a few questions to keep the conversation moving and information flowing your way. Questions which call for information about the three most predictive traits—socioeconomic background, satisfaction with life, and compassion—are always a good place to start.

Learn to ask the three different types of questions:

- Open-ended questions are an invitation to chat, and usually lead to longer, more informative answers
- Leading questions focus the response on a particular issue and help keep the dialogue on track, but may produce less spontaneous or complete answers

- Argumentative questions are usually your last resort, but may be necessary to ferret out the truth when you have to be confrontational

If at first you don't succeed—follow up: If you don't get an answer to the question you asked, either repeat it or rephrase it, but ask it again as soon as possible.

Why Did You Put It That Way?
Finding the Hidden Meanings
in Everyday Communication

Some conversations, particularly those about delicate subjects, remind me of scenes from the nature programs my kids watch: A small bird is sitting in a nest on the ground. As a predator approaches, she feigns a broken wing and hobbles off, leading the predator away from her young. Or the male frog puffs up his brightly colored throat to four times its normal size to reveal his irresistible charms to an available female, thus attracting her to him.

There are many parallels between how people interact and the dynamics that occur in the animal world. We humans advance and withdraw, distract and lure, as all creatures do. We lead others away from subjects we want to avoid, or pull them in the direction we want them to go. We accomplish this by using an arsenal of communication techniques developed for the sake of social survival: words and tone, actions, and even silence. Some are instinctive; others are conscious maneuvers.

As helpful as it is to know how to ask questions and listen to answers, not all questions are welcome and not all answers are forthright. We often tackle subjects that are unpleasant, humiliating, and even threatening. We steer conversations away from topics that would reveal our weaknesses or mistakes and usually try to avoid embarrassing others. We're socialized not to brag or lie. And most of us try very hard to respect those and other similar unwritten rules.

If we don't want to admit our shortcomings, openly boast about our accomplishments, or lie about our misdeeds, how do we handle situations in which we need or want to do just that? We rely on our stockpile of verbal and behavioral maneuvers. In this chapter you'll learn to recognize and interpret these maneuvers. The topics discussed here range from manipulative answers and other fairly straightforward verbal traits to typical conversational detours and more complex habits. Like all other traits and behaviors, these conversational maneuvers should always be viewed alongside other characteristics as you try to establish a pattern.

LOOK FOR THE MOTIVE

When I realize someone may be trying to direct or control a conversation, I always ask myself what he's trying to accomplish. By examining a person's behavior in the context of the broader conversation, I can usually identify his objective. When it isn't crystal clear from my observations alone, a few questions will generally bring the answer to the surface.

Even if there is no apparent reason for a person to manipulate a conversation, just the fact that he communicates in a particular way— volunteering information about himself, bragging, criticizing, or whatever—may have implications about his personality. If someone drops a name for a specific reason, for example, it may not say much about his character. But if he routinely name-drops, even when the name has little to do with the topic at hand, that points to insecurity, a need for acceptance, and a desire to call attention to himself.

People try to manipulate conversations for many different reasons both positive (to avoid embarrassing or hurting another person) and negative (to cover up a lie, to trick someone, or to pull someone into an argument). When you notice that someone is attempting to steer a discussion, ask: What does he have to gain? Does his behavior reflect an attempt to achieve a specific goal, for instance to gather facts or protect someone's privacy? Or does his maneuvering indicate low self-esteem or a need for attention? Pursue the conversation until you're fairly certain of the answer. You may have to watch and listen closely to spot some maneuvers; they may come and go quickly. Other techniques are easy to see, but their motivation is not as obvious. Whichever is the case, try to identify both the method and the motive. Once you do, you will gain tremendous insight into a person's character.

MANIPULATIVE ANSWERS

No matter how skillful you are at formulating questions, you're bound to run into people who are just as adept at sidestepping them. Some answers seem designed to avoid revealing anything, while others force unrelated information into the conversation. When you know what to look for, you can tell when someone is leading you toward or away from a particular topic, and why.

Nonresponsiveness

There are a number of ways to avoid responding to a question, from changing the subject to clamming up altogether. But before you place too much significance on someone's nonresponsive answer, make sure she heard and understood you.

I've seen many well-meaning and candid witnesses initially appear evasive, only to demonstrate later that they were trying their best to respond. Some people don't want to admit they don't understand a question, which is very often the case. Others are so preoccupied with another issue that they go off on a tangent without even realizing they haven't answered the question. Still others misunderstand the question, and sincerely believe they've provided an answer. Language and cultural differences can also make a person misconstrue a question and appear evasive or nonresponsive. In situations like these, nonresponsiveness is usually nothing more than a bump in the conversational road. With a few more questions, you'll be able to get the information you need.

However, if someone avoids answering several open-ended follow-up questions, you're probably on to something. He might be avoiding embarrassment, conflict, the truth, or an emotionally difficult subject. He might also be intent on talking about something totally unrelated, in which case his nonresponsiveness usually isn't an evasive tactic. Chances are, once he says what's on his mind, he'll be happy to discuss what's on yours. To determine what's going on, shift to leading questions or, if necessary, pointed ones. If that still doesn't work, you'll have to try to get the information elsewhere, or abandon the search altogether.

Before you launch into a full-scale assault, however, try to make an educated guess about the reasons for the person's reluctance to answer. Without having at least some sense of his motives, you'll be forging ahead at your own risk. Many people find it insensitive and rude when someone insists on discussing an issue they have plainly tried to avoid.

During jury selection, it's not uncommon for a lawyer to encounter this pitfall as he bores in unmercifully on a juror who is clearly embarrassed by a particular subject. In a recent breach-of-contract case, the attorney representing the man who filed the lawsuit was examining an elderly juror who obviously did not want to talk about his son. The attorney wanted to know why. His unrelenting and very public inquiries quickly became offensive. Initially, the man revealed that his son was "incarcerated." Further probing established that the son had been convicted of burglary. That should have been enough for the plaintiff's attorney to make his call regarding the juror, but he continued to pry, asking for details about the conviction, the length of the sentence, where the son was incarcerated, and the nature of the relationship between the father and the son. With each question, the father's answers became shorter, until finally he stopped replying altogether. He knew he'd be excused from the jury, so why bother responding? Throughout this scene I was acutely aware of the man's humiliation and distress, and wondered why the lawyer persisted in the examination, especially since these issues had nothing to do with a breach-of-contract case.

I later realized that the attorney was so curious about the man's reluctance to talk that he couldn't help but probe; his urge to know the facts got the better of him. In suggesting that nonresponsiveness should excite your curiosity and prompt follow-up, I'm not urging you to do it thoughtlessly. As much as you may want or need a certain piece of information, recognize when further questions will only alienate the other person, and try another approach later.

Not Denying or Explaining When It Would Be Expected

Just as people can protest too much, they can also fail to deny an accusation or explain an event, leaving the truth hanging there in the silence for anyone who cares to hear. The behavior is similar to nonresponsiveness but can be even more revealing.

Most of us are quick to deny any hint of wrongdoing and happy to explain ourselves if we have nothing to hide. That's why, in nearly every courtroom, judges instruct juries that they may draw a negative inference if one party has a chance to explain an important issue but doesn't. Keep this instruction in mind as you deliberate about people outside the courtroom as well.

Imagine a woman asking her boyfriend, "Did you have a good time last night?" after he's stayed out unusually late one evening. If he's normally talkative and quick to volunteer details about his evening's activities, but this time he averts his eyes and says simply, "It was okay," hoist the red flag. The more communicative a person normally is, the more significance you can place on his failure to explain or deny unusual behavior. To be absolutely sure he didn't misunderstand, raise the issue again. If he once more fails to explain or deny, it's time to consider possible motives.

Avoiding a topic by failing to explain or deny is especially significant because most of us want to be loved, respected, and understood. We also want to spare those who are close to us any unnecessary worry or heartache. When we deviate from these expected patterns, it's usually because honesty would hurt someone, or would cost us their respect, approval, and affection. We hope that if we just ignore the issue, it will go away.

But people aren't always hiding something when they fail to explain or deny. Someone may be defensive about an issue or angry because you keep pressing it. He may want to avoid confrontation, believing you're going to scoff at any explanation he does supply. He may be playing games, wanting you to be jealous or insecure. Or he may be trying to control you by keeping you off-balance. He might even be offended by your suggestion of impropriety and not want to dignify it with a response.

All of these are possible motives, but they're also the excuses typically pulled out of the hat by someone who really is hiding something. Whenever I hear them, I am suspicious, just as I would be if my teenager came home at two A.M. and, when asked where he'd been, replied, "What's the matter? Don't you trust me? I can't believe I have to explain my every movement to you!" That sounds like guilt. Don't let someone's aggressive response distract you from what you should be hearing.

Short Answers

There's nothing inherently suspicious about short answers. They're often refreshingly frank and to the point. Still, the person who constantly offers only very brief responses is rather unusual—and leads me to ask myself whether my questions called for more information than he provided. If open-ended questions that call for a narrative response are repeatedly met with a brief yes or no, my eyebrows go up.

To investigate, I look at the person's body language and listen to his tone of voice. An honest but succinct reply typically doesn't look the same as a dishonest one. By the same token, someone who gives short answers because he is nervous, afraid, defensive, or embarrassed won't use the same body language as someone who is no-nonsense but basically at ease. Short answers are just an early warning signal—what they mean must be checked against other clues. An excellent example is the prospective juror I mentioned earlier, whose son was doing time for burglary. The man's answers were very curt, his body language extremely defensive. I could clearly see that he was honest, but he sure wasn't happy about being forced to publicly discuss such a sensitive subject.

Long Answers

Long answers are more challenging to interpret. There are plenty of long-winded people out there with no motive except to get attention, and lots more who just have a hard time expressing themselves. But sometimes a long answer hides or distorts the truth. *People who want to avoid lying outright often try to spread the truth around in a long answer so that, in order to discover it, you have to pick out a piece here, a piece there.* The person may tell himself, "I'm not lying; all the pieces are there. If he can't find them, that's not my problem."

Don't place every person and response under suspicion, but you'd be foolish not to be on the lookout for possible hidden meanings in extra-long responses. To test an unusually long answer, first ask yourself if it's appropriate under the circumstances. Did it answer the question, if in a roundabout way? Or did the person respond like a politician, answering the question he *wished* had been asked? Did he reveal much of himself in the answer, in a candid manner? Did his body language and voice reflect honesty and openness? Suppose you *had* asked for a five-minute response, would his answer have been appropriate?

Next, ask yourself whether the answer was coherent, or rambling and disjointed. If it was incoherent, that might be a result of nervousness, social ineptitude, insecurity, or confusion. An answer that's coherent but seemingly uncalled-for may be meant to hide the truth, to control the conversation, to keep the floor in an attempt to push a specific agenda, to buy time to think of what to say, or to impress others.

Bear in mind that some people are simply more articulate than others. Someone who isn't used to speaking publicly may have more difficulty expressing herself, and as a consequence may take longer to do so. This doesn't mean she's insecure, confused, or lying. As always, look at the pattern that has developed before you draw any conclusions. A rambling and disjointed answer from a slick-talking salesman would suggest one thing, the same answer from a nervous recluse quite another.

Answering a Question with a Question

"So, what do you think of the new sales guy?"
"I don't know. What's your impression?"
"Well, didn't you have lunch with him yesterday?"
"Why do you ask?"

When someone doesn't want to commit himself, he will often answer a question with a question. He's waiting for more information from you, so he can tailor his answer accordingly. Is it safe to admit you think the new sales manager is terrific, or does your colleague disagree? What will he think if you confirm that you went out to lunch with him?

I often see this dynamic played out in the courtroom: "How do you feel about the death penalty?" "What do you mean, how do I feel?" The juror may want more information before committing herself. She may want to know how we think she *should* feel, or she may want to get some hint as to the most socially acceptable response. When she finds out, she can give the answer that will make her feel comfortable.

When someone answers a question with a question, stay alert. It doesn't necessarily mean she's being evasive; although sometimes that's the case. She may also be insecure, embarrassed, or eager to please; or she may just want clarification. The motive may be sinister or innocent. For example, assume an employer says to an employee, "I called the store yesterday afternoon and you were gone. When did you leave?" If the employee responds, "When did you call?" he may want to know so he can say he left as late as possible. On the other hand, he may have come and gone several times during the afternoon and have a perfectly good reason to ask for clarification. Don't be too quick to judge the answer harshly.

Another common reason people answer a question with a question is to redirect the conversation. "Want me to get two tickets to the ball game on Friday?" a man may ask his wife. "Did you know the Wilsons are going to be in town this weekend?" his wife might reply. A response like this usually means one of three things: the other person didn't hear you; she's trying to answer in a roundabout way, by giving you new information with her question; or she just doesn't want to answer. If she doesn't want to answer, it may be that she's avoiding something, such as the fact that she already made plans for Friday without consulting you. Or it could be that she hates ball games and wants to avoid a fight. You'll find out which with another question or two.

Some individuals with good people skills have figured out that by answering a question with a question they can get others talking and break the ice. These born socializers are naturally curious about other people; they shouldn't be viewed with suspicion. However, if someone consistently turns the conversation to other people and never reveals anything about herself, I usually assume she's secretive.

There are, then, a number of possible motives for answering a question with a question. To focus on the most likely, first ask yourself whether the information sought in the second question was necessary to answer the first—for instance, to clarify a point. If not, the person is probably probing for information so her answer won't seem stupid, trying to find out what you know so she can plot some sort of strategic response, or fishing for clues about what will win your approval.

Next, consider whether the second question is an attempt to redirect the conversation. If so, the other person either didn't hear you or wants to avoid responding. If she's trying to avoid a response, you've probably hit a sensitive issue. Cautious follow-up is definitely in order.

Once again, look for patterns. Review the exchange in the context of the entire conversation. If the person responding to your question with a question is otherwise candid, there's no reason to conclude she has an ulterior motive. If she consistently avoids responding by asking you questions, consider the possibility that she may have something to hide.

VERBAL CALLING CARDS

The words we choose to express our thoughts always do double duty. In addition to expressing our ideas, they reveal our perception of the world and our place in it. Certain verbal traits are particularly reliable as "calling cards," telegraphing basic data about a person's background and beliefs. Our use of slang, word themes, and titles may be so ingrained we're rarely conscious of them, which makes them all the more telling. Profanity, the final category in this section, is a more obvious and equally revealing trait. Each of these four verbal calling cards provides easy access to important information.

Slang

The term "slang" has a relatively broad meaning. It can include colloquialisms, bad grammar, and even the latest trendy sayings.

Colloquialisms can reveal whether someone was raised in a rural or urban setting and shed light on his cultural influences and socioeconomic background. Whenever I hear a particularly vivid colloquialism, I ask about its origin. The answer usually broadens my understanding of the person's upbringing and gets him talking about his past. This is particularly important since socioeconomic background is one of the three most predictive traits.

Rural slang is filled with colorful metaphors, whose meanings might not be instantly obvious to you if you're from another part of the country. I know a man whose parents were raised on a cattle ranch in Wyoming and who sprinkles his conversation with cowboy colloquialisms. To folks unfamiliar with ranching terminology, his slang sometimes comes across as a bit odd, if not offensive. During one business

meeting with a woman senior executive, he described a harsh and di-
sheveled woman as looking as though she'd been "rode hard and put
away wet." Seeing the shock on the executive's face, he was quick to explain: the idiom refers to the appearance of a horse that has been run until
it sweats, then put into its stall without being brushed. Judging by her expression, the executive understood him to mean something else entirely.

Bad grammar, also an aspect of slang, can reveal much about a person,
but never assume that because someone has bad grammar he isn't smart.
Poor grammar more frequently reflects someone's socioeconomic and
educational background. Some of the shrewdest people I've ever known
were not brought up using the Queen's English. When I encounter someone who is obviously intelligent but ungrammatical, I'm fairly comfortable concluding that his parents were not well educated and that he
himself has probably had little formal schooling. But having said that, I
must add that there are many exceptions to this rule. You can usually
spot them by tuning in to the context in which the bad grammar is used.

First, take a look at the person's human environment, the men and
women with whom he surrounds himself. Some people consciously use
poor grammar so they'll seem to be just one of the guys or blend in with
a certain peer group. For others, reverting to slang with family or close
friends is a way of relaxing or showing familiarity.

If someone can clean up his language at will, he may be intentionally
using slang to convey a particular image. Is he trying to play the part of
a good old boy or a street-smart hustler? Is he in an environment where
he doesn't want to reveal his level of education or sophistication? Does
he lapse into slang when he's excited and has perhaps lost some control?
The circumstances and context, coupled with the degree to which slang
is used, will reveal interesting shades of character.

Word Themes

The English language provides us with an immense menu of words to describe what we're feeling or thinking. Most of us order up our words
from many different sections of the menu, but some people routinely express themselves in themes.

For example, many lawyers habitually use terms of combat or aggression. Their vocabulary is sprinkled with terms like "won," "battle,"
"aggressor," "destroyed," "confronted," "maneuvered," "outflanked,"
"strategize," "in the trenches," and so on. Lawyers and nonlawyers who
use the language of battle reveal their aggressive, competitive, and often
combative nature. Nonconfrontational people do not usually use these

terms to describe a trip to the grocery store or the purchase of an automobile.

Other people describe life in sports terminology, peppering their speech with words such as "score," "goal-line stand," "touchdown," "at bat," and "bottom of the ninth." Sports analogies frequently reveal a competitive or aggressive nature. Sports talk might also reveal a person's avid interest in sports.

Every so often I encounter someone whose speech is laced with sexual innuendo and who is quick to point out any sexually suggestive meaning that might be given to what someone else says. Usually, this type of person is trolling to see the other's reaction; it's an extreme form of flirtatiousness. And it's not limited to men. While most of the men and women who engage in this practice would be quick to profess innocent intentions, in my experience their word themes are a good gauge of their intentions. They use sexual innuendo because that's exactly what's on their mind. People who are comfortable with their sexuality, and not interested in yours, don't constantly inject sexual innuendo into a conversation.

The "honesty" word theme can also be very enlightening. People who use it preface their remarks with terms such as "frankly," "to be completely honest," or "to tell the truth." I'm always suspicious of someone who feels the need to tell me when he's telling the truth. Am I to infer that when he *doesn't* say "frankly" I can't trust him?

As always, be on the lookout for deviations and extremes. The more a person relies on word themes, the more strongly he relates to some aspect of those favored words.

Use of Titles

The way a person uses titles can reveal his geographic background, life experience, and upbringing. For example, most lawyers refer to the "ladies and gentlemen of the jury," but I work with one who always refers to the "men and women of the jury." This usage reflects his military background: military officers, who are used to addressing the troops, don't refer to them as ladies and gentlemen but as men and women.

Many Southerners address women as "ma'am" and men as "sir"; it's a characteristic of that culture. If I heard someone I knew was from southern California consistently address men as "sir," I'd assume he'd been in the military. If I knew he was from the South, I wouldn't automatically make that assumption.

A title may also be used sarcastically or to show respect—or it may be purposely ignored. I came face to face with this technique the first time I was asked to testify as an expert witness in a trial. The issue was whether it would be possible to select an impartial jury from members of the community where the case had received substantial media coverage. The lawyer who called me as his expert referred to me as Dr. Dimitrius throughout my examination. But when the opposing counsel began to question me, he called me *Mrs.* Dimitrius. When I'm referred to as Mrs. Dimitrius at my sons' PTA meetings, I don't conclude that the speaker is trying to downplay my professional qualifications. In the courtroom, however, that is exactly what the opposing lawyer was trying to do.

Whether the use of titles reflects cultural background, respect, or some other state of mind is usually fairly obvious if you ask yourself: "Does he routinely refer to everyone in the same way?" If so, his use of titles probably reflects his cultural background. But if not, he is probably using titles on a particular occasion to convey a particular attitude—respect, disrespect, or sarcasm. Look to the context and his accompanying body language and tone of voice to see which.

Profanity

Several years ago, I worked with a very well respected jury consultant who by all indications but one was as prim, proper, and highly professional as you can imagine. The exception was her frequent and colorful use of profanity—she swore like a sailor. This was particularly remarkable coming from such an attractive and well-educated young woman, who socialized almost exclusively with other highly educated professionals. Profanity is more frequently used by those who are less well educated, come from a lower socioeconomic background, or work and live with others who also swear a lot. Language is greatly affected by peer pressure, since we all tend to conform to the behavior of the group with whom we spend most of our time. My colleague's use of profanity, a deviation from her normal behavior, proved key to predicting her independent and rebellious nature.

Profanity is much more common in the media today than it was fifteen or twenty years ago, but it is still usually perceived as a deviation from normal polite conversation. If someone curses frequently, especially on particularly inappropriate occasions, it suggests he is socially inept, insensitive to the reaction of others, or excitable. It's not unusual for someone who uses profanity when agitated to be aggressive and have a volatile temper as well. Excessive profanity is threatening. Those who indulge in it often are aware of the effect it has on others, and may use it as a method of intimidation.

Of course, most of us swear every now and then. Even someone with tremendous self-control might shout an off-color word or two when he hits his thumb with a hammer, wins the lottery, or feels some other sudden, intense physical or emotional stimulus. But when someone uses profanity regularly or inappropriately, it doesn't signal a temporary loss of control. Rather, it likely reflects more deeply upon his background and personality. *To gauge the significance of profanity, consider how often the person uses it and under what circumstances.* Don't be too quick to judge someone who occasionally lets loose with a curse word or two; rather, try to determine what inspired the outburst.

Recently, I met with an attorney whom I've known for some time. She's a petite, extremely well spoken, and very gentle person. Yet she let fly with a few choice expletives on this occasion, while describing an opposing attorney. As soon as the words escaped her mouth, she stopped and apologized. We both laughed and went on with our conversation. Her lapse told me that her anger and frustration were intense enough to have temporarily overrun her social graces. That was a significant observation, because it helped me understand her intense feelings about the case and those involved with it.

The attorney's outburst also revealed that she was becoming more relaxed with me. Those who usually avoid profanity will be more inclined to let dicey words slip once they have become comfortable with you. When two people are first dating, they'll typically avoid the use of profanity like the plague. Once the couple becomes more comfortable with each other and less wary of being judged, curse words might start slipping into their conversations.

CONVERSATIONAL DETOURS

The best discussions aren't laid out like train tracks across the plains. They take interesting twists and turns as information is exchanged and opinions expressed. Detours such as pregnant pauses, interruptions, and rambling are usually just a part of the flow. But sometimes, such detours aren't so much the natural product of conversation as conscious efforts by one participant to change the subject. When this happens, it's worthwhile to pay extra attention; what people *don't* want to discuss can be extremely revealing.

The Pregnant Pause

You're in the middle of a free-flowing and spontaneous conversation. You say something, perhaps something provocative, threatening, or off the subject. There is no response. The rhythm of the conversation has been broken—whatever you just said caught the other person off guard. He's derailed and taking a moment to get centered again.

Pregnant pauses are often accompanied by the "deer in the head-lights" look: someone freezes and panic or anxiety sweeps across his face. He doesn't blink. It's as if something in his brain has shorted out momentarily and he's thinking, "Oh God, what do I do now?" When this occurs we often assume we've caught him in a lie, but the reaction also could signal that he is surprised or offended by what you've just said. When I see this look I immediately ask myself what may have prompted it. Was it the question about why he left his last job? Was it the mention of lipstick on his collar?

Not all pauses are so dramatic. Brief pauses can reflect anger, frustration, or even disgust. Frequently someone who is upset will take a moment to regain control of his emotions before he responds. If this is happening, you'll see a quick look of anger, accompanied by a tightening of the jaw, a grimace, or a shake of the head. If he's frustrated, he'll show it by exhaling air, shrugging, turning his head, or exhibiting some other sign. And it's possible that the pause simply means he had a completely unrelated thought; he may have realized suddenly that he forgot to lock his front door or turn off his stove. If that's the case, you'll probably see a look of distraction, a faraway gaze, and a slacking of the facial muscles.

When a pregnant pause occurs, don't try to fill the void with another question or comment. Instead, look closely for clues in the person's face, eyes, and mouth. Think back to the flow of the conversation that was interrupted by the pause. What were the last words spoken, the ones that knocked this person off balance?

Interruptions

As the previous chapter pointed out, interruptions are often fatal to good conversations. Most of us want our companions to listen carefully when we speak, with their attention focused on our every word. But some interruptions are inevitable. It's natural for someone to interrupt when she's excited about what you're saying and wants to jump in, or when she senses you're groping for words. However, someone who interrupts consistently or at particularly annoying junctures not only derails the conversation but also reveals a lot about her own state of mind or personality.

Consistent or poorly timed interruptions may be motivated by impatience or boredom—you may be going too slowly for the other person, or pursuing a topic that doesn't interest her. You might be tempted to chalk up her behavior to intentional rudeness. But it may point to a family background in which conversations were highly charged and competitive, or rules of conversational conduct weren't very strict. If someone grew up in a big, vocal family where every dinnertime conversation was a verbal free-for-all, the habit will be hard to break.

People eager to push a specific agenda also often interrupt to steer the conversation their way. They want to persuade you, not listen to your point of view. These interruptions are often argumentative. The more heated and frequent they are, the more likely you've touched a nerve with the person, especially if she doesn't usually interrupt.

Chronic interrupters may also fall within the general category of attention seekers. They want to take the floor away from you so everyone will focus on them and what they have to say. People who have this habit are usually insecure and self-centered and will do whatever is necessary to direct the conversation. They may not hesitate to bring up an entirely unrelated topic in order to control the discussion, or they may be content to stay with the existing topic as long as they're the ones talking. If the interruption leads to an entirely different topic, it may signal that the person is uneasy with the subject at hand.

Sometimes it isn't clear whether someone has interrupted in an effort to control the conversation or seek attention, or simply because she's excited about the topic. If someone's body language speaks of enthusiasm, and an interruption contributes to the dialogue, there's probably no harm meant. But if someone interrupts with a comment that is completely off the topic, he is usually trying to control the conversation, either to avoid an uncomfortable issue or insert his personal agenda, or because he is bored, impatient, or anxious to move on to another topic or end the conversation altogether.

Rambling

It's important to distinguish between the rambler and the person who changes topics to control the conversation. Ramblers bounce from topic to topic and thought to thought, almost at random. Their conversations consist of many detours. Sometimes they seem incapable of pursuing an orderly line of thought for more than a few seconds.

I've found that most ramblers can't control their habit. They also don't usually have a conscious motive for rambling, except in the rare case when they may be buying time while they think of something else to say. Rambling usually reveals nervousness, confusion, insecurity, a need for attention, or a lack of mental or emotional focus. It's unusual for someone whose speech is normally coherent and organized to lapse into rambling. When that happens, look for signs of intoxication or severe fatigue or distraction. If you suspect that someone's rambling is nothing more than nervous chatter, look for the associated body language such as fidgeting, shifting of body weight, or glancing around the room to confirm your theory.

Changing Subjects

We don't possess Mr. Spock's flawlessly logical Vulcan mind. Our conversations meander a bit—which keeps them interesting. But occasionally someone will completely change directions in the middle of a discussion. A sharp turn is usually no accident.

When you spot someone changing the subject, ask yourself whether he was previously open to the topic but suddenly went cold on it, or whether he avoided it from the moment it was first mentioned. For example, assume a young woman asks her husband when he wants to start a family. He responds, "I'd love to have kids, but do you really think we're ready? Can we afford it? Is my job secure enough?" During the conversation that ensues, he then focuses exclusively on his problems at work. He has effectively changed the subject. The change, however, is a natural detour and relates to the original question, which he was willing to discuss. It's just that, in his mind, his job security is directly related to whether they are financially prepared to have children.

Compare this with how the wife might interpret the response if her husband doesn't even address the issue of children but instead responds, "Don't even talk about kids. It's all I can do to keep my head above water at work," and then launches into a detailed report on his boss, stalled projects, and staffing problems. Such an immediate shift sends a very different message. Here, his wife might conclude that her husband is actively avoiding the topic.

Whether someone is wandering innocently or with the intention of avoiding a topic altogether can usually be determined from the relationship between the original topic and the new one. Are the two connected, or has this person completely changed the subject? The only way you can find out is to listen for a while. Don't attempt to redirect the person immediately, but instead explore the new topic with him and see where the conversation carries you. He may eventually return to the original subject—revealing more information in the process.

I often see this in court. A witness will give what at first appears to be a completely evasive answer. When the attorney asks him to answer the question that was asked, the witness may express surprise, and even take offense, at the suggestion that he was trying to change the subject. As the questioning proceeds, it becomes obvious that he's being candid, but felt it necessary to preface his response with an explanation, which at first blush seemed irrelevant.

If someone is allowed to answer however he chooses, and still never returns to the topic at hand, he may be trying to avoid the original subject. There's also the possibility that he is so focused on an issue of particular importance to him that he has forgotten what he was asked in the first place. If you're talking to someone who wanders, gently nudge the conversation back in the original direction and see if the resistance continues. If it does, you know the detour wasn't accidental.

REVEALING HABITS

People use a variety of techniques to get their points across or sidestep delicate subjects, but certain maneuvers seem to be much more common than others. Maybe it's animal instinct; maybe we come equipped with only a limited number of tricks. The habits described in this section are those that crop up most frequently in everyday exchanges. Sometimes they're unconscious, but more often they are intended to provoke a specific response. Once you familiarize yourself with them, you'll start noticing conversational nuances you were never aware of before.

Defensive Behavior

Chapter 1, "Reading Readiness," described how defensiveness can hinder our attempts to view people objectively. We can learn to curb our own defensiveness, but what do we do when we encounter it in others? Defensiveness is extremely common and can put an end to a conversation in a matter of moments. If you see someone starting to get defensive, quickly try to diffuse his anxiety if you hope to keep the conversation going.

Defensiveness arises in a number of ways, some passive, some very aggressive. Most defensiveness is entirely understandable—if you're being attacked or criticized, it's natural to defend yourself. But even so, the defensiveness has to be dealt with before a meaningful discussion can continue.

The type of defensiveness that's most difficult to identify is defensive withdrawal. Someone who withdraws when she feels attacked will usually just grow silent. Withdrawal is hard to read; it can reflect not only defensiveness but also boredom, preoccupation, pensiveness, or even agreement. Usually the only way to find out which is to ask if "anything is wrong?" or "did I say something that upset you?". The tone and content of the response should provide the answer. If the person is just thinking of something else, he'll usually be quick to volunteer it. However if he has withdrawn out of defensiveness you'll probably be met with either an evasive response, or some level of hostility.

On the other end of the spectrum are people who aggressively attack as soon as they are threatened or challenged. "The best defense is a good offense," goes the old sports cliché, and many people live by it. The person who has adopted this coping mechanism has usually found that she can intimidate others into submission with the threat of a confrontation. A typical part of this tactic is to blame you or someone else in an effort to deflect the focus from herself. She may also try to make her "attacker" feel guilty by pointing out how hardworking she is, how much she's sacrificed, or how much personal pain she's endured on his behalf. "Where's the customer suggestion file? You said it would be on my desk by noon," a manager might ask his assistant. "Neither Susan nor Linda is in today, and I've been covering for them," the defensive assistant might reply. "I skipped my break and had to answer the phones, too. Plus I've got a cold. I dragged myself out of bed to come to work. I shouldn't even be here!" The assistant is hoping that her good deeds will outweigh the neglected file, or, at the very least, that her manager will back off rather than get into an argument.

Withdrawal and aggression are common defensive behaviors among animals. If cornered, most animals will either freeze or lash back. We humans use these strategies but have also developed a few more sophisticated methods of handling perceived threats. One of these is to profess our religious beliefs, our family values, or our high morals and ethics. Politicians are famous for this. Richard Nixon, accused in 1952 of taking illegal campaign contributions, declared on national television that the only thing he'd received was his dog, Checkers. "The kids, like all kids, love the dog, and I just want to say this, right now, that regardless of what they say about it, we are going to keep it." Nixon was trying to deflect criticism by professing the family values of a devoted and loving father.

The courtroom is a natural forum for such protestations. People accused of unethical or criminal behavior often retreat behind their religious commitment as a first line of defense. They are also loyal friends, devoted fathers, and loving husbands. They've recently found the Lord and are born again. We hear it all the time, even when the defendant is guilty of unimaginably brutal crimes.

Another uniquely human defensive behavior is to emotionally disarm the attacker by flattering him. The person on the defensive will respond to criticism by declaring, "You're really important to me, and it makes me feel awful that you're so upset about this. I value your opinion more than anyone's. I'm sorry you're so unhappy with me. If it weren't for your support, I'd be lost"—and so on until the critic is swept away on a wave of compliments. How can he criticize someone who is so fond of him? If he doesn't realize he's being manipulated, the guilt-stricken attacker may even end up apologizing for his criticisms.

Yet another sign of defensiveness is the unprovoked protestation of innocence. This is the tactic that elicited Shakespeare's "The lady doth protest too much, methinks." It's natural, and even expected, for someone to deny or explain accusations against him. But when someone launches into a long excuse for his conduct even before it has been called into question, he's acting defensively. Likewise, even if someone's conduct has been questioned, his response may be so overblown that you should wonder why.

The most common causes of defensiveness are embarrassment, anger, guilt, or being caught in a lie. But specific events aren't always to blame; some people are defensive about their very existence. Consider the stay-at-home mom who refers to herself as "just a housewife," or the corporate employee who calls himself a "wage slave." Even if these people believe they're doing the right things with their lives, they apparently don't feel that the rest of the world respects them for it. A sort of free-floating defensiveness seeps into their personalities. The housewife may express her political opinions defensively because she fears no one will take her seriously. The wage-earner may get snippy with a car salesman who, he thinks, isn't treating him with enough respect. If you didn't know about their defensive streak, you wouldn't understand their behavior.

When you recognize the signs of defensiveness, ask yourself what the cause might be. If the person is probably reacting out of guilt, embarrassment, or anger, or to cover up a lie, stick to your guns. Don't let someone's various defensive maneuvers distract you. If she seems to have no obvious reason to behave defensively, consider the possibility that her attitude has more to do with her basic insecurity than with anything you said.

Braggadocio

"I'm not bragging—it's really true." Whether it is or not, someone who inserts self-glorifying comments into a conversation is usually doing so for a reason. Braggadocio typically takes the form of interjecting one's accomplishments when they're not relevant, name-dropping, or exaggerating one's successes.

To recount your accomplishments or mention someone's name for a good reason is not braggadocio. During a job interview, for example, it's appropriate to stress your achievements and offer impressive references. Similarly, there's nothing wrong with responding truthfully when asked "How much do you earn?" or "Were you a good student?" If you make a million dollars a year and were a straight-A student, so be it. You didn't volunteer the information but merely answered a question—so you're not bragging.

Before we examine jurors in open court, we often know a tremendous amount about them from their questionnaires. But we have few clues about who will be a braggart, because the questionnaires usually don't give the jurors much chance to boast. It's always telling when, during oral questioning, someone launches into a self-aggrandizing speech about his fairness, superior intelligence, or stunning accomplishments.

Bragging is a color- and class-blind trait. It occurs in people from every walk of life and at every level of success. Sometimes they have a lot to brag about. Sometimes they don't. Sometimes what they brag about is true. Sometimes it is clearly fictional. *But over the years I've noticed one consistent trait among braggarts: they nearly always lack true confidence.* They boast because they need approval and recognition. Confident, secure people who are satisfied with their position in life don't need to steer the conversation to themselves and their achievements.

When you see this occurring, first ask yourself whether the horn-blowing was called for, as in a job interview, or volunteered out of the blue. If it was called for and handled appropriately, I wouldn't attribute any significance to it. If the boast was gratuitous, try to determine whether it was true, exaggerated, or totally false. If it was true but inserted at an inappropriate moment, you can usually interpret the behavior as a sign of arrogance, lack of confidence, or need for approval.

Claims that are greatly exaggerated or altogether false shed a very different light on the person. Someone who falsifies her achievements reveals deep unhappiness and dissatisfaction with her life, as well as an obvious lack of candor. This behavior points to a sense of inadequacy far greater than that of the person whose boasts are gratuitous but true. In rare instances, the fabrications are so extreme I have to wonder whether their maker is delusional, if only because she actually thinks people believe what she's saying.

I recently conducted a mock trial in a case that involved the design of a piece of machinery. Among the jurors was a fifty-five-year-old man who had been one of thousands of engineers with a large aerospace company for many years. He was asked about his job. One could have inferred from his answer that he had been a key player in the development of the American space effort over the past two decades. For a number of reasons, I had the impression that he was grossly exaggerating.

After the presentation of the evidence, the jury began its deliberations. The aerospace engineer was extremely opinionated and egotistical. He quickly rejected opposing views and constantly reminded the other jurors of his vast experience with product design. Everything from his words to his body language reeked of his dissatisfaction with his life. He cut people off in mid-sentence, was sarcastic toward those who disagreed with him, and shook his head and rolled his eyes in frustration and contempt if someone voiced a view different from his. Without a doubt, this was a man who had not achieved the degree of professional success he had hoped for. The bitterness in his voice led me to believe that he would be quick to blame his lack of success on someone or something other than himself.

Ultimately, as I would have predicted, this man's opinions swayed most of the other jurors. They allowed his aggressive, boastful approach to intimidate, subdue, or persuade them. Had they been reading him correctly, they would have realized he was the last person whose lead they should have followed: he was motivated by his need to be important, not by the desire to listen to all points of view and reach a fair decision.

Exaggeration

Imagine a conversation between Little Miss Sunshine and Eeyore, the gloomy donkey of the Winnie-the-Pooh stories. Little Miss Sunshine's statements would be laced with words like "wonderful," "the best," "perfect," and "fabulous," while Eeyore's would be loaded with "awful," "horrible," "disgusting," "depressing." There would be no room for shades of gray.

We all encounter Little Miss Sunshines and Eeyores in life. Sometimes we run into someone who gets equally worked up about positives and negatives. This sort of exaggeration often signals the person is insecure and trying to be noticed. If you had a bad experience at the dentist's a few years back, she had an even worse one. If you know a great Italian restaurant, she knows the world's best. Besides being insecure, people who engage in this sort of exaggeration are often trying to control the conversation and the behavior of those participating in it. If a group of friends is pondering which restaurant to try, aren't they likely to choose the one that's "absolutely the best"? Who wouldn't shy away from a movie that is "the worst piece of junk I've ever seen"?

Some people express themselves in extremes not because they want to control others' behavior but because that's how they see life. The positive thinkers include those who are sincerely thrilled to be alive and who express their enthusiasm at the drop of a hat. But there are also people who adopt a jovial attitude in an attempt to disguise a deep disappointment with life, or in an effort to change, or at least ignore, their fate through sheer force of will. "If I act as if I'm happy, I'll be happy," they tell themselves. It can be very difficult to distinguish between the person who is truly joyful and the one who has constructed a sunny façade. Occasionally someone who's overcompensating will let down her guard, revealing her anxiety or sadness in a passing comment or facial expression. But often, only time will tell. By watching and listening to her and perhaps asking questions, you'll eventually learn whether her cheerful disposition is genuine.

More distressing are people who are intensely pessimistic and critical. They're not happy with life and are quick to let you know it. What's worse is that they often seem to want to infect everyone around them with their own misery. There's a natural inclination to recoil from these naysayers, but I try not to. When I'm speaking with someone like this, I try to be sensitive to why he has chosen this form of communication. Is he reaching out for me to soothe his misery? Has he recently been overwhelmed by a tragic loss?

As this book has emphasized throughout, the benefits of reading people aren't limited to protecting yourself in a sometimes harsh, competitive, and dishonest world. These techniques also enable you to make the world a little better for those around you. When you understand what motivates people and learn how to listen to them, you'll be a better friend, a more effective boss, even a more compassionate stranger. So although your instinct may be to run from the Eeyores in your life, try to connect with them at least once or twice. At the very least, you'll learn a little bit more about human nature.

Ingratiating Behavior

Ingratiation is generally interpreted as blatant manipulation. The many colorful nicknames for this trait—"kissing up," "sucking up," and "brown-nosing," to cite three of the tamest—testify to the contempt in which the behavior is commonly held. But there are times when people ingratiate themselves with others out of innocent motives. So before you judge someone a brown-noser, consider the context.

Someone may try to please out of a desire to make you feel comfortable, intelligent, and accepted. Sympathy is another possible motive. If you've recently gone through an ordeal, your friends may offer such utterly unconditional support that it seems they're yessing you to death. Whether or not you like the behavior, their intentions are good.

People who lack confidence in their own ideas sometimes offer unwavering support to those they admire. They are followers, too timid to make their own choices. Their actions may resemble brown-nosing, but they aren't truly manipulative.

Then there are real brown-nosers—the ones who *are* manipulative. They typically fall into two categories: those who ingratiate to gain a personal advantage, and those who do so to win your approval.

I recall an interview I held with a candidate for a research position at my office a few years ago. She had excellent qualifications, a pleasant appearance, and an engaging manner. But as the interview progressed, I started to get the uncomfortable feeling she was too good to be true. When I told her the job involved a lot of fieldwork, overseeing mock trials, conducting community attitude surveys, and so forth, she assured me the tasks I described were exactly what she wanted to do. When I asked how she felt about working in a small company, she said it was perfect given her temperament. No matter where my questions headed, she followed with enthusiastic answers. Either this was a match made in heaven, or the woman would say anything to get the job. I decided to find out which.

Having already established that what this young woman supposedly longed to do more than anything else was assist me with my fieldwork, I asked how she felt about the clerical responsibilities that came with the job. She was quick to respond that she loved to type, organize files, and handle phones. When I asked how she felt about the prospect of my small company merging with a large national firm, she apparently forgot that just twenty minutes earlier she'd said working in a small, informal office was extremely important to her. Now she gushed that the merger was "an incredibly exciting possibility"; and she "looked forward to the opportunities it would present." She did not get the job: her ingratiating behavior was clearly a means to an end.

To determine whether an apparent brown-noser is trying to manipulate you for her own gain or just seeking approval, take a close look at her other traits. People who use ingratiation to control or manipulate will usually demonstrate some of the other controlling, manipulative traits discussed in previous chapters. They'll show signs of self-centeredness that will be absent in the person who just wants your approval. That person will tend to be quiet and unassuming, perhaps even nervous. If his demeanor, appearance, and other clues point to a passive or timid nature, he probably isn't trying to control you in the strict sense, but to gain your acceptance.

Self-criticism

The ability to poke fun at yourself is an admirable quality. We all do it from time to time. Extremely self-deprecating behavior, however, makes a powerful statement about a person's self-esteem. Whenever you hear somebody make more than one or two self-critical remarks in the course of a conversation, you should wonder why.

The first question to ask is whether the comments are meant as ice-breakers or good-natured social gestures. "I'd forget my head if it weren't screwed on" is clearly a casual remark, unless the person repeats similar sentiments so often you feel compelled to respond to them. However, when an obese person says, "I'm such a pig, I can't say no to a meal," there is a lot more going on than lighthearted self-mockery.

In my experience, people who make biting self-critical remarks are very insecure and (obviously) have low self-esteem. Their motives are often complex. They may be hoping you'll disagree with them, or they may be looking for encouragement, support, help, or sympathy. Some self-deprecating comments are an effort to deliver the first strike: by addressing the topic themselves, they don't have to worry that someone else will bring it up. Some people even use self-critical remarks to put their companions at ease. By laughing at a flaw of their own, they hope to send the message that it's not a big deal to them and shouldn't be to anyone else.

How someone responds to others' remarks about her is a good test for whether she is harmlessly poking fun at herself or is truly sensitive about a particular subject. For example, if a man bristles whenever someone comments on his receding hairline and also makes self-deprecating jokes about "pitiful old bald guys," that tells me this may be a very touchy issue for him. While it may not point to overall low self-esteem, it probably indicates he feels uncomfortable about his appearance.

If a person doesn't handle others' criticisms well, but criticizes himself when you're around, it is a safe bet he's reaching out to you. People who repeatedly make such comments want a response. They are watching carefully to see whether you agree or disagree, whether you approve or disapprove of them. There are many ways to respond, but be aware that avoiding the topic altogether is in itself a response, which will probably be interpreted by them as your agreement with their self-criticism.

The Broken Record

We all have favorite conversational themes, chords we like to strum over and over again. We have stories we like to tell, good times we like to re-call. Now and then, however, you'll encounter a person who returns to one particular topic with tiresome regularity, until you want to cry out, "Enough, already! I get it." Unless he's repeating himself because of a mental condition such as senility, such repetitiousness usually means one of two things. Either he is nervously trying to fill space in the conversation rather than suffer through awkward silences, or he's sending a loud, clear signal that something is on his mind, and he wants you to acknowledge it.

I saw a glaring example of this during jury selection in a case in downtown Los Angeles. One of the jurors, a middle-aged and significantly overweight woman, mentioned early in her questioning that at the tender age of eighteen she had become a grand master in a card game similar to bridge. A few minutes later, she let us know her IQ was at the "genius level." It wasn't long before we heard about her prowess at the card game again, and then another reference to her high IQ. The topic of someone's IQ rarely comes up during jury selection, and when it does, it doesn't come up half a dozen times. This woman was clearly trying to impress us with her repeated references to her intelligence. The repetition, especially when coupled with such blatant braggadocio, revealed she was obviously insecure, probably as a result of her weight, and was seeking acceptance and respect.

Whenever you encounter somebody obsessed with a particular matter, look for the reason. What is causing them anxiety, bringing them joy or satisfaction, or striking them as funny? Whatever it is, it weighs so heavily on their mind that there's no room for anything else. If you ignore it, it usually won't go away. No matter how unimportant the subject may be to you, they're crying out for you to acknowledge it. And until you do, don't expect them to focus completely on anything else.

Gossiping

"I really like Diane, but . . ." "Did you hear that Jim got fired?" "Could you believe how Joe and Mary behaved at the party last night?" Gossip is the tool of the insecure, unhappy, vicious, and manipulative. Whenever someone tries to draw me into a gossipy conversation, I wonder what she says about me behind my back.

People who love to gossip are seldom comfortable admitting it, so they often disguise their rumor-mongering as concern for others or idle chitchat. No matter how it's packaged, gossip has a few distinguishing characteristics. First, gossip is nearly always negative. Even if the person begins on a positive note, the conversation will soon degenerate into a critique. Second, the person who gossips usually wants to persuade you to her way of thinking or ferret out your opinion about the gossip's victim. Finally, the person who instigates the gossip session is often trying to boost her own ego by demeaning someone else.

The best way to figure out the motives for gossiping is to consider the target and the context. If the target is a social or job-related competitor, jealousy and resentment are frequent motives. If the topic is a mutual acquaintance, the gossip may want to learn how you feel about her, or to influence you to dislike her. Occasionally the person who is gossiping is strictly hunting for information: gossip usually begets gossip. It's also a way for the person who knows a juicy tidbit or two to feel important and get attention.

Volunteering Information

Throughout, this book has made a point of how important it is to reveal information about yourself. Self-disclosure makes others feel comfortable, encourages them to open up, and leads them to trust you. But there's a difference between being open during the give-and-take of a conversation and forcing information about yourself into the dialogue, particularly at inappropriate times. Whenever someone volunteers information, listen carefully. What they're telling you is significant to them and should be to you as well.

It's one thing for someone to tell me she is a recovering alcoholic if I ask her why she doesn't drink. It is quite another for a virtual stranger to approach me at a cocktail party and volunteer that she's drinking soda water because she's a recovering alcoholic. Likewise, if I ask someone whether he played sports in college and he tells me he was on the football team, I don't draw the same inferences as I would if he volunteered this news out of the blue.

People commonly volunteer information to make a connection with you by telling you what they think you want to hear or what they believe will impress you. During jury selection, we're always on the alert for people who talk at length about how fair and unbiased they are. They're clearly trying to sell themselves, which is always cause for concern. Maybe they really are fair, but if so, it's going to be revealed in their attitudes about a host of issues. We're not just going to take their word for it. The fact that they volunteer the information only excites our suspicions. Anyone that eager to serve as a juror may be saying whatever he thinks we want to hear, not what he really thinks.

People also volunteer information as a way to cover up what they don't want to reveal. If the saleswoman volunteers how religious or ethical she is, take note. She may be proffering the information to disarm you. Anytime someone touts any aspect of their character *without being asked,* I wonder why. Volunteered personal information about someone's beliefs or habits is often inaccurate or exaggerated. These self-disclosing statements are like flashing neon arrows pointing to areas you should watch carefully.

Often people will volunteer personal information about their accomplishments. When they do, it's usually because they're feeling a bit insecure and need to brag to boost their ego, or maybe they're hoping to influence your opinion of them. There's always the possibility, too, that they're just trying to get the conversation rolling.

Another reason people volunteer information is to gauge your reaction to a sensitive subject. They want to avoid investing their energy in the relationship if whatever they volunteered is going to create a problem. Several years ago, when the AIDS epidemic was most highly publicized, a friend revealed to me that he was HIV-positive. As he did this, I watched him closely. He was not glancing down or trying to avoid my gaze; rather, he was studying me intently. It was clear he cared very much how I responded; he was testing me. Would I judge him or withdraw from him? Similarly, I've known a number of single mothers who very early in a new relationship with a man reveal that they are divorced and have young children at home. They broach the topic at the start because they know there's no future in a relationship with someone who isn't sympathetic to the burdens of single parenthood.

A similar tactic can work in business situations. For example, when meeting with new clients I frequently volunteer that I have young children at home. When I disclose this, I usually learn more about the client, who will almost always reveal whether he or she has children. I also communicate my need to schedule meetings in advance, since the demands of parenthood sometimes keep me from dropping everything on a moment's notice. If I make this clear up front, the client and I can establish rules that work for both of us.

People may volunteer information about themselves to set limits, gauge your response, sell you, or create intimacy. Always keep your ears open for these statements, and give them special attention.

Humor

Humor has many faces. It can be biting and sarcastic, subtle, slapstick, genuine, or insincere. It can be used to bring people closer, or to maintain distance. Scores of books have been written on the topic, and still some aspects of humor are too subjective ever to be explained fully. But a basic understanding of how it's used in communication is essential to accurately reading people.

Humor can be employed as a weapon or a shield. It can be a powerful tool of aggression, used to hurt and humiliate. It can be used to deflect criticism or defuse a crisis. People frequently use humor to disguise their true feelings; if they don't dare lodge a serious complaint, they'll toss off a humorous but pointed remark instead. As with self-criticism, humor can also be a means of self-protection. The woman who jokes about her height may be introducing the topic to guard against someone else bringing it up, or to suggest to others that she is comfortable with it.

Always ask whether humor is directed at a particular person and, if so, whether it has a critical element. If the employee who arrives late is met by a supervisor who says, "I'm glad you could join us," he should take that comment seriously, no matter how lightheartedly it was delivered. Similarly, whenever I hear someone follow a critical but humorous remark with the phrase "Just kidding," I take note. Usually they're not kidding at all. They're just trying to disguise their message.

If I decide the humorous remark wasn't a veiled criticism, I look to the other most likely motivations. The best way to determine the motives behind someone's use of humor is to evaluate the nature of his jokes (harsh or warm, for example) and gauge its impact on the dialogue.

- Does the humor redirect the conversation? If so, it may be the speaker's preferred method of getting control or attention. Or perhaps the person is trying to distract you from a subject he would prefer to avoid.
- Does the humor take a serious topic and attempt to turn it into a casual or lighthearted one? Consider whether the joke is an attempt to avoid confrontation.

- Does the humor reflect a compassionate attempt to show empathy or understanding?
- Does the humor disguise emotions the person may not want to reveal—fear, disappointment, embarrassment, jealousy, anger?
- Does the humor add meaning or enjoyment to the conversation? People who are happy and comfortable with life often just naturally use humor. They have no particular motive. But if this is the case, the joke will not be at someone else's expense.

Sarcasm

Sarcasm is one of the most powerful ways to communicate. Like humor, it can take various forms, but unlike humor it is rarely harmless. Nearly always, people use sarcasm to express a strongly felt opinion, belief, or emotion when they don't want to come right out and say it.

Whether I'm selecting a jury or choosing a friend, I'm always very alert to sarcasm. Cutting and harsh, or mild and funny, sarcasm says a tremendous amount about a person. It speaks of anger, hostility, bitterness, jealousy, frustration, and dissatisfaction with life. Someone who resorts to sarcastic remarks, no matter how charmingly they are delivered, is saying, "Watch out, I bite." He almost always ends up at the hard end of my personal "hardness scale."

No matter how confident they may appear, people who make sarcastic remarks rather than communicate more directly are often insecure. Confident people usually express their feelings directly. They don't need to attack from the flanks. The sarcastic person is also usually manipulative; he attempts to influence the action from the sidelines instead of approaching it head-on.

Sarcasm can be extremely hurtful. It's usually aimed at an individual rather than a group or event, which means that for nearly every sarcastic remark, there's someone who feels its sting. With very few exceptions, sarcasm is a cruel and insensitive way to get a laugh or make a point at someone else's expense. Always be alert to someone who favors this method of communication.

KEY POINTS

Always ask why someone is leading you toward or away from a topic of conversation: Is it a noble effort not to brag, criticize, hurt, or embarrass you or another? Or is it an attempt to cover up a lie, self-promote, or grab attention? Or is it just a coincidence?

Be on the alert for common ways people use their answers to direct conversation:

- *nonresponsiveness.* An isolated occurrence doesn't mean much, but if there's a pattern, there's a reason.
- *failure to deny or explain when it would be expected.* If you're certain they heard you, their silence usually means your concerns are well-founded.
- *short answers.* The consistent lack of a normal amount of detail should make you question "why?"
- *long answers.* They're often used to disguise the truth, by deflection and distraction.
- *answering a question with a question.* Unless more information is really needed to answer the question, someone who uses this technique is usually probing for information from which he can tailor a response.
- *pregnant pauses.* Something derailed the person. It's usually the last thing you said.
- *interruptions.* The motive may be to control the conversation, get attention, or just excitement or enthusiasm.
- *rambling.* It's usually a nervous habit or lack of focus.
- *changing subjects.* Watch to see if the person is abandoning the subject or just approaching it from a different direction.

Watch for verbal calling cards and revealing habits: They're usually laced with meaning.

- *slang.* Colloquialisms, bad grammar, and trendy sayings are good indications of personal background. But before you reach any conclusions about someone, look to see if they can turn it on and off at will.
- *word themes.* Our interests, values, and temperament are revealed by the word images we favor.
- *use of titles.* Sarcastic, respectful, or just the way someone was raised, there's often meaning behind their use.
- *profanity.* To gauge its significance, consider how frequently it is used and under what circumstances.
- *defensiveness.* Remember the best defense is often thought to be a good offense. Don't be knocked off the scent by someone's aggressive behavior.
- *braggadocio.* Unsolicited boasting reflects not just the obvious arrogance, but an insincere streak as well.
- *exaggeration.* Watch for other signs of dishonesty and low self-esteem, as one of those traits is usually at the core of this behavior.

- *ingratiating behavior.* Brown nosers want approval, but don't assume evil motives.
- *self-criticism.* Humility is great. But in the extreme it reflects deep insecurity.
- *the broken record.* Whatever warrants obvious repetition by someone is very important to her. Don't ignore it.
- *gossip.* Consider it the tool of the unhappy, insecure, mean-spirited, and manipulative.
- *volunteering information.* Unsolicited self-disclosure, especially in large doses, signals an attempt to connect, impress, persuade, brag, test, or deceive.
- *humor.* As a sword or shield, it's a powerful tool. Identify whether it is lighthearted or cutting, and you'll be well on your way to discovering what it says about the jokester.
- *sarcasm.* With few exceptions, sarcasm is a way to get a laugh or make a point indirectly—usually at someone else's expense.

Actions Speak Louder Than Words: Recognizing the Revealing Nature of Behavior

The McMartin Preschool trial taught me many things about human behavior. Oddly, one of the lessons that has stayed with me the longest has nothing to do with the defendants, the children, or the media circus that surrounded that trial for years. Instead, it has to do with one of the jurors, a quiet, analytical Asian man with a college degree in engineering. When we first interviewed him, he seemed the very essence of the anonymous engineer: nondescript, neat, clean clothing; bland hairstyle; quiet voice; controlled, precise mannerisms. As I watched him in the jury box and listened to his calm, intelligent responses, nothing about him suggested he'd be anything more than a quiet follower type once he got on the jury.

But his behavior toward the other jurors cast a whole new light on the man. As they entered and left the courtroom, he graciously held the door for them. He organized groups for lunch, and on Monday mornings was always the first one to ask how everyone's weekend had been. In addition to being smart, he was clearly a caretaker. Intelligent caretakers take charge. He became the foreman.

This experience reinforced just how closely we have to watch the way people behave toward others if we want to get the fullest sense of who they are. All the other factors covered in this book—appearance, body language, environment, voice, even the words people speak—must be viewed alongside their actual behavior in the real world. Life isn't just a series of one-on-one interviews between you and other individuals. In order to understand people well, you must see them in action and learn to recognize when their actions are speaking louder than their words.

Character is ultimately revealed by what a person does, not what he says. A few of the most highly evolved among us may achieve perfect consistency between what we say about ourselves and how we behave, but with most of us there's a gulf. This is by no means always sinister. Sure, there are times when people pretend to have good qualities that their actions prove aren't there. But there are also diamonds in the rough whose real beauty is hidden beneath their modest, self-effacing ways. Very often the people least likely to blow their own horns are the most loyal friends, the hardest workers, and the most dedicated parents. And it's their actions that prove it.

Honesty, compassion, confidence, egotism, commitment, and many more key personality traits can be seen in people's behavior toward you and others. Sometimes the *only* way you'll learn of certain traits is by observing people's behavior. This chapter will cover some of the most common ways important traits are revealed by actions. If the behavior matches the pattern you've already seen develop, you'll know you're on the right track. If the behavior points in a far different direction, I suggest you believe the behavior.

HOW PEOPLE TREAT OTHERS

Unless you live in a remote farmhouse, you encounter dozens of people every day. The encounters can range from a three-hour heart-to-heart with your girlfriend to a friendly wave to the guy who lets you merge in front of him on the freeway or a nasty gesture to the one who doesn't. A bit of our character is revealed in each of these exchanges. To a remarkable degree—over time, and through the hundreds of encounters we have each week—most of us are consistent. We may put on an especially genteel face for a first date or a job interview, but eventually our real character peeps through the curtain, then boldly steps out.

As you meet new people and try to get a better sense of your older acquaintances, you have lots of opportunities to watch the way they treat other people, not just you. Three groups are especially revealing: co-workers, children, and "everyday" people.

Interaction with Co-workers

Whether it's an office tower or a gas station, the workplace is like a mini-kingdom. There's his highness the boss, the knights of the realm, and the serfs. Which is to say that unless you're at the very peak of the pile or its extreme bottom, you deal daily with superiors, co-workers, and subordinates. Those dealings are often political, and always delicate. The way people handle them reflects many facets of their character.

How a supervisor treats his employees is tremendously telling. Power is intoxicating, and many people handle it poorly. The supervisor who is kind, respectful, and friendly with his employees tends to be self-confident, compassionate, generous, outgoing, and concerned about the way others perceive him. The supervisor who treats her subordinates like servants is typically insecure, domineering, insensitive, and uncaring, not only in the workplace but in every aspect of her life. People don't flip a switch and consistently treat their employees in one way and their spouse or friends in another.

When we select jurors, one of the most important questions we ask is whether they are supervisors at work and, if so, how many people report to them. People who spend much of their time in a position of control and responsibility over others typically take those workplace attitudes home. Not surprisingly, they also often become the foreperson of the jury.

An employee's attitude toward his boss is just as revealing as the boss's attitude toward her employees. Some employees are sullen and bitter, resentful, dissatisfied with their lives, angry, frustrated, and even jealous. Others are eager to please, sometimes to the point of kissing up; that points to insincerity, a manipulative character, and a need for approval. Still others are respectful, responsive, and cooperative; that reflects security, high self-esteem, and comfort with their role in the workplace. Usually, those who are at ease with their position at work are also comfortable with their lives in general.

Pay particular attention to how people treat their peers at work. Some are supportive, helpful team players. Others seem to believe that their success at work depends on their co-workers' failure. They are unsupportive and critical; they typically don't socialize with their co-workers. The better the relationship between a person and his co-workers, the more likely that he is self-confident, comfortable with his situation in his life, and considerate. On the other hand, if he's competitive, unsupportive, jealous, and selfish at work, why should you expect him to behave any differently at home?

Interaction with Children

Children are unique objects of our attention. Some people are instantly at ease with them, while others, even if they themselves are parents, never quite get the hang of communicating with kids. It would be unfair to assume that the latter type is uptight or uncaring; to a great degree the rapport one has with youngsters is a nonelective trait. But the way people treat, and train, their own children can be very helpful when you want to gauge their values and their attitudes toward others.

I have friends whose two young sons are always included at the beginning of any dinner party. Their parents introduce them to each of the guests, who are met with an exceedingly polite "Good evening, Ms. Dimitrius," or "Good afternoon, Mr. Mazzarella." When it's time to eat, the adults withdraw to the dinner table. Meanwhile, the children enjoy something special apart from the grown-ups, who can then engage in lively, uninterrupted conversation. My friends are proud of their children and sensitive to their need to be included—but equally sensitive to the fact that many adult guests will enjoy the evening much more if dinner isn't dominated by squirming youngsters, tipped glasses, and incomprehensible descriptions of the latest video game.

I know another couple whose three young children are allowed to run wild not only through their own dinner parties but at homes where they are guests. This insensitivity to guests and hosts alike reflects egocentricity and a lack of consideration for others. It also reflects a failure to take personal responsibility.

Between these two extremes lie the rest of us. Do we caution our children not to touch objects in a souvenir shop? Do we ask them to be quiet at the movie theater? Are we playful with them? Do we include them in our conversations, rather than follow the "speak only when spoken to" approach? Affirmative answers to these and similar questions may reveal consideration, thoughtfulness, sensitivity to others, compassion, patience, and even playfulness and good humor. A negative response may reveal just the opposite. There's so much to learn, it's well worth paying attention.

Interaction with "Everyday" People

I recently went out to dinner with a friend and her new beau. She had been raving for weeks about what a kind, considerate, and engaging person he was. He had truly swept her off her feet. Within minutes of meeting him I thought, "Boy, has he got her fooled." At the restaurant, he curtly announced his reservation to the hostess without so much as a glimmer of courtesy. He proceeded to interrogate the waiter about the menu, as if he were conducting a criminal investigation, then glared at the busboy who brushed against him as he served his water. Meanwhile, he was exuding charm and grace to those of us at the table, whom he obviously deemed worthy of his attention and good humor. It was clear to me that he was a nice guy only when it served his purposes. The "little people" obviously didn't rate.

I have made the same observation about many jurors during the course of my career. It is not unusual for a juror to be polite, solicitous, and respectful to the lawyers and judges, then downright rude to his fellow jurors and to court personnel. He may let the door to the courtroom close behind him even though a fellow juror is right behind, or push through the crowd as he enters or exits the courtroom, or bump thoughtlessly against other jurors' knees as he heads for his seat in the jury box. Since assessing a person's position on the "hardness scale" is so important in evaluating character, every time I see someone act thoughtlessly or rudely, I take note.

As for the lawyers in the courtroom, very frequently they display completely different attitudes toward the judge and other court personnel. Sometimes they will be respectful and friendly to the clerk, court reporter, and bailiff when the judge or jury is present, but rude when no one "important" is watching. A lawyer's mistreatment of court personnel reveals his arrogance, controlling nature, and possibly even insecurity. It also reveals his poor judgment: in most courtrooms the judge has an excellent relationship with his staff. They are quick to report to him any abuses by the attorneys—usually during the very next recess.

Whenever I'm evaluating someone's character, I pay careful attention to how she relates to the clerk at the grocery store, the teller at the bank, the gas station attendant, the waitress at the local diner, and whoever else she meets. Does she always walk past the Salvation Army volunteer without reaching into her pocket? Is she the type of person who always writes thank-you notes and sends get-well cards or thoughtful gifts? Does she glare at the clerk who's having trouble with the cash register, or give her a comforting smile?

Truly kind, thoughtful, and confident people do not treat others in dramatically different ways depending on their mood or their perception of what someone can do for them. As a result, *watching how someone acts toward "everyday people" can give you a pretty good idea how he or she will act toward you once the bloom is off the rose of your relationship.*

READING THE GROUP

Certain situations are tailor-made for people-watching. In these settings you can observe how someone deals with people he likes, people he can't stand, family, co-workers, and strangers. You've been a participant in scenes like these many times, but the next time you're there, take a moment not only to watch the people around you but to read them.

The Family Dinner

In many famous films, the crucial scene takes place around the family dinner table. It's the perfect forum for drama, and it's fun and informative to watch, especially if the family isn't your own.

The family dinner can be extremely revealing, especially if it's attended by someone's parents, spouse, siblings, and children. For one thing, you can get a good feel for the person's background. As was noted in chapter 2, someone's background is a key predictive factor. How someone was raised, and by whom, will have a tremendous influence on the type of person she is. Psychologists often point out that when it comes to child-rearing, what goes around comes around: those who are raised with criticism become critical, those who are raised with love become caring, and those who are raised with encouragement become supportive. By watching how someone's parents treat her and her siblings, and how she treats them, you can get a good feel for the way she was raised and how she's likely to treat others.

A person's relationship with his spouse is also very telling. Does he expect to be waited on, or is he quick to offer to fill empty glasses, set and clear the table, and wash the dishes? Does he lead the discussion, or passively sit by and watch? Is he affectionate or distant?

The dinner table is also a good place to watch how a person treats her children. Does she draw them into the conversation? Does she keep an eye on their manners? Is she warm and affectionate? Is she relaxed and comfortable around her kids, or critical and tense? Patient or quick-tempered? Take note of the subtleties, and how the children behave toward their parents. Are they timid or confident? Polite or disrespectful?

If you spend time with the family before or after the meal, keep your eyes open. Is there laughter and playfulness in the home? Does the family sit motionless in front of the television until dinner is served, or do they chat? If so, what about? Can you spot evidence of family projects—a jigsaw puzzle, art projects, a plate of kid-decorated cookies? Are there any pets, and if so, how do the family members interact with them?

The first time you have a meal with the family of someone important to you—a prospective mate, a new friend, a business associate—you're often too nervous about the impression you'll make to notice much of what's going on. If you can summon your concentration and really look around, you'll get a priceless preview of what's in store should your relationship grow.

A Workplace, Not Your Own

I love going to my dentist's office. It's not that I have a masochistic streak
that attracts me to Novocain and dental drills. It's just that I always feel
uplifted in that environment. My dentist and his assistant, hygienist, and
receptionist have all been together for years. There is constant laughter,
joking, and friendly inquiries about the events in one another's lives. I'm
inspired by the competence, good cheer, and kindness with which the
people in the office interact with one another and with patients. This is
how all dentists' offices would be in a perfect world.

Even before I learned more about the individual personalities in my
dentist's office, I could guess a lot about them just because of the environment they have created together and the way they treat one another.
The laughter tells me they're friendly, open, and don't take life too seriously. It also suggests that they're content with their jobs and with life in
general. I've never heard any of them gossip, about anyone. While all of
them are very professional and competent, no one appears oppressed or
fixed, nose to the grindstone, at his or her station. The overall feel is one
of ideal equality, respect, and teamwork. In fact, if I didn't know that in
a dentist's office the dentist is typically the boss, I would probably pick
the receptionist as the one in charge, since she's always directing traffic.

What can I tell from a workplace like this? The person whom it reflects
most strongly is the dentist. He picked the staff, and he nurtures the environment. While the other members of the team are equally dedicated
and cooperative, he gets credit for creating and maintaining this atmosphere, because he has the most control over it. The fact that his staff has
stayed with him for many years indicates not only that he's a nice person
and good manager, but also that he probably pays them a fair wage. He's
generous not only with his praise but with his pocketbook—an all too
uncommon trait.

You can learn several important things when you enter someone's
workplace. First, the atmosphere will tell you what kind of person is running the show. This can be an important clue about the person you're
evaluating: Why did he choose this workplace, and this boss? Does he
enjoy the atmosphere, or dread coming to work each day? Are the other
workers cheerful or grouchy? Are they tired and overworked, or energetic? After sizing up the atmosphere, take a look at how your "readee"
fits in. If it's a healthy atmosphere, does he appear to be contributing to
it, or cynically staying on the sidelines? If it's a tense, unpleasant atmosphere, does he seem to notice and mind, or does he shrug and say,
"That's life in the big city"?

When someone is willing to work in a tense, high-pressure atmosphere, it's essential that you look for reasons. For instance, many large law firms have reputations for being sweatshops. The attorneys, particularly the young ones, work incredibly long hours and have little time for themselves or their families. If the only thing I know about someone is that he works in one of these firms and is happy and satisfied there, I know he is probably aggressive, hard-charging, confident, intelligent, and strong-willed. I can also reasonably assume that his family is not his highest priority; he's ambitious and probably self-centered. Once again, there are always exceptions, but this is my bias, and it has been borne out many times as I've gotten to know people who thrive in this environment.

The Company Picnic

A company party or picnic is an excellent occasion to watch your co-workers. Maybe you see them every day at the water cooler or in staff meetings, but larger events can give you a different, and often more revealing, view. Frequently those in attendance are so busy partying they don't spend much time people-watching. But where else can you see someone interact with his boss, colleagues, subordinates, friends, spouse, and children (other people's as well as his own)?

Watch to find out who organizes games and who joins in. Who are the socialites and who are the recluses? Do people spend their time mingling comfortably with superiors, co-workers, and subordinates alike, or do they keep to their own? How do they relate to the children present? How do they treat their spouse? Who spends time with his mate, and who abandons her in favor of other pursuits?

If you apply what you've learned from previous chapters, you'll be able to pinpoint the leaders, the followers, and the loners. You'll find out who is confident and who's insecure; who is happy and who's discontented; who's friends with whom, and who is no one's friend. So don't back out of the next company event. Go to it, watch, and learn.

The Crowded Room

If you've never gone to a party, wedding, or other big event where you don't know most people, and played the observer with the intent to read them, try it. A bash like this is a great opportunity to try to peg different types.

Find the person with the loudest voice and watch how he moves around the room. How closely does he approach the people he talks to?

How frequently does he sit down with them? Does he dominate discussions? Observe the observer. Watch how she reacts when someone approaches her. See how she holds her drink, and whether she sips it nervously or takes long, slow sips as she peers over the glass across the room. Watch the line at the bar or the buffet table, and see who pushes in and who graciously makes room for others. Identify who's taking the lead by organizing activities, making toasts, introducing people, or assuring that everyone's needs are met.

This is, in essence, what we do as we pick juries. We don't just observe physical appearance, ask questions, and listen to the answers; we watch how people interact. An excellent example comes from a case in which the defendant was charged in a murder-for-hire scheme involving the Hare Krishna religion. The juror was a middle-aged, heavyset white woman. There was nothing in particular about her appearance, background, or answers during jury selection that suggested she would be sympathetic to the defendant or the Hare Krishna movement.

But she frequently looked at the defendant almost maternally with warm, kind eyes, and smiled gently whenever he looked toward her. Unlike most of the jurors, while walking in and out of the courtroom she did not give the defendant the widest berth possible, but instead seemed almost to try to engage in contact with him by walking close by.

This woman's actions told me loud and clear that she somehow connected with the defendant. And as it turned out, she was an excellent juror for the defense. In fact, after the trial she befriended the defendant.

Practiced observation like that will reveal much about the personalities you study in a crowded room. Some people will seem intent on dominating the group. They will position themselves at the head of the table, or wherever the most people are. They will be loud and control virtually any discussion in which they participate. These people, while seemingly confident, may actually be the most insecure. Undeniably, they are seeking attention.

There are also observers. They will typically position themselves at the edge of the room, where they can watch everything. They usually speak with people one on one, and while talking they continue to survey the environment. Observers may withdraw to their observation posts because they are uncomfortable in large groups. It's just as likely, however, that they are perfectly comfortable but would rather sit on the sidelines. I can usually tell which: If an observer is approached and withdraws at the first opportunity, he reveals that he's uncomfortable and has staked out his observation post for that reason. If, on the other hand, he engages in conversation for a reasonable period of time, but then graciously excuses himself to find another secluded post, he shows that he is not particularly uncomfortable with large groups but for whatever reason has chosen on that evening to remain on the sidelines.

Those who are generally uncomfortable in large groups will typically shift nervously and change locations frequently. They will avoid contact with others. They will resist when someone attempts to draw them into whatever activities are under way. I know a man who frequently seeks out a television to watch, even when he's a guest in someone else's home. Others will disguise their retreat as an excursion to look at the art down the hall or check out the landscaping in the yard. This type of reaction in a group environment may reveal a number of different things. Perhaps the person is preoccupied with other matters and simply wants to be alone for a while. He may also be very uncomfortable and trying to escape.

I know one very well known attorney who has the disconcerting habit of looking over people's shoulders as he greets them in a crowded room. He's scanning for anyone more worthwhile on whom to focus his attention. This obviously reflects arrogance and earns him a poor score on my personal "hardness scale."

Other people will quickly attach themselves to someone and spend hours without mingling at all. Maybe these two have a lot of catching up to do. But if not, they probably feel uncomfortable in groups.

Still others will work the room, going from person to person as if prizes were being awarded to whoever shakes the most hands. Generally speaking, more confident and outgoing people will be much more sociable in large groups but won't feel the need to flit from person to person.

You never need to evaluate these interactions in isolation. The general observations I've offered here may be confirmed by physical appearance, body language, voice, and other clues. But if those other clues persuade you that the person's interaction in a crowd doesn't fit his overall pattern, you may choose to give it little weight. But make sure you add it to the mix.

IS WHAT YOU SEE WHAT YOU GET?

We'd all like to believe other people when they tell us how honest, caring, and committed they are. We may even feel a little guilty for doubting what people say about themselves, especially if they are close friends or family. Personal experience has taught us, however, that we can't always take people at face value.

A few basic characteristics are important no matter what your relationship is with someone. Honesty is usually at the top of the list. Whether you're looking for a mate or a repairman, you want to know that what you see is what you'll get. Here are a few areas to keep in mind as you're assessing what someone's really like.

Consistent Honesty

It's amazing how often a person who professes to be honest, and maybe even believes it herself, will reveal a certain level of "candor flexibility" in her everyday actions. It's easy to spot a lack of basic honesty if you keep your eyes and ears open.

Does the person call in sick when she wants to take the day off to go shopping or extend her weekend? Does she stretch the facts when she's trying to make a point? Does she acknowledge that she's late because she misjudged her schedule, or does she tell a little lie about bad traffic, car trouble, or alien abduction? Does she fabricate stories about her past accomplishments to impress others? When the clerk at the market gives her too much change, does she bring it to his attention? I watch for these behaviors, and I watch for them very carefully.

Just as we all want other people to believe we're honest, we want to believe others are honest with us. But why should we think that someone who lies to others when it's convenient or profitable won't behave the same way with us? *True honesty, like other character traits, is marked by consistency.*

If someone is dishonest with you, she'll go to some lengths to disguise the fact from you. But, astonishingly, she often won't bother to hide her dishonesty toward others! It's as if dishonesty doesn't count if it's directed elsewhere. Don't be foolish enough to think you're so different and special that no one would dream of fibbing to you. *Assume someone's exactly as honest with you as she is with others.*

Talk Is Cheap: Recognizing People's Values and Priorities from Their Choices

Life is full of choices: free time versus career success, family versus friends, commitment versus freedom. Someone's choices normally carry more weight with me than his professed beliefs. If his choices are inconsistent with his stated values, I'll go with the values reflected by the choices. *Choices reflect what a person's values are; words reflect what he wants you to believe his values are—or what he wishes they were.*

Talk is cheap. It should be tested against actions, if possible. If you want to know whether your spouse really places your marriage before his or her job, you might ask yourself how frequently dinner plans, trips to the movies, vacations, or watching the kids' Little League games are sacrificed to the demands of work. If you wonder whether you're really on your most important vendor's "preferred customer" list, don't rely on what the salesman says, recall what happened the last time a product was in short supply and he had to decide which of his many customers were going to receive a shipment. If you want to know whether your best friend still feels as strongly about your relationship as you do, set aside what she says and ask how frequently she gets in touch. Does she invite you to join her in the activities she once did? Is she now spending her free time with others?

Before you begin evaluating any given action, make certain there were no extenuating circumstances. People *usually* make choices on the basis of what they want, need, or value, but sometimes they act under duress, or out of fear, anger, or misinformation. If you hold someone strictly accountable for her choices without taking circumstances into account, you may judge her too harshly, or even be completely off target.

One, Two, Three Strikes—You're Out

How many chances do you usually give your friends and loved ones? Do the second chances really amount to tenth or eleventh chances? If so, you're not alone. But this habit can leave you involved with people who are never going to live up to your expectations. Everyone makes mistakes, but when someone does the same things over and over again, they are no longer mistakes; they are conscious choices reflecting probable future behavior. You might be justified in overlooking a single questionable action, but when the odd behavior repeats itself, that's not a coincidence. It's a compass, and it should guide your decisions.

Not long ago I couldn't suppress my urge to tell a friend just how incredibly naive I thought she was. She was dating a man who professed to want a committed relationship and assured her he was not seeing anyone else. She wanted to know whether I thought he was cheating on her.

When she told me he never allowed her to answer the telephone at his house, and that he screened calls privately while she was there, I thought, "This doesn't sound good." She then added that he'd changed his phone number several times during the four months she'd been dating him. "Even worse" was my reaction. Then I found out he often went for long walks alone—except for his cell phone! I thought: "It's getting worse all the time." She added that he was always careful to pick up his mail and tuck it away before she could see it. When she told me that he frequently went off in the evenings and declined to tell her where he'd been, I thought: "What next?" There was one more thing: when he traveled alone, he'd put the telephone in his hotel room on "Do not disturb" mode at night.

This guy was either seeing someone else, or he was a criminal. Whatever he was up to, it wasn't good. Any one or two actions might have been understandable, but there was no innocent explanation for the whole pattern.

Likewise, it may be possible for an industrious, responsible employee to sleep through his alarm once, or even on a couple of occasions. But if an employee shows up to work late several times a month, it's fair to assume that he's the opposite of industrious and responsible. If you want to effectively incorporate a person's actions into your analysis of his character, at some point you have to acknowledge what you're seeing and say, "Enough is enough."

What's in It for Me?

The interview goes something like this:

BOSS: What I'm looking for is a team player who is going to spend his time at work worrying about the company and not focused on himself.

APPLICANT: I've always been a team player. I believe if you remain focused on what's best for the team, everything else will take care of itself.

BOSS: Do you have any questions about the company or the responsibilities that come with the job?

APPLICANT: Well, I was curious about how long it would be before I'm eligible for a vacation, and how many weeks of vacation I would get each year.

Putting aside that the boss hopelessly tainted the first response with very poor questioning, this applicant has revealed a "What's in it for me?" personality. The true team player wouldn't have focused immediately on himself. There is nothing unusual about wanting to look out for your own interests; we all have a natural instinct for survival. In fact, someone who constantly sacrifices her own interests for others and becomes a doormat is showing very little self-esteem. But some people take self-interest too far, steadfastly pursuing their own goals to the exclusion of everything and everyone else.

This type of person keeps track of favors and never gives one without expecting at least as much in return. He pursues personal opportunities at the expense of family, friends, and co-workers. Frequently the "What's in it for me?" type is critical of others and jealous of their success. Oddly, he is often the one who most loudly proclaims his commitment to the team. The last thing he wants to do is admit to his selfishness: to do so would defeat his primary goal, which is personal gain. Moreover, many "What's in it for me?" types seem oblivious to the fact that they possess this trait, or else they write it off as assertiveness.

Spotting a "What's in it for me?" person is relatively easy. Does the individual ever give up something important to him without exacting some kind of payment in return, emotional, financial, or other? When he hears of a good opportunity, whether it's tickets to a play or a chance to become involved in an interesting project at work, does he try to hoard or trade on the information, or does he attempt to include others in his good fortune? Is he always looking for an angle, asking questions that relate to how he might benefit from a situation? If you notice a pattern like this, you're probably dealing with a "What's in it for me?" personality.

Remember, level of compassion is among the key predictive traits. "What's in it for me?" people are not usually considerate or compassionate. They may pretend to be, in order to achieve their objectives, but their concern is usually only for show. The "What's in it for me?" person tends to be selfish, jealous, insecure, petty, excessively competitive, and egocentric.

When I am selecting a jury I make note whenever one of the jurors expresses inordinate concern about such things as the number of days he'll need to be off work, whether he can get a note for his employer excusing him for a full day even if he served only half a day, and whether lunch is provided. This person is not focusing on his opportunity to participate as a citizen-judge. He's concentrating on what's in it for him. As a juror, he's likely to be closed-minded and opinionated. I almost always suggest he be excused.

Performance Under Fire

It's relatively easy to be kind, generous, gracious, and witty when all's right with the world. It's a lot more difficult when you're in crisis, under stress, ill, or otherwise tested physically or emotionally. Some psychologists believe that only a thin layer of socialization prevents our id—the animalistic, instinct-driven child within us—from grabbing what we want and throwing tantrums when we don't get our way, just as we did as little children. How someone handles adversity is the ultimate test of his character.

Working in the judicial system has given me the chance to see how people react under extremely stressful circumstances. Some rise to the occasion, the internal animal reined in by self-control, manners, and strength of character. Others break down, go ballistic, or lose all sense of ethics and become abusive and dishonest. You don't know how someone will take the heat until you see her perform under fire.

In the military, those who performed well under fire are recognized and promoted. In business, the dispatcher who calmly meets the crisis presented by a large and unexpected order is equally revered by her boss. In private life, the man who suffers financial or personal loss without blaming others and with honesty, dignity, strength, and a resolve to overcome adversity and move forward should also be respected and admired. Most of us don't weather the storm so nobly.

It's tempting to excuse bad behavior by attributing it to stress, illness, or temporary anger. Sometimes these excuses are valid. But by the same token, it's life's highly charged situations that reveal a person's strength of character. If you have the opportunity to be with someone who is in a state of crisis, stress, or illness, watch him carefully. His actions may not tell you exactly how he'll behave in everyday settings, but you *will* learn how he's likely to react when similar pressures surface in the future. That's invaluable information if you'll be depending on the person either at work or in a personal relationship. My friend's mother used to tell her, "Never marry a man until you've seen what he's like sick, stressed, and angry." It's good advice.

"That's Not Like Him"

This book has emphasized throughout that any deviation from the norm is worth noticing. People are creatures of habit: they develop routines, have a certain repertoire of responses to life's daily challenges, and tend to act the same way over and over again. When someone's behavior deviates dramatically from usual, there is almost always a reason. Occasionally the deviation can be chalked up to one of the exceptions to the rules discussed in chapter 9. But more often the deviation has specific significance. Even if the person denies its importance, you should take note. The deviation may be the first sign that a major change is about to take place.

For example, let's assume a coffee salesman always calls on Le Coffee Beanery on the first day of the month and receives its order on the spot.

Then one month when the salesman shows up, the manager says, "I'll get back to you." While it may be tempting to take the manager at his word, chances are that something's up. Is the Beanery having financial problems? Is the manager talking to another supplier? Is he thinking about leaving the company and thus not tending to business as usual? Whatever the explanation, the fact that there has been a deviation from the norm is significant, even if the manager says, "Don't worry, everything's fine."

I'm not suggesting there's a sinister reason whenever someone's behavior deviates from normal practice. Perhaps when your close friend declines to go on your customary Saturday morning walk, it's because she's just not feeling well. So don't be paranoid—just alert.

People Do Change—Sometimes

An entire generation of hippies in the 1960s transformed itself into the yuppies of the 1980s. The pot-smoking free-love flower children put on their three-piece suits and Rolex watches and jogged to their Wall Street offices.

People change, particularly over long stretches of time. But there's a difference between the decades-long evolution of a personality and the sort of dramatic changes we often wish we could inspire in certain friends or acquaintances. In the typical situation, someone fervently wants his or her mate to change overnight—to be more committed to the relationship, a better parent, more romantic, or harder-working. Many psychologists will tell you that anyone can change "if they really want to." But how can you tell whether someone really has changed, and whether that change is permanent?

First, consider how long someone has behaved in a way that reflects specific beliefs. Back to the hippie-to-yuppie example: a person who spent four years in a hippie phase at Berkeley is less likely to retain those values than someone who spent twelve years living in a commune. *The longer a person engages in a particular type of behavior, the more likely it reflects a core belief or quality, not just a temporary phase or mind-set.*

Another important criterion is how recently the person exhibited the behavior. If I find out that thirty years ago a juror helped his fellow students take over the dean's office, but that since then he's lived a fairly "establishment" life, I don't conclude he'll be antigovernment. But if I find out he picketed the governor's mansion last year, I'll assume he still feels a certain amount of hostility, or at least suspicion, toward the government. *The further in the past an action took place, the less significance you should give it when predicting future behavior.*

If a person's past actions conflict with the way you're reading him today, you should consider how long it took the change to occur and why. Some people really do change their behavior practically overnight, but there's usually a compelling reason: alcoholics stop drinking, abusers quit abusing, some sinners really do find religion. Most often, however, genuine change is an evolutionary process. It takes time. For that reason, when you evaluate someone who has dramatically changed his behavior, try to find out why he changed and how long the process took.

It's natural to want to give people the benefit of the doubt and believe they won't repeat whatever unpleasant deeds they've done. But such generosity can be costly. If you want a clear-eyed view of somebody, temper your goodwill with a little healthy skepticism. Ask yourself:

- How long did he engage in the behavior?
- How recently did he engage in the behavior?
- If he changed his behavior, did he do so overnight or was it an evolutionary process?
- Why did he change?

WHY DID YOU DO THAT?

Most traits and behaviors are fairly easy to understand once you start paying attention and have learned what to look for. Those discussed in this section are no exception. Why does your girlfriend make promises she doesn't keep? Why is your assistant avoiding a simple task that someone with half her abilities could polish off in an hour? What should you make of "preachers"—those annoying folks who feel compelled to lecture you on everything from exercise to parenting to financial planning? What about people who make a big deal out of every act of kindness they perform? Why does money sometimes inspire grand gestures—acts of stunning generosity or appalling chintziness? Finally, what about excuses? Is it possible to tell a sincere apology from an empty one? All of these actions command your attention, and all of them can teach you something useful about a person.

Unkept Promises

We all make commitments we don't keep. We say we'll follow up on that customer order we missed yesterday, and we don't get around to it. We promise to call someone back later in the day, or to stop by and visit soon, and somehow it just doesn't happen. Most of the time we have every intention of following through on our promises, but life interferes.

A child gets sick, the car breaks down, or we simply forget. That's normal, and if it happens only now and then, it doesn't mean much.

However, when someone consistently forgets, has "something come up," or neglects commitments, it does mean something—usually, that she says what sounds good at the moment without thinking or caring about whether she'll be able to deliver. This doesn't necessarily mean she's dishonest or has some evil motive. She may just not consider what it will take to keep her promise. But whatever her motive, you can't count on her—and you shouldn't expect her to change.

Some promise-breakers do have an evil motive. They tell you whatever will get them what they want, then keep the promise only if it's convenient or beneficial. Sometimes they have no intention of following through. They're just saying what they need to as part of some larger strategy to achieve their personal objectives. The trick is knowing the difference between the person who makes a promise without thinking it through and the one who makes a promise with no intention of keeping it.

When evaluating a promise-breaker, I find it helpful to ask four questions:

- Did something unanticipated happen that explains why the person didn't follow through?
- Was the promise made quickly—perhaps too quickly for the person to think it through?
- Is this the type of promise the person has made and broken frequently in the past?
- Did this person have any reason to pacify me with a promise he or she had no intention of keeping?

Someone who breaks her promises frequently but seems to have nothing to gain by it is probably just a people-pleaser who finds it difficult to say no. Once you realize this, don't expect her to keep her promises, but don't judge her too harshly. But if you can identify some selfish reason for her to have made a commitment and failed to keep it—and again, if it happens frequently—watch out. Such consciously misleading behavior points to a self-centered, insensitive, and dishonest character.

Sometimes What You Don't Do
Speaks Louder Than What You Do

If you've ever gone to one of the many clinics on how to reduce stress in your life, you probably received the following advice: make a list of all the tasks you've been avoiding and, one by one, complete them. It's very stressful to avoid duties or neglect your commitments. People normally put up with the stress of putting things off only when they find the task even more unpleasant than the stress.

The things people avoid can be extremely revealing. Of course, there are a lot of chronic procrastinators around who put off virtually everything. But when someone who's usually reliable stalls like a mule over a particular job, especially when it would make a lot more sense for him to simply do it, it's important to look for the cause.

First, before you assume that someone is purposefully avoiding a task, make sure there is no other explanation. Maybe she's just approaching the job in a roundabout way or is overwhelmed by other tasks and not specifically avoiding anything. If, however, the circumstances point toward intentional avoidance, ask yourself what the reason could be. It is usually because she

- lacks confidence and fears failure
- is uncomfortable about doing the task but unwilling to acknowledge that
- is embarrassed
- is offended or put off by some aspect of the task
- is not getting along with the other people involved in the task
- is not personally interested or motivated
- is trying to avoid revealing something that will be disclosed if she acts
- is trying to avoid confrontation

In a fraud case I worked on a few years ago, the passive partner in a restaurant business suspected that the partner who was actually running the restaurant did not properly account for all income and expenses. He asked for an accounting and got a lengthy response detailing the history of the eatery and all of the managing partner's efforts. The response also recounted the restaurant's past successes, included glowing newspaper reviews, and predicted even greater glories in the future. But lo and behold, it did not include the only thing the passive partner wanted: an accounting.

The managing partner's evasiveness only increased the passive partner's curiosity and resolve. Why hide the ball? After a lengthy battle, the passive partner eventually obtained all the pertinent records. Not surprisingly, he found the managing partner had been skimming for years.

In court and in everyday life, I've found that if I know what someone is actively trying to avoid, I can learn much about how she is thinking and feeling. If an employee is putting off a project, odds are she feels overwhelmed or intimidated by it, does not want to deal with the other people involved with it, or is bored with it. But (unless she's a habitual procrastinator) there will be a particular reason. Likewise, if a man has promised his girlfriend that he'll ask his old flame to quit calling him, but he never seems to find the right time or opportunity, there's a reason. He may be embarrassed or offended by the request, or still attached in some way to the old girlfriend. In these cases, as in most, once you've realized the person is avoiding the task, you'll be on your way to unearthing the reason.

Preachers

Some people are quick to tell you what you should think, how you should feel, and how you should behave. They may tout a strong work ethic, aggressiveness, frugality, compassion, attention to detail, or just about anything else. They deliver their message with such intensity it seems reasonable to assume that they possess whatever value it is they're advocating.

Unfortunately, many people preach values that are totally foreign to them. Preaching goodness does not make someone good; preaching hard work does not make him diligent; and preaching compassion does not make him kind. His actions do. Regardless of the passion with which someone delivers a sermon, and despite the fact that he might genuinely believe he practices what he preaches, don't be fooled. When evaluating someone's character and attempting to predict his behavior, focus on actions, not words.

And whether or not someone seems to practice what he preaches, I always wonder why he felt the evangelical urge in the first place. Is he "selling" himself? Trying to control me? Or just rambling to get attention? What is important to keep in mind is that the preacher always has an agenda. If you want to understand him better, look hard for his motive. You'll usually find it, and when you do, you'll find another important clue about him.

Why All the Fanfare?

I was sitting in a small coffee shop one night when I heard a man proudly announce, "This one's on me." I looked up and saw a well-dressed couple in their early fifties. He had his arm rigidly around her waist in a nervous but excited way that indicated they were on a first or second date.

Apparently afraid she hadn't heard his generous offer the first time, he turned to her again and with a reassuring nod of his head, repeated, "This one's on me." True to his word, he sprang for her coffee. I wondered, "Why all the fanfare over a cup of cappuccino?"

I see fanfare not just in personal relationships but in all areas of life— in the man who makes a big fuss when he picks up the check, instead of quietly slipping the waiter his credit card; the boss who parades around the office at bonus time handing out checks as if his employees, after kissing his ring, should bow deeply as they back out of the room; and the woman who is sure to let her friend know just how inconvenient it was to run an errand for her.

When someone insists on making a big deal out of something he does for you, he is sending a message: "I have just done something nice for you. I should be recognized for it. You should be grateful, and you should do something nice for me in return." It's a way to give with strings attached. In some cases, people aren't satisfied with the attention they receive at the time, and continue to remind you afterward of what a generous gesture they made or how much they sacrificed.

The person who insists on fanfare feels he needs to buy your affection, and thinks he has. He's insecure and doesn't believe you'll appreciate him properly if left to your own devices. To ensure your gratitude, he makes certain you realize you're indebted to him. When you repay the debt, you'll prove how much you care.

Now consider those unassuming people who quietly pick up the check, go out of their way to run an errand for you, fill in for you in a pinch at work, bring you chicken soup when you're ill—all without asking for any recognition, let alone payback. Even when you thank them, they're quick to remark, "It was nothing!" They are not trying to win or buy your approval. Their actions spring from a generous and caring nature, and they're confident enough of their own worth and their relationship with you not to worry about how much you appreciate them.

The next time someone does something nice for you or someone else, watch him. As a gauge of confidence, self-esteem, and a caring nature, the fanfare test is very reliable.

Big Spenders and Scrooges

A few years ago I worked on a case in which a dispute arose between the beneficiaries of an elderly woman who had recently died. The woman was partially blind and lived a very isolated and simple life in the same small house she had called home for twenty-five years. When she went to the market she bought what was on sale. If she could use a coupon as well, even better. Her friends and family knew she'd bought a few apartments over the years, and that after her husband died almost twenty years earlier she had managed the apartments herself. They thought this was more of a hobby than a profession.

She left an estate worth more than $33 million.

A much more common personality type is the big spender. Whatever the big spender does, he does first-class: buying expensive clothes, eating at expensive restaurants, staying only at five-star hotels, or always flying first-class. Big spenders are not always rich. People with modest incomes may be big spenders in relative terms. They're the ones who always buy the most expensive gifts, drive cars that cost more than their colleagues', and flaunt wardrobes and jewelry that likely eat up half their salaries.

What moves people to such extremes—frugality to the point of self-sacrifice, or extravagance to the point of financial ruin?

Most people who are frugal to a fault have been poor at some time. As was pointed out in chapter 2, socioeconomic background is a key predictive trait, likely to have a huge impact on a person's outlook and behavior. Many people saw their worlds, or their parents' worlds, crumble during the Depression. These people lived for a decade without any luxuries. For many of them, any personal extravagance is unacceptable. It violates their need to store acorns for the winter that they are sure will come again. Some extremely frugal people also have very low self-esteem and don't feel they are worth spending money on.

The big spender often shares the frugal person's low self-esteem but expresses it in the opposite way. He has a need to impress people, and therefore when he does spend money he likes to make sure everyone knows about it. It's vitally important to him to be seen as a "first-class person" because, in his mind, being first-class buys him the credibility and respect that an unassuming lifestyle will not. Many big spenders cannot truly afford their extravagances but feel compelled to keep spending because they think it ensures them the approval of others.

A useful test in evaluating why someone is a big spender is to ask whether she pampers herself the same way whether or not others are aware of it. Most big spenders will be quick to explain that they simply enjoy the finer things in life and can afford them. If they quietly treat their mom to a trip to Hawaii every year, have an expensive coin collection no one knows about, or engage in any other pricey, but private, activity, their self-indulgence does not reflect a need to impress others. But if they spend only when others are looking, they are trying to buy more than just things. They're purchasing approval. Knowing that about them is a great asset when you're trying to predict their behavior.

"I Can't Help It—It's How I Was Raised," and Other Common Excuses

It's rare to hear an honest, heartfelt apology. What we most often get after someone has behaved badly is a halfhearted "Sorry," followed by an excuse: "I was angry" (or "drunk," "upset," "not myself," "confused," "hurt," "jealous"). "I didn't know any better." "It's just the way I am." "The devil made me do it."

Our behavior, including our bad behavior, is usually a matter of choice. When someone offers an excuse for what was clearly voluntary behavior, I always try to determine whether the excuse suggests that the behavior was an isolated incident that won't be repeated. It's often a very tough call to make. If you reject someone's excuse there may be a confrontation; ultimatums may be issued, and conflict can erupt. So before you decide someone's excuse doesn't fly, ask yourself the following:

- Does the behavior reflect a lapse of judgment, a temporary loss of inhibitions, or a more deep-seated lack of fundamental values?
- Did the behavior continue for a long time?
- Did the person attempt to cover up the behavior?
- Was the behavior inconsistent with the person's usual pattern?
- Was the behavior entirely voluntary, or was there some other factor at play?

If someone has control over his behavior, his excuses are usually less persuasive. It's one thing for an employee to explain that he was late to work because an accident on the freeway closed the traffic lanes for an hour. He couldn't help that. It's quite another to blame his tardiness on running out of gas. He could have avoided that with a little advance planning. The same can be said of most excuses. Someone who fails to take responsibility for his own mistakes or bad judgment, hiding behind lame excuses, isn't being honest, either with you or with himself. Listen carefully. *The quality of a person's true character is often closely tied to the excuses he favors.*

THE GOLDEN RULE OF HUMAN BEHAVIOR

"Do unto others as you would have them do unto you." The Golden Rule, with a few minor modifications, is the last secret shared in this chapter. Here's the revised version: *"Others do unto you as they expect or want you to do unto them."* People want to see themselves reflected, and therefore validated, in those around them.

We all want to have a good image of ourselves. As a result, we tend to assign the most importance to whatever strengths we have and to devalue our weaknesses. Highly intelligent but less attractive people will generally value intelligence over looks. Athletes will value physical prowess. Artists will value taste. Those who pride themselves on being prompt will value punctuality in others. The hardest workers in the office will value effort over results, while those who are able to achieve their goals without much effort will place more importance on the end product and award little credit for how hard someone works.

In every aspect of life, the equation is remarkably reliable. If you know someone who loves to give flowers, you are probably safe in assuming the one gift she'd really like to receive is—you guessed it—flowers. If she likes to say "I love you" at the end of each phone conversation, she wants to hear you say it, too. Keep this simple principle in mind, and you'll be well on your way to understanding what others want and expect from you.

KEY POINTS

Remember, character is ultimately revealed by what a person does: How someone acts reflects his true values. His words, if inconsistent, tell only what he wants you to believe or wishes his values were.

Focus on how someone behaves toward others: True character is marked by consistency. People who are truly honest, compassionate, and kind won't just behave that way toward those who have something they want. Notice how they relate to "everyday people." And don't expect them to act any differently toward you once the bloom is off your relationship.

We all make mistakes: But repetitive behavior isn't a "mistake." Don't blindly accept excuses. Recognize repeat behavior for what it is—a clear sign of a person's character.

People do change—sometimes: To gauge the chances that change is real and permanent, ask:

- How long was the behavior set?
- How recently did it change?
- How quickly did it change?
- What motivated the change?

Look for patterns of behavior: Identify patterns such as:

- *selfishness.* We all have needs, but someone who always asks first, "What's in it for me?" tends to be selfish, egocentric, jealous, insecure, petty, and excessively competitive.
- *performance under fire.* We all have our breaking points. But remember, it's life's highly charged situations that reveal a person's strength of character.
- *unkept promises.* Sometimes their motive is evil, sometimes it's not; but whatever the motive, don't expect to be able to rely on them.
- *avoidance.* Sometimes what someone doesn't do is as important as what they do.
- *preaching.* Preachers always have an agenda—persuasion, control, attention. But don't assume they practice what they preach.
- *fanfare.* It's a sure sign of insecurity. As a gauge of confidence, self-esteem, and a giving nature, the fanfare test is very reliable.
- *spending habits.* Some people become scrooges, others big spenders, but any extreme in spending habits usually arise from deep seated insecurities.

Question why someone has deviated from a set routine: The more consistent the habit, the greater the significance of a change in the routine.

Remember the golden rule of human behavior: "Others do unto you as they expect or want you to do unto them." People want to see themselves reflected, and therefore validated, in those around them.

Sometimes Things Aren't What They Appear to Be: Spotting Exceptions to the Rules

Josh was getting harder to handle each year. It began in preschool, where his teacher chalked up his behavioral problems to a low tolerance for frustration. In kindergarten things only got worse. He sometimes lashed out in anger at his teachers, and often ignored them altogether. He behaved better at home, but was also very short-tempered there. By the time he entered first grade, his distraught parents were ready to take him to a psychologist to be tested for learning disabilities. Luckily, the city's hearing program arrived at Josh's school in time to discover the real problem: Josh was hard of hearing. Who wouldn't be frustrated if he couldn't hear half of what was being said?

Even though teachers and parents today are more alert to signs of hearing impairment than they once were, this scene is still replayed thousands of times each year. It's a good example of what can happen when all the pieces but one fit a particular pattern, and that one critical piece goes unnoticed. Most of the people you meet who display a particular pattern of traits won't surprise you. But be careful not to leave out that one critical piece of the puzzle.

There are a few characteristics that can shed an entirely different light on what you thought was a crystal-clear image. I think of them as exceptions to the rules, because if you don't take them into account you may reach distorted or incorrect conclusions, even if everything else seems to fit.

I've found nine exceptions that occur more frequently than others. Some are completely involuntary. Others are elective, and often an attempt to manipulate.

- the "elastic" person who attempts to mold himself to meet your requirements
- the person who has carefully rehearsed his presentation
- the liar
- the delusional thinker
- the person who is mentally or physically disabled
- the person who is ill, fatigued, stressed, or otherwise "not himself"
- the person who is under the influence of drugs or alcohol
- the person who is strongly influenced by his or her culture
- coincidences—they do happen

THE ELASTIC PERSON

Engineers use the term "elasticity" for the tendency of a material to deform under pressure and then return to its natural state when the pressure is off, like a rubber band. People are naturally elastic, and from time to time, most of us consciously or unconsciously alter our appearance, behavior, or words to meet others' expectations or desires. But the person who consistently molds herself to be what she thinks you want her to be is, in essence, providing you with false information. If you're not getting the facts, you can't make a reliable judgment.

Slobs can be tidy, at least for a while, if the motivation is there. Lazy people can appear industrious—temporarily. Opinionated people can appear open-minded, and selfish people can seem giving. But these people will tend to "change" as time passes, relationships mature, and the desire to please decreases. The kind, considerate, understanding new boyfriend becomes insensitive, overbearing, and jealous. The hardworking, helpful employee becomes lazy and uncooperative as he settles in to the job.

In truth, the boyfriend and the employee were never really what they at first appeared to be. They always were insensitive and uncooperative. They were demonstrating the principles of elasticity: once the pressure or motivation that caused them to change eased, they reverted to their true form.

Don't assume that attempts to please always spring from a conscious desire to manipulate. They can be an unconscious and very well meaning attempt to gain acceptance or approval. We naturally put on our best manners when we meet a new beau's parents for the first time or go out to dinner with the boss. But whatever someone's motives may be, it would be a mistake to see her under those unique circumstances and assume she always has impeccable manners. You need to see her over a period of time and in several different situations before you can tell which behaviors are real and which are elastic.

Once the bloom is off the rose of either a personal or professional relationship the pressures that caused the elastic behaviors will subside, and the person will revert to her normal state, good or bad. Until then, it's wise to reserve judgment.

THE REHEARSED PRESENTATION

I have seen many witnesses who are articulate, forceful, and poised on direct examination by the lawyer who called them to the stand, only to crumble when the opposing attorney cross-examines them. Sometimes this is because a particularly skillful attorney has dished out a brutal cross-examination, but in many cases it's simply a matter of exposing the actor who has rehearsed his role. In daily life, if you're not alert to the rehearsed presentation, you run the risk of misjudging someone. You might find him more articulate and witty—or less imaginative, creative, or flexible—than he actually is.

Not surprisingly, you're most likely to encounter a canned presentation when someone is trying to sell you something. It doesn't have to be a car or a time-share. The "salesman" can be trying to persuade you to "buy" an idea, a point of view, another person, or himself. There is probably one "sales pitch" that he's found particularly effective, so he repeats it in order to achieve the best possible result.

Sometimes, too, people deliver a rehearsed story because they're trying to make a good impression and don't have the confidence to speak spontaneously. The insecure or nervous often find it easier to practice a speech in advance, like the high school boy who writes down a list of things to say to the girl he's about to call for the first time. People also tend to repeat the same stories if they've had positive experiences with them in the past. Others have laughed, been persuaded, or been charmed by the story. They hope you will be, too.

It isn't too difficult to spot this type of behavior. Often the presentation seems too perfect and utterly unspontaneous. When delivering a prepared shtick, people are in their comfort zone. If you want to find out how they behave when they haven't had the opportunity to prepare, take away the home-field advantage. Take them out of their comfort zone and put them in yours.

If someone is delivering a sales pitch, ask a pointed question that he'll have to respond to spontaneously. If he keeps dodging you, stay after him until he either answers or makes it clear he's unable or unwilling to, which in itself will tell you something. If someone you've just met is trying to wow you with her intelligence by discussing world politics, see if she's a one-trick pony. When the conversation allows, ask what she thinks about the latest movies. See if she knows anything about sports. What you choose to discuss isn't important. Your goal is to see how she reacts as you try to lead her away from her comfort zone. Does she speak willingly about other topics? Is she at ease and articulate even if she knows little about the subject? Does she ask intelligent questions? Or does she consistently try to lead you back to where she feels comfortable and in control?

Over the years I've seen some almost comical exchanges in the courtroom when lawyers, busy delivering a carefully prepared presentation of what they no doubt believe to be inspired arguments, are interrupted by a judge who wants answers to other questions. Even a casual court observer knows the courtroom is the judge's turf: whatever he wants to know takes precedence over whatever a lawyer might prefer to discuss. Even so, it's not unusual to see lawyers try to stay within their comfort zone by telling the judge they'll "get to that," or "That's not the point," or even "I don't think that's relevant." I can assure you that a lawyer's reluctance to deviate from his canned presentation doesn't bolster his credibility in the eyes of the judge. After all, if he were truly comfortable with his position, he'd be willing to examine it from any perspective.

In everyday conversations, we have to be a bit more careful about how we test someone outside her comfort zone. People try to stay with what they know because it's safe and familiar. It can be disconcerting to be forced off one's home turf, so your mission is to proceed gently. Make the transition with tact and diplomacy, not abrasively. The objective is to get to know the other person when she isn't just delivering a rehearsed presentation, and you won't achieve it if you alienate her. Instead, you'll see how she reacts when she's angry and offended.

THE WILD CARDS: LIARS

If people were all honest with one another, reading them would be a lot easier. The problem is that people lie. I'm not talking about those who are wrong but sincerely believe they are correct, or about the delusional few who genuinely can't tell fact from fantasy. Rather, I'm referring to the one characteristic that is probably the most important in any relationship: truthfulness. And if we assume it's there when it's not—watch out!

Much of the information we gather about someone comes directly from the horse's mouth. If he is lying, the information is wrong, and we're likely to misjudge him. That's why it's so crucial to identify liars as soon as possible, and, if you have reason to doubt a person's honesty, to continue to test it until you're entirely at ease with your conclusion.

I have found that most liars fall into one of four basic categories: the occasional liar, the frequent liar, the habitual liar, and the professional liar.

The Occasional Liar

The occasional liar, like most of us, will lie now and then to avoid an unpleasant situation or because he doesn't want to admit doing something wrong or embarrassing. Also like most of us, he does not like to lie and feels very uncomfortable when he does. Because he's uncomfortable, he'll usually reveal his lie through his appearance, body language, and voice. The stress lying causes him will leak out through such things as poor eye contact, fidgeting, or a change in the tone, volume, or patterns of his speech.

The occasional liar often gives his lie some thought, so it may be logical and consistent with the rest of his story. Because it's well thought out, you probably won't be able to spot the lie by its content or context, or by information from third-party sources. In fact, the occasional liar will seldom lie about something that could be easily verified. Consequently, when dealing with an occasional liar, you need to focus on the various visual and oral clues he exhibits.

The Frequent Liar

The frequent liar recognizes what she's doing but doesn't mind it as much as the occasional liar does, so she lies more regularly. Practice makes perfect: the frequent liar is much less likely to reveal her lie through her appearance, body language, and voice. Also, since it doesn't bother her as much to lie, the typical stress-related symptoms won't be as obvious. Any clues in her appearance, voice, and body language might be rather subtle. Often a better way to detect a frequent liar is to focus on the internal consistency and logic of her statements. Since the frequent liar lies more often, and tends to think her lies through less carefully than the occasional liar, she can get sloppy.

The Habitual Liar

The habitual liar lies so frequently that he has lost sight of what he is doing much of the time. In most cases, if he actually thought about it, he would realize he was lying. But he doesn't much care whether what he's saying is true or false. He simply says whatever comes to mind. Because he doesn't care that he's lying, the habitual liar will give very few, if any, physical or vocal clues that he's being dishonest. But because he gives so little thought to his lies and they come so thick and fast, the habitual liar doesn't bother to keep track of them. As a result they are often inconsistent and obvious. So while it's hard to detect the physical and vocal clues in a habitual liar, it's easier to spot his inconsistencies. Listen carefully and ask yourself whether the liar is contradicting himself and whether what he's saying makes sense. Asking a third party about the liar's stories will also help you confirm your suspicions.

The habitual liar is fairly uncommon, so most of us are temporarily taken in when we encounter one. An acquaintance of mine told me she worked with a woman for several months before her suspicions that the co-worker was a habitual liar were confirmed by an obvious and quite ridiculous lie. The liar, a brown-eyed brunette, came to work one day sporting blue contact lenses of an almost alien hue. When my friend commented on her lenses, the liar said, "These aren't contacts. They're my real eye color. It's just that I've always worn brown contact lenses before."

More than once, a client has told me that his adversary lies all the time and will undoubtedly lie on the witness stand. I counsel my client not to worry: the habitual liar is the easiest target in a lawsuit. In real life, she can run from one person to another, from one situation to the next, lying as she goes, and no one compares notes. There are no court reporters or transcripts of testimony; no one reveals what every witness has said to every other witness, and nobody pores over everything the liar has written on the subject to see whether it's all consistent. But in litigation, that is exactly what happens—and suddenly the habitual liar is exposed. It's very rewarding to see.

The Professional Liar

The professional liar is the hardest to identify. He doesn't lie indiscriminately, like the habitual liar. He lies for a purpose. For example, a mechanic who routinely cons motorists about their "faulty" transmissions will have his diagnosis carefully prepared. A real estate salesman who doesn't want to acknowledge a leaky roof will respond quickly to an inquiry about the stains on the ceiling with a rehearsed, very spontaneous sounding statement: "That was old damage from a water leak in the attic. All it needs is a little touch-up paint."

The professional liar has thought the lie through and knows exactly what he's going to say, how it will fly, and whether the customer can easily verify it. Such a well-practiced lie will not be revealed by the liar's voice, body language, or appearance. The lie will be consistent, both internally and logically. The only sure way to detect it is to check the liar's statements against entirely independent sources. Have the roof inspected. Get a second opinion from another mechanic. Take nothing for granted.

Before you make a definitive call about someone who is truly important to you, always ask yourself whether the information you have about him is reliable. Is he being truthful? If your goal is to accurately evaluate someone, you can't afford to skip this step.

THE DELUSIONAL THINKER

Every once in a while I find myself staring at someone, a look of disbelief on my face and my mouth ajar, wondering, "How can anyone be so clueless?" We've all encountered people who have lost touch with reality, if only in one specific area. This is a blind spot, as in "She's just got a blind spot where her sister is concerned." Some people have one or two blind spots. Others have enough to weave a complete set of blinders.

If you think you're immune, consider this: after participating in the questioning of over ten thousand jurors, I could count on one hand (well, maybe two) the number who admitted to having any racial bias. I don't need to refer to any surveys to say without fear of contradiction that more than one in a thousand people harbor some racial bias. But it seems that only one in a thousand is willing to admit it in open court. Some are simply lying; they know they're racist but aren't about to say so in a courtroom. The majority, however, really do believe they are bias-free, and for many that amounts to delusional thinking. If I took the word of every prospective juror who declared, "I don't have a prejudiced bone in my body," a lot of bigots would have sat as jurors in the cases on which I've worked over the years. But I don't accept that type of information at face value, because I can't. It is too important to my client.

For the same reason, when a particular issue is important to you in evaluating someone *even if you believe she is fundamentally honest,* don't assume you can take everything she says as gospel. Ask yourself: Is there any evidence that she may be fooling herself? Have I stumbled across a blind spot?

Delusional thinking can be the result of someone else's suggestions, or we can develop blind spots ourselves. In working on the McMartin

Preschool case and other child-molestation cases, I saw how easily the children could be persuaded that they had been asked to participate in sexual acts—not only with their day-care providers but, in one prominent case, with large animals that couldn't even have fit into the room. The youngsters' reality was altered by suggestions—they were brainwashed. Similarly, some of the blind spots I've seen in adults were probably the result of odd ideas implanted by their parents from an early age.

More often than not, however, adults brainwash themselves. Some behave dishonestly, and, rather than admit it, create elaborate justifications for their misdeeds. Others take credit for someone else's ideas or accomplishments. As time passes, perhaps they tell the story of their achievement over and over. With each successive telling they become more comfortable with it, until eventually they delude themselves into believing it.

This type of delusional thinking can be difficult to spot. But you can't afford to miss it. You may have correctly concluded that in most respects someone is exceedingly honest and reliable, and you may have dismissed the potential that she would mislead you intentionally, even though her story feels wrong or doesn't add up. In view of her past honesty, the possibility that she's lying doesn't make sense: how could this essentially truthful woman make up such a story? In cases like this, consider the possibility that you've run into her blind spot—she's having a bout of delusional thinking.

THE PHYSICALLY DISABLED

Years ago, I had a client who suffered from a nervous twitch. The twitch worsened when he was under stress: he would grimace and his head would jerk sideways. His attorney decided to explain this during jury selection, so that the jurors wouldn't misinterpret his neurological problem as a dishonest man's psychological response to tough questions.

Anytime you're evaluating someone who is disabled, it's critical to identify the disability and how it affects him or her. People with physical disabilities may not display the pattern you would otherwise expect. Make no assumptions about what the impact of a disability might be. It differs tremendously from person to person, often depending on whether the disability is lifelong or developed in childhood or adulthood, and on how much support the disabled person has had in coping.

I see many disabled people in my line of work. They're involved in lawsuits concerning their disability, and they often act as jurors, witnesses, lawyers, and judges. I've seen how differently people handle the loss of a limb or bodily function. On one end of the spectrum was a woman who suffered a severe and debilitating injury to both her legs in an automobile accident. She came from a very wealthy family and was bright, attractive, outgoing, and well-educated. But because of her injuries, she had become surprisingly bitter and angry. Apparently feeling that something vital to her had been unfairly taken away, she developed a sense of entitlement. Without recognizing the significance of this woman's physical disability in her life, it would have been very difficult to truly understand her and predict her behavior. Her disability proved to be the trait that in many ways trumped all others.

On the other end of the spectrum was a juror in a case on which I recently worked. He was born with a deformed right arm, which was no more than a foot long; and his hand wasn't much bigger than a large walnut. This obvious physical disability must have made him the brunt of vicious teasing in childhood.

After learning the basics about this man—his educational background, job history, family background, and life experiences—I was fairly confident that he would be a good juror for the defense, on whose behalf I had been retained. However, I was a little worried that because of his disability he might harbor some bitterness and hostility, which generally would not be good for the defendant in a criminal case. Also, because of the severity of his handicap and the effort undoubtedly required to overcome it, I thought he might not be particularly sympathetic to the defendant's plea for understanding and leniency. Because of these concerns I paid very careful attention during questioning to his body language and voice, as well as to his answers.

Everything I saw and heard suggested to me that he was a very well adjusted, compassionate, and open-minded man: a good juror for this case. We left him on. I felt even better about this decision when I saw him confidently raise his small right arm and hand to be sworn in as a juror. That degree of comfort with his disability reaffirmed my faith in him. Clearly, he had long ago come to terms with his disability and it did not negatively color his worldview.

With careful attention, you can determine what impact someone's disability has probably had on his view of the world. How does he refer to his handicap? Does he talk about it freely and comfortably? Excessive joking about it may reveal a deep-seated discomfort, but the ability to poke fun at oneself occasionally is always a good sign. Look to see how easily he moves among others and copes with physical obstacles such as stairs and doors. The more someone has mastered his environment, the more probable it is that he's integrated his disability into his life rather than letting it dominate him. Watch also for signs that someone prizes independence and has worked to achieve as much of it as he can. If he seems comfortable with himself and is as independent as possible, chances are his disability hasn't negatively influenced his worldview.

Often, however, a person's disability colors many aspects of his behavior and beliefs. You can identify such a person by a number of clues. Often he'll withdraw even from activities he could perform. He may be bitter toward others and toward life in general. He may expect to receive special treatment beyond that which is appropriate to accommodate his handicap. And he may use his disability as a rationale for his failures or unhappiness. Remember, satisfaction with life is a key predictive trait. If someone believes he has not achieved what he should have because of his disability, its impact on him will be that much greater. In such cases, the disability may overshadow the person's other traits and may be the driving force behind his character.

Any significant physical disability—whether it's heart problems, paralysis, epilepsy, or a stutter—needs to be viewed with special care. It would be unwise to assume that a disability defines a person, but by the same token, it would be naive to ignore the unique influence a serious disability may have on someone's life experiences and attitudes.

"I'M NOT MYSELF TODAY": THE EFFECTS OF ILLNESS, FATIGUE, AND STRESS

If you had met me in the winter of 1979, the fall of 1981, or the fall of 1987, you would have found me morose, humorless, unimaginative, weak, needy, weepy, and altogether quite debilitated. My appearance, body language, voice, words, and conduct would have been completely consistent. I was a mess.

But if two months later I ran into a friend of yours to whom you had described my pitiful condition, she would have thought you were crazy. I would have seemed very independent, outgoing, and happy.

So what happened? Like many women, after the birth of each of my three children, I suffered severe postpartum depression. My entire personality was altered by the physiological changes taking place in my body. Without knowing what was going on, you would have completely misinterpreted who I was and how I was likely to react under "normal" circumstances.

People's personalities can be severely affected by postpartum depression, PMS, chronic stress, and similar conditions. Personality can also be affected by the flu, a nagging cough, a toothache, or an upset stomach.

But because most people try not to complain too loudly about their ailments, it's easy to miss the signs that someone is ill or under stress. If you didn't know he was nauseated, you might perceive someone suffering from a touch of the flu being quiet, inattentive, perhaps even rude. Similarly, you might think someone who is exhausted is bored, grouchy, not very intelligent, or possibly under the influence of drugs or alcohol.

Some medical problems are more obvious and last longer than others and it's usually not hard to see their impact on someone's behavior. When someone breaks a leg or suffers a bout of pneumonia, you'll probably attribute many of their grouchy moments to their condition. But temporary or less obvious conditions, like stress and fatigue, are easier to miss. You need to be on the lookout for them, however, because almost everyone's good humor and social graces take a backseat under these circumstances.

My friend Robert recently came very close to making a disastrous decision because he didn't realize one of his partners was under significant stress. Robert is an attorney in a small law firm, whose handful of partners have all shared strong personal friendships as well as professional ties over the past several years. Not long ago, one partner, Gary, suddenly became cold and distant. He and Robert had had some disagreements about a few minor issues in the previous weeks, but such differences of opinion never jeopardized their friendship before, and Robert didn't understand why they should now.

After two weeks of progressively more tense exchanges, the awkwardness escalated to open hostility at a firm meeting. Afterward, as Robert sat in his office sulking, Gary knocked on the door. Gary began by apologizing for his behavior, and told Robert how much he cherished their friendship. Slumping in his chair, Gary then dropped a bombshell: he and his wife were getting divorced. Gary was devastated.

Robert had neglected to look for possible explanations for his partner's odd behavior, even though there were strong indications that one of the exceptions to the rules was involved. Gary's actions were so out of character—and after all those years of friendship, Robert knew Gary's character well—that Robert should have realized that whatever was bothering his friend had nothing to do with their normal interaction.

When you see a sudden change in someone's behavior, look for signs of stress, illness, or fatigue. If you think his behavior is influenced by any of these, try to find out what exactly is wrong. You'll be able to tell by paying close attention to his body language and voice—and, if you're close to him, by simply asking.

THE IMPACT OF DRUGS AND ALCOHOL

Much of what has just been said about illness, fatigue, and stress applies equally to drugs and alcohol. They can produce symptoms of depression, anxiety, or hyperactivity. In some people drug or alcohol abuse is an illness, and might be considered nonelective. Others are recreational users, in which case the situation is totally elective. When evaluating people who sometimes seem to be under the influence, try to determine two things: How often do they use? And how does it affect their behavior?

Drugs and alcohol always affect behavior, but unless you know what a person is like sober you'll have a tough time knowing exactly what that effect is. Therefore, it's pretty foolish to make a judgment call about someone you first meet over a heap of empty champagne bottles at a New Year's Eve party. You need more information.

The most important thing to learn is whether the person has a substance-abuse problem. If so, it's a critical mistake to ignore the impact it will have on her behavior. Sometimes it's difficult to accept that a normally hardworking, considerate, intelligent person cannot be relied upon because she abuses drugs or alcohol. But in many cases, even when everything else you know about someone points in one direction, if she is a drug or alcohol abuser, one of the exceptions to the rules is at work. If you want to know the significance of that exception, just talk to the families, friends, co-workers, and employers of drug and alcohol abusers.

If, on the other hand, someone is just a recreational drinker, the most important thing to bear in mind is that what you see when he's been drinking is not necessarily what you'll get under normal circumstances. Alcohol can make people jovial or belligerent, aggressive or passive. The outgoing, witty life of the party and the loudmouthed party pooper may have very similar personalities when they're sober. Unless you recognize that drugs or alcohol may substantially change behavior, you may completely misjudge the traits you see when somebody is under the influence.

CULTURAL INFLUENCES

Many people think only of race or ethnicity when they consider someone's "cultural background." In fact, cultural background is much more. It is the influence of any peer group. Certainly race, ethnicity, and national origin influence us, but so do our religious background, age, regional origin, economic background, and sexual orientation. There are even professional cultures—among athletes, doctors, truckers, actors, the military, academicians, and almost every other identifiable group.

Attributing certain traits to certain groups is stereotyping. It's true that many stereotypes have some basis in fact, and that *some* stereotypes may accurately reflect characteristics of *some* members of the group: some Frenchmen are romantic, some Englishmen are witty, and some Scots are frugal. But reading people based on stereotypes is extremely unreliable. I can assure you, when I'm working for the defense I don't lean toward Scottish jurors on the theory that they will award lower damages.

As chapter 2, "Discovering Patterns," pointed out, you need to look beyond stereotypes to how someone's cultural experiences may have influenced her. The weight you should give a person's cultural background depends on just how deeply immersed in that culture the person has been. What role did her culture play in her youth? And how much contact has she had with it since then?

- Did she go to school with other members of the same culture (for example, Hebrew school, Catholic school, Greek Orthodox school)?
- Does she regularly attend religious services?
- Was she raised, and does she still live, in a community populated mostly by members of that culture?
- Were her family's friends predominantly of the same culture?
- Do her current friends have the same cultural background?
- Does she patronize doctors, lawyers, shopkeepers, and others who have the same cultural background?
- Does she use cultural colloquialisms?
- Does she watch television and movies in her native tongue?
- Does she speak her native tongue at home?
- Does she wear clothing and hairstyles that reflect her culture?

Much the same line of inquiry is helpful when evaluating the influences of *any* culture. Imagine how someone may be influenced by a lifetime of emphasis on sports. Did your new boyfriend grow up living and breathing sports? Do he and his friends spend a significant amount of time playing in adult sports leagues? Is he an avid fan? When he's watching or playing a sport, does the rest of the world (including you) disappear? If so, his immersion in the sports culture may be a driving force in his behavior. Even if other characteristics don't suggest it, he is probably competitive, tough, macho, and able to concentrate. I know law firm recruiters who give high marks to applicants—male or female—who are successful athletes: the traits prized in jock culture frequently translate into success in the courtroom.

If your new brother-in-law was in the military, does he keep his hair short even though he's left the service? Years after retirement, does he still say "Yes, sir," or "Yes, ma'am"? Does he still carry himself with a military bearing? If so, the military mind-set undoubtedly had a profound impact on the way he views the world. He's probably disciplined, authoritarian, and conservative.

Whenever I'm involved in selecting a jury, I am very attuned to how someone's cultural experience may affect his other characteristics. One good example of this involves a man who had been immersed in two powerful cultures. I was working on a case in which a former police officer was the defendant. Those of us on the defense team were looking for jurors who did not have a bias against police officers or other authority figures. The juror at issue was a former Marine about thirty years old. He earned a master's degree in computer science after he left the Marine Corps, and was now working for the Department of the Navy. He still wore his hair very short and held his weight-lifter's body as stiff and erect as if he were still in the Marines. "Yes, sir" and "No, sir" were typical responses to the questions put to him. Everything about this man pointed to a law-and-order, no-nonsense, support-your-local-police-department mentality. Except he was African-American. And the sad reality is that in southern California, if not the entire United States, most young African-American men have had an unpleasant experience with the police, or are close to someone else who has.

Our jury questionnaire asked about confrontations with the police. This juror had replied simply, "I was stopped by the police one time with some friends." When asked to explain the situation further during the oral questioning, he replied, "You mean the incident where I was detained." As he said "detained," his jaw tightened. He snarled the word through gritted teeth. Without knowing that he obviously believed the police had treated him unfairly, we might have left him on the jury. As it was, I believed that his personal negative experience with the police would override all the other traits that would have suggested a sympathetic mind-set.

Recognition of cultural influences was also a factor in my recommendation to dismiss the Hispanic woman juror in the Simi Valley trial of the four officers accused of beating Rodney King discussed in chapter 5. Although she herself appeared to be unbiased, she acknowledged that her husband felt very strongly that the officers were guilty and should be severely punished. While I would never presume that all Hispanic marriages are dominated by the man, I am certainly aware that many are (and that this is not unique to Hispanic cultures). After further questioning, I was satisfied that the juror's husband dominated their relationship. For this reason I believed that whatever other positive traits she might have from the defense perspective, she should not be retained as a juror because she would have a difficult time overcoming her culturally induced bias.

I did not act upon a cultural stereotype in either of these examples. I tested it. Only after I was able to verify that the black Marine really had had an alienating experience with the police, and that the Hispanic woman really did have a traditional patriarchal marriage, did I conclude that those cultural influences might drive their behavior.

In some cases, investigation reveals that such conclusions are unfounded. For example, I recently participated in a program for the Ontario Bar Association in which one of my co-panelists was a middle-aged, highly respected woman judge. At first, she seemed all business—confident, direct, and no-nonsense. At the podium, she typified the rather harsh, humorless professional culture in which many businesswomen, particularly in the field of law, are immersed.

After the program, I had dinner with the judge, and found that while her appearance and demeanor on the panel had pointed toward a strong "professional-woman cultural influence," once she was off that podium, it just wasn't there. She was warm, friendly, self-effacing, and funny. She talked of her children, not of her professional successes. She was not at all self-important or uptight, even going so far as to casually take a puff off another judge's cigarette during the cocktail hour. This is definitely not something I would expect from an uptight, all-business career woman.

Examples of cultural influences abound in everyday life. Here are a few, inspired by events I've witnessed over the past several months. All of them demonstrate how important it is to consider culture when you're reading people.

If you saw two men embracing each other and kissing on the cheek, would you assume they were gay? If you knew they were heavily influenced by a European culture in which men typically show such affection for one another and were comfortable with it, you would realize that such a conclusion is probably unwarranted.

If you saw a young woman dressed in a short skirt, four-inch platform shoes, a spaghetti-strap blouse that revealed both her belly button and her bra straps, dark lipstick, and long, multicolored fingernails, would you conclude she was loose and sleazy at best, and more probably a "working girl"? Not if you were aware of contemporary fashion culture. If every girl who dressed like this were a hooker, that category would include half the girls in southern California between the ages of fifteen and twenty-one. Even "good girls" dress that way these days.

Recently—only two days apart—I heard an elderly white man and an elderly white woman refer to African-Americans as "Negroes." Are they bigots? Disrespectful? No, they both grew up during an era when that was how polite, respectful whites referred to African-Americans—and the word "black" was considered insulting.

You see a young couple proudly displaying their assortment of tattoos and exotic body piercings. Are they freaks? Social outcasts? Rock musicians? No, they are members of the MTV generation. Ten years from now, likely as not, they'll be teaching your children calculus or ringing you up in the grocery store.

Cultural influences are extremely complex and often difficult to recognize. Still, there are a few simple rules that can help you correctly identify when they are most likely at work.

- Remember that race and national origin aren't the only cultural influences. Also consider religion, age, geographical origin, sexual orientation, economic background, and profession, as well as the person's other peer groups.
- Never make decisions based on cultural stereotypes. Always test them against the life experiences of the person you're evaluating.
- When someone appears to be subject to a particular cultural influence, learn about the nature and extent of that influence, and from that information try to gauge its importance in shaping the person's perspective.

COINCIDENCES DO HAPPEN

Sometimes seemingly significant events are entirely meaningless. While a healthy skepticism is essential for reading people effectively, it's just as important to keep an open mind to the possibility that something is just an innocent coincidence.

In an earlier chapter I relayed the story of the woman juror who wore black gloves to court every day during the federal prosecution of the four officers for the beating of Rodney King. Had the woman been white and had the trial involved something other than an allegedly racially motivated beating, I might have assumed either that the woman was cold or that she just liked to wear gloves. Everyone on the legal team certainly wouldn't have wondered whether she was making a racial statement. The fact is, the racial background of the people involved in the case was purely coincidental.

Just because you see someone at the opera does not mean he is cultured or sophisticated, or even that he likes the opera. Maybe a friend gave him the tickets and he felt obliged to attend. Likewise, while it may be natural to assume that someone you run into at a baseball game likes baseball, maybe he's on a company outing or is courting a customer who enjoys the game. In either case, meeting that person in that setting is just a coincidence.

If someone has an obvious stain on his tie, can you assume he's a slob? Maybe. On the other hand, perhaps a waiter spilled some soup on him twenty minutes earlier and he hasn't had a chance to change. He may be the most obsessively fastidious person you'll ever meet. The spot on his tie may be meaningless—or worse, misleading.

In the continuous process of gathering and weighing information, you will catch a few red herrings. Don't assume anything. Look for patterns; and expect to come across coincidences now and then.

KEY POINTS

Always consider whether you're missing a key piece of the puzzle: Some single factor can drastically alter an otherwise clear picture.

Be particularly alert for:

- *the elastic person.* With time and exposure he'll revert to his natural state.
- *the rehearsed presentation.* Take her out of her comfort zone and see how she handles herself.
- *liars.* Most people are uncomfortable when they lie. That discomfort usually leaks out somewhere. But the more frequently one lies, the less it bothers him and more difficult it is to spot the lies from voice and mannerisms. You'll need to focus more on what he says and does, or verify his statements independently.
- *the delusional thinker.* Sometimes we unwittingly fool ourselves, not just others. It's not a lie, but a blind spot.
- *the physically disabled.* Don't assume someone who is physically challenged will see and react to the world as the able-bodied do.
- *illness, fatigue, and stress.* Don't judge too harshly, but realize that what you see is what you can expect to emerge under similar circumstances in the future.

- *drugs and alcohol.* They can change behavior so dramatically from moment to moment that they should always be considered.
- *cultural influences.* Before you jump to any conclusions, determine if someone's culture deeply impacts him. If it does, learn as much as you can about the culture before you draw any conclusions.

Never forget, coincidences do happen: Sometimes seemingly significant events are entirely meaningless. Don't assume too much.

CHAPTER 10

Listening to Your Inner Voice:
The Power of Intuition

The African-American defendant weighed more than 275 pounds and acted as if he had a serious "attitude." Even in a suit and tie, he looked menacing. The prospective juror, on the other hand, was a young, petite, well-educated white woman from a wealthy family. It was a murder case, so the attorneys took their time interviewing the woman. We questioned her for hours, and she said nothing in all that time to indicate that she would be particularly charitable toward our client. In fact, the more we learned about her background, the more she seemed to fit the profile of a person who would probably vote to put our client in prison for life—or worse.

At the end of the day, the lead attorney on our team turned to me and shrugged. "Well," he said, "she's history, right?"

"I'm not sure," I replied. "We may want to keep her. Something still tells me that she may have an open mind." I knew from the look of skepticism on the attorney's face that he was going to need a much more specific reason than that to keep the woman on the jury. No way would he bet his client's life on a mere hunch.

That night, I lay in bed and tried to figure out why my intuitive feeling about the woman seemed so much stronger than the objective facts I had learned about her in the courtroom. Where did my hunch come from? Why did I have such a powerful feeling that it was right?

Of course, the evaluations of jurors that I make for my clients are much too important to depend on guesswork. *I never guess* about who should sit on a jury. But intuition is not guesswork, and it has always played a major part in my work. Over the years, I have learned to pay close attention to my deeper feelings about people and situations. Often, sudden flashes of intuition have led me to conclusions about people that appeared, at first, to be totally at odds with the rational workings of my mind. And on most occasions, these intuitive conclusions have turned out to be right.

As a result, I have become totally convinced that intuition is both *very* real and *very* powerful, and I know that it can be very useful in reading people. At the same time, I have become convinced that there is really nothing mysterious about how intuition works. Contrary to what many people will tell you, I believe that intuition is a normal part of our mental equipment that most of us simply don't understand very well. If we understood it better, we could use it more often and more effectively.

In the eyes of many, intuition is some kind of special mystical gift that is given to only a few chosen people. But I believe that we *all* have natural intuitive abilities—and that we can all improve our intuition enormously by working at it.

I was flattered some years ago when *The American Lawyer* called me "the Seer" because of my ability to understand jurors and predict how they will act. And I sometimes wish that I did, in fact, have second sight. It would make my job, not to mention the other parts of my life, a lot easier.

But I am definitely not clairvoyant. My ability to predict human behavior is based not on some mysterious sixth sense that only I possess, but on *the use I make of the ordinary five senses that every human being possesses*. It is not "second sight" but curiosity, focus, observation, and deduction that lead to effective intuition.

WHAT IS INTUITION?

The very word "intuition" carries a strong charge of mysticism, suggesting some mental voodoo that defies analysis or description. Professional psychics are said to use it to perform astounding feats, from predicting who somebody will marry to forecasting the fate of the world. I admit that some of the things that psychics do look impressive at first glance.

But what is it, exactly, that psychics *do*? When you strip away all the show business, *what is the process* that lends them to seemingly astounding conclusions? When you look closely, you can see that psychics are simply people who are very good at reading people. They have trained themselves to be especially sensitive to the signals that people send out about themselves. Over time, they amass a great deal of information about human nature, and they become very adept at pairing certain types of human signals with certain types of human behavior.

The information they gather is stored in their brains in two different ways. Part of it remains *conscious* knowledge, which they draw on and use with complete awareness of what they are doing. But most knowledge slips down into the *subconscious* mind, and psychics call upon it without being fully aware of the process that permits them to use it.

This is why some psychics are undoubtedly sincere in their belief that "voices" are speaking to them when they make intuitive predictions. They are simply not fully aware that the information that allows them to make accurate decisions about people was originally gathered by their own conscious minds and stored away in their subconscious. Their "gift" is their natural ability to gather and store information, and to retrieve it from the subconscious.

The average person doesn't pay such close attention to his or her perceptions and experiences. We don't even notice most of them. Consequently, most of our experiences about life and people are deposited behind the opaque curtain of our subconscious within a few days, or even moments, after we are exposed to them.

But even though we may not be consciously aware of these experiences, they become part of our stored knowledge. If certain events led to a bad or good experience once, when similar events occur again something inside us may hoist the flag we call intuition. This flag may come in different guises: déjà vu, free-floating anxiety, getting a sick feeling in the pit of our stomach when something feels wrong, or becoming excited when something feels right.

Thus, *what we call intuition is nearly always the surfacing of a submerged memory, a barely noticed event, or some combination of the two*. The "feeling" doesn't come to us over the cosmic ether, but drifts up from our own subconscious. This means that all we have to do to greatly improve our intuitive abilities is find new ways to gather information, store it, and retrieve it from the subconscious.

SEARCHING YOUR MIND

Our subconscious holds thousands of experiences and observations, much as a computer stores information in its hard drive. However, when we use a computer, we can click on the "Find" button and instantly retrieve any information we want. Access to our subconscious is much more haphazard, particularly if we weren't paying much attention when the information was loaded.

I've always been very attentive and observant, and I've also been fascinated by how particular aspects of a person's appearance, actions, voice, or behavior forecast his thoughts and actions. As a result, I've amassed a very large subconscious database of various human characteristics and what they are likely to mean in various people under different circumstances. This vast database is the foundation of my intuitive responses to people and situations.

By the time jurors enter the courtroom, are called to the jury box, and ready themselves for the first question, I've usually formed an initial impression of each of them. As I watch them more closely and listen to their responses to the lawyers' questions, this impression is almost always borne out. There is nothing psychic about that. It's simply that the way each of these jurors look, talk, and act fits the pattern of one or more segments of the thousands of other jurors I've seen walk through the doorways of hundreds of other courtrooms. Sometimes I'm hard-pressed to say what it is about someone that leaves me with a particular impression. But in most cases, by the time the decision is made to accept or reject the juror, I've discovered the source of my intuition and can logically explain myself to counsel.

Let's return for a moment to the juror we mentioned at the beginning of this chapter. The lead attorney agreed to have her return for a second day of questioning, though he let me know he was going to be a hard sell. My hunch that this young white woman would be good for our client remained unshakable—though still mystifying—until the afternoon recess of the second day, when I realized what I must have subconsciously noticed about her.

The courtroom was arranged in a fashion common in courtrooms across the country. The jury box was on one side of the room. The counsel table, where the defendant sat with me and his lawyers, was near the middle of the room, just a few feet in front of the low swinging doors to the aisle that runs down the middle of the spectators' seats and ultimately out to the hallway. Every time a juror comes or goes, he or she must pass by the counsel table. Most jurors, not surprisingly, cut a wide path around the defendant, particularly if he's a large, gruff-looking man charged with murder. This jury was generally no exception. Some of them looked as if they were tempted to jump over the railing next to the jury box rather than come anywhere near the accused.

But the young woman who had been the subject of my attention and frustration for the past two days didn't veer away from our client. She seemed to go out of her way to walk close to him—close enough that he could have reached out and grabbed her. Furthermore, unlike most jurors, she didn't take her eyes off him but seemed intent on scrutinizing him "up close and personal." This was truly extraordinary behavior under the circumstances.

As I've watched thousands of jurors walk by—or, more accurately, around—defendants charged with violent crimes, my subconscious storehouse was full of such images. While I had not consciously registered that this woman's behavior was dramatically unusual, my subconscious had raised a flag. Her behavior made it apparent that she was not afraid of the man, as most jurors would be if they had already judged him guilty of murder. Also, she was plainly inquisitive and had not formed a rigid opinion about him. Her attentive looks as she passed him revealed that she wanted to know if he'd really committed the crime, and would want to gather as much information as possible about him if she were asked to decide that question. What more could we ask of a juror?

BUILDING YOUR DATABASE

Since your intuition depends on the quality and quantity of your information, your first step is clear: *Improve the database.* A valuable database is filled with useful information, not random impressions. Chapters 1 and 2, "Reading Readiness" and "Discovering Patterns," showed you how to gather information and tell the important traits from the inconsequential ones. Other chapters have illustrated how to interpret various characteristics. If you consistently practice these techniques, you'll automatically fill your database with useful information.

You'll accumulate data a lot faster if you pay attention to everyone you meet, not just the people who are most important to you. If you're naturally curious about even strangers or casual acquaintances, you'll be way ahead of the game. Don't be shy about tactfully asking about someone's clothing, jewelry, or hairdo. If you don't feel like commenting, simply notice. Your inquisitiveness can be put to good use.

The more closely you observe everyone with whom you come into contact, the quicker you'll build up your database. I can illustrate the point with a fashion statement that's proliferated around the country the last few years: the eyebrow ring. I first saw one on the street in downtown Los Angeles, worn by a young man who looked like the lead guitarist in a grunge-rock band. My first thought was "How weird." My second was "Boy, that must have hurt." My curiosity was aroused, and I began noticing other people who wore eyebrow rings. Whether the person was a clerk at the market, a teller at the bank, or one of a group of young men and women hanging out at a coffeehouse, I paid attention. I was curious to know why each particular person might have chosen to pierce an eyebrow. I noted whether each seemed conservative, arty, a little on the wild side, intelligent, well-educated, flaky, respectful, dirty, whatever.

Since then, I've seen hundreds of eyebrow rings. They're often worn not by scruffy teenage men but by young girls who otherwise look like daughters of the middle class. Unlike tattoos, eyebrow rings can easily be removed, so they indicate a less fundamentally rebellious nature. Most of the young people with pierced eyebrows seem to be arty, individualistic, expressive types, who are making a fashion statement rather than a political or cultural one.

In recent years, I've accumulated a substantial store of knowledge about eyebrow-ring wearers. I don't expect to retrieve it very often. In fact, much of this knowledge may remain in my subconscious forever. But if a young woman with an eyebrow ring came into my office tomorrow to apply for a position as a file clerk, my intuition would probably tell me to keep an open mind—it might look odd, but if everything else seems in order it's no cause for alarm.

If you have always simply recoiled from people who wear eyebrow rings, assuming they're all unemployed, unwashed druggies, don't expect much help from your intuition if you find yourself needing to accurately evaluate a person who wears one. You simply won't have accumulated a sufficient database to warn you to look beyond the stereotype.

The next time you get a haircut, wait on a customer, or walk down the street, stop, look, and listen. Be attentive. Engage people, or at least look at them. Note any unique characteristics. If you're going to develop your intuition, you need to keep looking and listening until you get a sense of the whole person, until a pattern develops. Every time you do this, you'll be filling your database with valuable information.

TUNE IN AND TURN UP YOUR INTUITION

No matter how unobservant you may have been in the past, your database is still stocked with thousands of experiences. Improving the quality and quantity of the information in your subconscious storehouse will help you use your intuition more frequently, but you can also make better use of the data you already have. You can begin to tune in and turn up your inner voice right away by following four steps:

1. Recognize and respect your intuition.
2. Identify what your intuition is telling you.

3. Review the evidence.
4. Prove or disprove your theory.

Recognize and Respect Your Intuition

Before you can hear your inner voice, you have to turn on your receiver. You have to believe your subconscious may be reaching out to tell you that you are either on the right track or headed toward a cliff. When you find yourself thinking "This rings a bell," or "Something isn't right," or "I have a good feeling about her," stop and listen. Usually you'll have time to step back from the situation and reflect on it before making any decisions.

If you have a hunch, *do not* just go with your gut instinct. As much as I value intuition, it is not some pure, unimpeachable knowledge from beyond. Intuition can be influenced by your own often faulty memory. You should know why you're reacting to a person as you are before you let a hunch dictate your actions. Something about the current situation might be stirring up a recollection, but who knows what? You may have an adverse reaction to a man named Ralph for no better reason than that your next-door neighbor when you were six was a bully named Ralph— and you haven't known a Ralph you liked since. That's hardly a good reason not to go to work with someone named Ralph or hire a mechanic named Ralph.

The first step in the process of learning from our intuition, then, is simply to recognize and respect it. *Don't ignore or dismiss it, but don't follow it blindly either.* Think of yourself as a dog who hears a noise in the distance. You stop, become alert, and turn your ears in the direction of the noise. By doing that, you'll be turning on your intuition receptors.

Identify What Your Intuition Is Telling You

Simply recognizing that you have a funny feeling isn't very helpful if your objective is to make intelligent decisions. With a little self-examination you should be able to identify not just that you have a hunch, but what that hunch is.

If, for example, a woman has an uncomfortable feeling when she leaves an interview for a job as a cashier for a man who runs an auto-parts business, she should try to identify her concern. Is she afraid he is going to sexually harass her? Is she worried about the amount of over-time he expects? Is she afraid the business isn't doing well, and she may be looking for another job no sooner than she takes this one? If a man has just met a woman and decides to ask her out because he has a good feeling about her, what exactly is that feeling? Is it that she is going to be fun? Is his intuition telling him that he has met the future mother of his children? If a woman has an aversion to the new bookkeeper after passing him in the hallway for the first time, what might account for her reaction? Did he seem arrogant? Unfriendly? Sleazy?

Identifying your hunch is usually a matter of replaying the chain of events that led up to it. At this point, you're not trying to find the factual evidence that supports your feeling, you're just trying to identify what the feeling is. If you can, try to pinpoint the first time it occurred to you that something was wrong, or right. Free-associate. Ask yourself who the person or place reminds you of, and then reflect on the first image that pops into your head, no matter how absurd it may seem. At some point you'll feel the click of recognition:

"I think the store owner is attracted to me."

"I'll bet that woman has a great sense of humor."

"That new bookkeeper struck me as a real jerk."

It's important to focus on exactly what your intuition is saying, rational or not, because without focus you can't move to the next steps in the process and test the validity of your hunch.

Review the Evidence

Once you've identified what your hunch is, the next step in using your intuition is examining the evidence—that is, all the information already at your disposal. Mentally rewind the encounter and play it back in slow motion, carefully evaluating physical appearance, body language, environment, voice, words, and actions. As you review what happened while your intuitive response was forming, you will be tuning in to its source.

In the case of the fellow who got a good feeling about the woman he just met, he may recall seeing a calendar on her desk featuring his favorite cartoonist. Can he rely on that alone to conclude that he and the woman would have a great time together? No. But at least he has identified the evidence that led him to that initial gut feeling.

As for the woman who took an instant and seemingly inexplicable dislike to the bookkeeper, she may recall he wore the same aftershave favored by the creep her mother used to date. As soon as the woman realizes that her aversion to the new bookkeeper is simply an association between his aftershave and her mother's ex-boyfriend, she can dismiss her intuitive warning bell as a false alarm. She may or may not end up liking him for other, more rational reasons, but at least she won't get off to a bad start just because of a misleading gut instinct.

If the woman who interviewed with the owner of the auto-parts store has identified her hunch as a concern the boss might harass her, she now must look at the available evidence to see if it supports her suspicion. As she replays the interview, she might recall that the man approached her with a swagger and a smug smile when she first entered the room, maintaining only brief eye contact before looking her up and down. As he escorted her to her chair he touched her first on the arm and then in the small of her back. Once the interview began, he lowered his voice like a late-night disc jockey on a local jazz station. This pattern, coupled with a few suggestive remarks such as "I'm really, really, looking forward to working closely with you," created a fairly solid body of evidence that harassment was a possibility.

As you become more familiar with the clues to reading people, you will be able to better evaluate the evidence available to you. Knowing, for example, that an attempt to come within someone's personal space (touching the arm and back) often signifies sexual interest adds weight to your intuition. Without that knowledge, you might doubt your instincts and chide yourself for being too uptight about physical contact. As you evaluate the events that produced your intuitive response, remember that self-censorship is an obstacle when you're trying to tune in to your intuition. Don't be sabotaged by insecurity or political correctness. At this point in the process, let your intuitive response to a person's looks, environment, voice, and demeanor be your guide.

Prove or Disprove Your Theory

Once you've recognized that your subconscious is reaching out to you, identified what it's trying to tell you, and reviewed all the available evidence, you will probably have formed a theory about the origin of your intuitive response. Sometimes you don't need to take the process any further, as in the example of the woman and the bookkeeper with the unfortunate choice of aftershave. But when you haven't reached a comfortable conclusion, the final step is to test your theory.

Maybe you didn't have enough clues to make a call. Or there may have been plenty of clues, but you didn't notice them as carefully as you wish you had now that you know their importance. When we first meet somebody we are bombarded with new data, and it's easy to overlook details. There's also the possibility you encountered someone on a bad day, or think you may have, and want to see if your concerns are borne out. Now, having carefully reflected on your first impression, you can approach him again with your attention fully focused on the specific additional information you need to test your intuition.

The man who wants to know if his new acquaintance really does share his sense of humor might begin his investigation with a casual chat. He could start by asking her about the calendar. A ten-minute conversation should let him know whether there's a rational basis for believing they're on the same wavelength.

The woman considering the job at the parts store might conclude that she doesn't need any more information to know that the owner may come on to her if she takes the job—there's plenty of evidence pointing in that direction. But if she really needs the job and doesn't want to turn it down unnecessarily, she could ask for a second interview. This time she can consciously tune in to aspects of the man's appearance and behavior that might indicate a lecherous nature. She should be able to gather enough information to make the call now that she's focused on the possible problem. She can scrutinize the environment for such items as wall calendars, posters, and cartoons that might offer clues to the owner's tastes. She could look for family photos or other items that might shed some light on his personal life. She might also speak with female employees and, as tactfully as possible, ask how the boss treats them. This time she'll watch his gaze even more carefully; if he touches her, she'll be alert to whether he does so in a sexually suggestive way.

When you're out to test your theory, plan in advance. Prepare a few pertinent questions and ask yourself what character traits might reveal the most about the issue you're concerned with. Be very alert this time around, in case a second chance is all you get before you have to make a decision.

THE FOUR-STEP PROCESS IN ACTION

I vividly recall an experience in O. J. Simpson's criminal trial in which I followed each of the four steps in this process. A young Hispanic woman had been selected to sit on the jury. Our pretrial research, questionnaires, and the oral questioning led us to believe the woman would be receptive to the defense theory of the case and not particularly swayed by the prosecution's theories, especially its emphasis on spousal abuse.

The morning after the jury was selected, the young woman caught my eye. I had a strong feeling something was very wrong. I knew better than to ignore my intuition, even though no one relished the idea of further evaluating the jury that had been selected after months of effort.

After a little thought, I realized I was concerned that she had been abused herself. Once I had identified what my intuition was trying to tell me, I was able to focus on what had raised this red flag. Very quickly, I saw the basis for my concerns.

Previously, this juror had been very attentive in court. She frequently looked at the attorneys, the judge, and Mr. Simpson. She was absorbing everything in the courtroom. She was involved. But that morning she sat with her face turned away from us, staring off into space. When I looked at her more closely, I saw a small bruise on the side of her face, which she was either consciously or unconsciously trying not to reveal to us. When I brought this to the defense team's attention, everyone's red flags rose to full mast.

Someone can get a bruise on her face in a number of ways that have nothing to do with an abusive husband or boyfriend. But my intuition, calling upon my years of experience and stored knowledge, was telling me that if any of those other circumstances applied, the woman would not have been so preoccupied. What's more, if she had merely suffered an innocent bump, she wouldn't have averted her face: she was embarrassed, or trying to hide evidence of a home life she probably realized would cause her to be excused from the jury, or both.

The last thing any of us wanted to do was shame or alienate the juror by asking the judge to allow further questioning, especially of such a personal nature. But eventually the defense team agreed we had to take that risk. During the questioning that followed in Judge Ito's chambers, the juror acknowledged that her boyfriend had hit her the night before. Judge Ito excused her.

This time, my intuition was consistent with the most obvious interpretation of the facts. But that isn't always the case. Many times intuition flies in the face of other, more obvious evidence. When that happens, it's crucial that you know how to think through your hunch to the facts underlying it. I've experienced this many times during my career, and I'm often the lone voice trying to convince a reluctant legal team to keep or dismiss a juror. One of the most memorable occasions was the trial of an English cabdriver accused of killing four people, whose bodies were never found.

The defense team in that case included the defendant, who was very actively involved in the jury selection process. We were all wary when one of the jurors revealed that he had accompanied police on several "ride-alongs" in their squad cars. Wouldn't he be partial to the police if he had requested to ride around with them? The knee-jerk reaction was to dismiss him. The lawyers and the defendant assumed that anyone who wanted to see the police in action was a staunch supporter of the force. But something told me the man would be a favorable juror.

One of cabdriver's principal defenses was that the police had not followed appropriate procedure in the investigation and that as a result, their conclusions were unreliable. A second defense contention was that both the police and the prosecutors had made up their minds that the man was guilty without objectively evaluating the evidence themselves.

When I asked myself what my intuition was telling me, I decided it was saying that this juror would be critical of the police *if* the defense was able to prove the investigation was not handled properly. If the sloppy police work was due to the detectives prejudging the defendant before the investigation was concluded, I thought, this juror was even more likely to be critical.

Knowing what my intuition was telling me, I carefully evaluated the information I had about this prospective juror. First, it was clear that he was at least vaguely familiar with normal police procedures and the importance of following them. This meant he would understand why a deviation from proper procedures could taint the investigation and, consequently, the prosecution's case. Also, even though he had ridden along in a patrol car on a few occasions, he was not an auxiliary or volunteer police officer, and had no aspirations to become one. He was simply curious about the process and wanted to experience it himself. This suggested he had an inquiring nature and would be open-minded as we presented our case, even if we were critical of the police investigation.

Finally, and perhaps most significantly, the man was openly gay. I believed that an openly gay man who had undoubtedly been judged on the basis of his sexual orientation alone would be critical of the police if we could prove they prejudged the defendant. I hadn't focused on this issue at first, but on reflection, it became vital to my final analysis.

In this trial we hoped the jury would see that the prosecution had likewise made an unfounded judgment, which they were not willing to reevaluate despite any evidence that might contradict it. This stubborn refusal to objectively evaluate the evidence applied not just to the detectives but also to the district attorney's office: this was actually the third time the defendant had been tried for this alleged crime. The first trial resulted in a hung jury, the second in a mistrial. Nonetheless, the prosecution doggedly pursued the defendant a third time.

As I tuned in to this information, I became more satisfied that the juror would evaluate the investigation with an open and analytical mind. I believed he would also be receptive to the argument that the defendant was the victim of prejudgment, if we could prove it.

We decided to "turn up" the volume on my intuition by asking more about the man's experience as a gay person and his views about the state's possible prejudgment of the defendant. The more we questioned the man, the more certain I was that he'd be good for our side. The defense team, including the defendant, was extremely reluctant to leave him on the jury, but eventually deferred to my judgment. The man became an active participant in the jury deliberations that resulted in our client's acquittal.

HEEDING YOUR SECOND THOUGHTS

It's not unusual to get a strong feeling about someone from the moment you first meet him. But sometimes a gut feeling will emerge only after weeks or months, as a result of more information you've acquired over time. The "Discovering Patterns" chapter cautioned you to constantly test your first impression against new information. An intuitive response to a person should always be viewed as new information and never ignored, no matter when it finally emerges. Heeding your second thoughts can make the difference between a missed opportunity and an inspired decision.

An example of this occurred during the McMartin Preschool trial. All the prospective jurors had filled out extensive questionnaires weeks before in-court jury selection began. One juror, an African-American woman, made a number of comments in her written questionnaire that strongly suggested she would be very pro-prosecution. She acknowledged having read or heard much of the extensive media coverage that preceded the trial. She admitted that, on the basis of everything she had read and heard about the case, she believed the defendants were guilty. Everyone on the defense team, including me, had crossed her off the list of potential jurors.

The oral questioning took place about two weeks after the written questionnaires had been turned in. When she sat before us answering the lawyers' questions, this woman recanted much of what she had written two weeks earlier. She claimed to have reflected further on the case, and on the defendants' right to a fair trial. She apologized for being so judgmental and assured us she would be open-minded. Normally I would not even have considered selecting her. These words and actions suggested that she wanted to sit as a juror in a high-profile case and was trying to sell us on her ability to be fair. But for some reason I believed her. Something was telling me she really would be open-minded.

After coming to this realization, I began the process of reexamining everything she had said as well as how she looked and acted. I noticed that when she spoke to us, she made very direct eye contact. She leaned forward slightly in her chair. Frequently she sighed as she acknowledged the comments she made in her questionnaire. She expressed her regret at being so judgmental. She seemed to be struggling with the realization that she had passed judgment on others, just as so many had judged her as a black woman. She spoke slowly, sincerely, with an even cadence. It was as if she were searching her heart and soul for the absolute truth about how she felt.

By this point in my career I had seen many people misrepresent themselves just to get on a jury in a high-profile case. I knew how they looked and acted when they were trying to sell themselves to the judge and attorneys. Their body language, tone of voice, and speech patterns were stored in my subconscious data bank. The gut feeling I had about this woman was based on the fact that she didn't fit that pattern. We left her on the jury, which found my client not guilty.

ARE WOMEN MORE INTUITIVE THAN MEN?

We end this chapter with a question, the answer to which we believe validates our view of intuition.

Many of us know someone who truly seems to have a gift for understanding people or even predicting the future, and that person is usually a woman. When I tell people my definition of intuition—that it's basically a subconscious message percolating up from the storehouse of information gathered by our five senses—I'm often challenged to explain the psychic powers of somebody's grandma, aunt, or mother: "She knew when one of her friends was going to catch a cold two days before it happened," or "She predicted the car crash that killed little Jimmy Smith," or "She could always tell when I was lying to her."

Maybe there are some people, somewhere, who actually *do* sense vibrations, can describe the character of someone they know nothing about, and see into the future. I have never met one. As we explained earlier in the chapter, I chalk up these powers to observation and deductive reasoning. I have noticed, however, that true to conventional wisdom, women do tend to be more intuitive than men. There's a straightforward reason for this, and it's as obvious as the reason Mom always knew when you were lying.

More so in previous generations, but even today, most moms spend more time than most dads closely watching their children's behavior and mannerisms. Almost everyone looks different when he or she lies, even if it's a subtle difference that a stranger might not notice. When you were a child, the smallest change in your expression was instantly apparent to your mother. She wasn't psychic. She just had an enormous database on the topic of *you*. The moment you made a move that differed from your standard "honest" pattern, her subconscious picked up on it. Maybe it was something as minor as the angle at which you were standing. Maybe even she would not have been able to tell you exactly how she knew you were fibbing. But the fact is, your pattern was different. As you grew up and spent less time with Mom, her intuitive powers probably started to decline—at least when it came to you.

Today, this dramatic disparity between the roles of men and women has diminished, and in many families has disappeared altogether. But women still more frequently assume the role of caretaker, communicator, observer, and peacemaker in the family. And women typically are raised to be more sensitive to their own and other people's feelings. They're also socialized more to notice clothing, haircuts, shoes, jewelry, and other aspects of personal appearance. They read fashion magazines far more than men do, and they key in on who's had plastic surgery, who's wearing a wedding ring, and who's gained five pounds. They watch. They notice. If you have any doubt, ask how much the men and women you work with remember about what the boss's wife (or the boss) wore to last year's holiday party. If the women don't win hands down, I'll be amazed. Larger database, better intuition, it's as simple as that.

Is this a generalization? Absolutely. We all know men who are more attentive, observant, and sensitive than most women. And I'll bet they're more intuitive as well. As women's roles in society have moved toward parity with men's, the intuition gap has also closed. Mr. Mom, not his wife who works outside the home, is now the one who knows intuitively when little Johnny isn't feeling well or the dog needs to go outside. And that is as it should be, given the nature of intuition. Personal and social experience, not chromosomes, give rise to intuition.

And what about the woman who knew when her friends were ill, or the one who predicted a car crash? If I had the time, I'd relish investigating those stories. I'll bet those sickly friends looked different, or smelled different, or asked for a cup of hot tea instead of the usual coffee. I'd also wager that the corner where little Jimmy Smith died had been a death trap for years. One bet I'd certainly make is that most of those psychic aunts and grandmas have sterling memories, great eyesight, and a keen interest in other people's business.

KEY POINTS

Intuition isn't a mysterious sixth sense: It's the whisper of your subconscious memory of forgotten or barely noticed events. To maximize it, build your subconscious data bank by paying closer attention to everyone.

Tune in and tune up your intuition: Follow this simple approach when you hear that whisper of intuition:

- *recognize and respect your intuition.* But neither follow it blindly, nor reject it outright.
- *identify what your intuition is telling you.* If you have a "hunch," ask yourself what it is. Are you afraid? Nervous? Excited?
- *review the evidence.* Play back the events which immediately preceded your gut feeling, and try to consciously spot what you noticed only subconsciously the first time around.
- *prove or disprove your theory.* Once you've identified a plausible basis for your intuition, gather additional information from which to consciously test your theory.

Don't just listen to your intuition as you form first impressions: Keep alert to intuitive messages that might emerge months or years after you've come to know someone. "Second thoughts" are often intuitive voices, too.

Looking in the Mirror: Reading How Others Are Reading You

My work as a jury consultant often leads me into the role of image consultant: I advise my clients, their lawyers, and witnesses how to present themselves in the best possible light. Jurors and judges scrutinize the appearance and conduct of everyone involved in a case, particularly those on the witness stand. But the need to project the best possible image doesn't start or stop there, which is why, before trial starts, I have a brief chat with everyone involved in the case. It goes something like this: "Once you get near the courthouse, someone's eyes will be on you every second. The person watching you may be the judge, a juror, a court worker, another lawyer, or a witness. But every moment, someone will be sizing you up. What the judge or jury sees in your body language and demeanor, overhears in the hallway, or picks up in the restroom at the end of the day may be more important than what happens in open court. Someone will always be watching you, so prepare to be seen."

The same thing happens in sales meetings, boardrooms, the grocery store, job sites, or the ball game. Sometimes, as during job interviews or blind dates, you expect it. Sometimes you don't. But make no mistake— someone is almost always looking and listening.

How people read you will make a tremendous difference in your life. Every clue we've given you about reading others and every trait we've described applies to you as much as to the people you're reading. *What you've learned from these pages is equally valuable whether you apply it to others or to yourself, and it's most effective if you do both.* This chapter will offer some tips on fine-tuning the impression you make: how to prepare to be read; gauge your audience; plan your approach; and react to shifting circumstances. Think of this as an exercise in self-awareness—a commitment you consciously make to leave behind a positive impression.

PREPARE TO BE READ

Preparing to be read doesn't have to be a complex process. It can be as simple as washing your car before you pick up a customer or your new girlfriend, or taking a few extra minutes to change into more appropriate clothing before you head off to dinner or to a meeting. It may involve nothing more than thinking of a few intelligent questions to ask during a job interview.

Preparation is an invaluable habit because, as the saying goes, "You only get one chance to make a first impression." And important first encounters often occur when we least expect them. You never know when you might meet someone who could change your life. A man hoping to meet the woman of his dreams should think twice before he leaves the house in old, baggy sweatpants and a faded T-shirt. When he finally bumps into that perfect woman, she may take one look at him in his raggedy sweats and walk the other way. And who's likely to stop and say hello to a woman at the supermarket if she's racing around like she's late for a bus and wearing curlers in her hair? And the day you decide to wear that poorly fitting old outfit because you didn't make the time to do the laundry will be the day your boss invites you in to meet the company's biggest customer.

I am always acutely aware of how people may read me, always conscious of the impression I'll make—not just when I first meet someone, but even as my relationships develop. Getting off to a good start is important, but even great first impressions can tarnish if they're not maintained. In time the process becomes second nature. But if you're unaccustomed to this sort of forethought, make a list of what you can do to present yourself in the most positive light in any given situation. You can begin by asking yourself these questions:

- Who will I see?
- What is my objective?
- How should I look?
- How do I get there and back?
- Where should I go and what should I do?
- How should I act?
- What should I say?

Who Will I See?

To be read in the most positive light, start by considering your audience. I'm not suggesting you transform yourself, chameleonlike, to suit everyone else. I'm simply recommending that you take a moment to find out exactly who you'll be dealing with and take that into consideration.

Before you run out and buy a new suit for a job interview, find out who will be interviewing you and learn as much as you can about the company he or she works for. Is the company formal or informal? Is it progressive or conservative? Will you be meeting with a man or a woman? Is he or she young or old? How long has he or she been there? Will this person be your direct supervisor, the one who hires you, or simply the first stop in a series of interviews? Perhaps you've spoken with the interviewer over the phone. Have you detected an accent that points to a particular geographic region or country? Is an information package or company brochure available?

Let's assume you learn the person you're meeting with is a college-educated woman in her early thirties who has a Southern accent and that you will be working directly under her. You also discover that the company is run by two brothers in their late thirties who are very casual and progressive. When you picked up the application, you noticed everyone in the office was dressed casually. How might this affect your preparation?

How would you prepare differently if you learned the interviewer is a sixty-five-year-old man who had been with the company for thirty-five years? He's in charge of personnel and will have nothing to do with supervising you once you're hired. He does, however, have the final say in whether you will be hired. He has a strong New York City accent. You also learn the company is an old-line, publicly traded, conservative outfit run by a former head of General Motors.

In the first instance you should be particularly alert to the personal impression you make. How you'll relate to your co-workers and the woman who's interviewing you, and how you'll fit in to the office environment may be as important as your work experience. In the second example, you might conclude that your most conservative suit and demeanor would be appropriate and that the emphasis in the interview is going to be on your résumé, not on your personality or ambitions.

In any situation, a moment to consider your audience is time well spent. Even if you're just going to pick up your kids at school, bear in mind that the teachers, the staff, and the other children will be checking you out. You can show up scruffy and haggard, or you can run a comb through your hair and change out of those old sweats. It all adds up.

What Is My Objective?

Several years ago I attended an annual gala sponsored by a group of at-torneys with whom I worked regularly. The organization had several hundred members, perhaps four hundred of whom were present.

On the way, I picked up a friend, who was also a woman in the legal business. When she came to the door, I was surprised to see her in an ex-ceedingly revealing evening gown. She was poured into it, and pouring out of it. A single woman, she was obviously trying to look as sexy as possible in the hope of attracting the men who would be at the party. What she didn't consider was that most of those men would have their wives or girlfriends in tow.

When we arrived at the party, we noticed immediately that my friend was the only one who had chosen to make this particular impression. The rest of the women were dressed conservatively, in suits or sophisti-cated dresses. They were obviously trying to look their best, but they were not trying to impress anyone with their sexiness.

The men with whom my friend worked—and upon whom she de-pended for her livelihood—avoided her like the plague. The last thing they wanted to do in front of their wives and girlfriends was pay atten-tion to a scantily clad woman who often worked with them late into the night. For my friend, the party was a disaster. While looking sexy was important to her, she quickly regretted sacrificing her professionalism on that occasion. She learned her lesson the hard way.

Almost every event is an opportunity to make any number of different impressions. At a company picnic, you can maintain your usual buttoned-down image, or loosen up and let people see your more play-ful side. If there's someone at the office in whom you're interested ro-mantically, you can use the company picnic as an opportunity to get her attention. Or this may be your big chance to get to know your boss bet-ter on a personal level. *What you hope to achieve in an encounter should dictate how you prepare for it.*

Your effort to plan to leave a great impression shouldn't be restricted to face-to-face encounters. Remember, people also read us when we write letters, send faxes or e-mail, and make telephone calls. Yet most of us don't give much thought to these communications. We fire off let-ters more extreme or confrontational than anything we'd say in person or even over the telephone. Your message doesn't have less impact just because you don't see the recipient react with shock, offense, or anger to your letter or your remark over the telephone. In fact, a "nasty-gram" can often do more damage than the same statement made to a person's face, because you don't have the opportunity to respond spontaneously if the other person's reaction is not what you anticipated or wanted.

Most of us spend more time thinking about what we're going to have for dinner than about the impression we want to make on the person with whom we're eating. Don't make this mistake if you want to harvest as much as possible from each encounter. And don't think making a good impression is hard work and burdensome. It's not.

How Should I Look?

Most of us pay *some* attention to our personal appearance *most* of the time. But often we make the same mistake my skimpily clad friend did: we don't think it all the way through. Chapter 3 introduced you to the many aspects of our personal appearance that can affect the way we are read. Chances are, you focus regularly on only a few of them. Maybe you carefully comb your hair but don't shine your shoes? Perhaps you give some thought to your clothing but very little to your makeup. Maybe you put on your fanciest cowboy boots and best shirt but neglect to get a badly needed haircut.

You should give thought to every aspect of your appearance if you want to project the best possible image. Remember, a significant deviation from an otherwise flattering pattern may be the one trait someone finds most important. If you're trying to create a professional, conservative, businesslike image with your freshly polished shoes and pressed suit, lose the cartoon-character tie.

You alone can determine how much energy you're willing to put into your appearance, but the critical point is that you should think about it. Reflect on what's generally expected of people in your position at work. For a woman to have her nails done every two weeks may seem like an annoying waste of time and money, but she might decide it's worth it if she's in a profession where such things matter. If you'll be attending an event, whether it's a political rally or the rodeo, think: how would you react to someone who appeared the way you do? Set a standard for yourself, and make a conscious decision to live up to it.

If during the day you will be seeing different people whom you want to impress differently, bring a change of clothes. You may not be able to cut or style your hair between your lunch meeting and your evening date, but there's a lot you can do to present an appropriate appearance on both occasions. Wear your conservative business suit to lunch, then put on your most stylish outfit before you leave work for that date. There's no reason why someone who works in a stuffy office all day needs to wear the same conservative clothes out to a dance club that night. And there is no reason to wear inappropriately casual clothes to work in preparation for the evening festivities. Do some advance planning for how you want to look during the course of the day, and you can always look your best.

How Do I Get There and Back?

The Fairy Godmother provided appropriate wheels for Cinderella's big evening out. You, too, should think about the impression you'll make with your vehicle. Is your car big enough to hold everyone? Can you clean it up so it won't leave a bad impression? If not, can you borrow someone else's car?

I'm not suggesting you rent a limo every time you want to impress a young lady or a client, nor am I implying that anyone who doesn't drive a new Mercedes should keep her car parked in the garage. But people often judge others by their cars, and I don't mean just the make and model. Some people do place a lot of emphasis on how new and expensive a vehicle is, but just as often they look at its upkeep. To show up for an important event in a car that's dirty and littered with trash makes a bad impression. It's almost like a peek into your house or a glimpse into your psyche. An unkempt car delivers the message that, while you may have spiffed yourself up for this one evening, the rest of the time you probably dress the way your car looks. If you doubt that people judge you by your car, ask yourself what *you* think of people who consistently drive dirt-streaked, dusty vehicles. It may not always be a fair or accurate way to judge another person, but we all do it. Be aware of that, and remember the location of the nearest drive-through car wash.

Where Should I Go and What Should I Do?

Think back to the last time you gave a dinner party: You pored through cookbooks, planning the meal. You thought about the location: In the dining room? On the back porch? Under the trees in the backyard? You planned the music, the lighting, the way the table would be set. When events take place on our own turf, we plan them carefully. By applying some of the same forethought to other events, you can get a lot more out of them as well.

Several years ago Robert Shapiro represented Christian Brando in connection with his prosecution for the fatal shooting of his sister's boyfriend. Mr. Shapiro held a press conference with Christian's father, Marlon Brando, in a very casual, friendly outdoor environment. The setting appeared carefully orchestrated. I presume that Mr. Shapiro wanted Marlon Brando outside in natural lighting rather than indoors under the harsh glare of fluorescent lights, and wanted plants and sky in the background—elements that personalized the actor. The choice of a natural environment instead of a sterile, cold one made Marlon Brando seem more like an ordinary guy, for whom, as a grieving father, compassion and understanding were in order.

The same concept applies to our everyday encounters. If you have an important client or customer you want to impress, consider all the possible places you might have lunch or hold the meeting. Different locations—café or upscale restaurant, large meeting room or your own office—will leave different impressions. You should even consider how you'll appear to the other person within that setting.

This was brought home to me years ago, when a friend told me about a meeting she attended with a group of businessmen from Japan. There were about twelve people in all, having lunch at a very expensive restaurant. My friend's boss reserved a table with an outstanding view of the nearby mountains. As the group was ushered toward the table, my friend was surprised to see her boss guide the head of the Japanese contingent to the seat that backed the window, where he wouldn't be able to see the view at all. Later, my friend's boss explained to her that in Japan, the most important person at the table is supposed to be framed by the view, so that everyone else sees him against a beautiful background. The boss's detailed planning impressed me—and no doubt the Japanese businessmen, too.

Always consider how the environment in which you choose to meet others reflects on you. If you want to make a good impression, don't interview a potential employee or speak with a customer from behind a disorganized desk piled high with papers and files. If you want someone to relax and view you more casually, turn off the fluorescent lighting and switch on a table lamp that casts a warmer, more flattering glow. If all the world's a stage, you are the director, actor, and prop master of your life. Set your stage in a way that will make you look good.

To make sure there will be no surprises in the courtroom, lawyers generally avoid demonstrations they have not had a chance to rehearse beforehand. Christopher Darden clearly demonstrated to the world why advance planning is a good idea when he asked O. J. Simpson to put on the bloody glove in front of the jury. Don't make the same mistake. If you can't actually set the stage and choose the props for your encounter with someone, at least learn enough about them to make sure there are no surprises.

I still chuckle at a story an attorney friend told me several years ago about an evening he planned for a prospective new client. The client and his wife were very conservative, formal, religious, and family-oriented. Without any independent investigation, my friend planned a meal at a highly regarded local restaurant, to be followed by an evening at one of the best-regarded theaters in the city.

The dinner went extremely well. The conversation was wonderful and the food was terrific. Everything was coming together exactly as planned. As the evening progressed, my friend's first impressions were confirmed: the client and his wife were conservative and perhaps somewhat judgmental, but basically friendly, salt-of-the-earth types.

After dinner, the group drove to the theater. The play had been advertised in the local paper as a modernistic interpretation of a classic Greek drama. The ads said nothing to suggest that anything untoward might occur during the course of the evening. Then came the five-minute orgy scene, complete with full frontal nudity.

Even months later, as my friend recounted the story to me, he kept shaking his head and saying, "That was the longest five minutes of my life." He certainly didn't want his guests to think he delighted in shocking others or enjoyed a good nude play every now and then. With just a bit more planning, he could have chosen another play and more successfully controlled the evening. The time it takes to read a review or get a recommendation from a friend is well worth the effort.

How Should I Act?

It isn't difficult to plan how you're going to behave. If you're going to a wedding, you can consciously decide how you'll relate to the people who will be there. If you want to use the occasion to mend fences with a cousin with whom you've been feuding, decide in advance whether it will feel more comfortable to treat her civilly but keep your distance initially, or to walk right up and say, "We've got to talk." You can plan in advance whether you're going to drink or remain completely sober; whether you're going to let your hair down or maintain a cool and collected demeanor; whether you'll stay on the sidelines or offer the first toast; and whether you'll mingle with strangers or take the opportunity to catch up with your favorite uncle.

Since weddings usually include so many guests, you can be sure someone will be watching you nearly every moment, and your actions will leave an impression. Why not give them a little advance thought? If you're starving and don't want to make a pig of yourself at the buffet line, have a snack before you go. If you know you'll have to leave early, make a point of apologizing in advance so you won't seem rude when you head for the exit as the bride and groom get ready to cut the cake.

Sometimes a little forethought can do more than just leave behind a good image, it can smooth your way through a potentially difficult situation. I forgot my passport on a recent trip to Toronto. It wasn't a problem going from the United States to Canada, but I learned it was going to be a problem getting back. I knew I'd be given the third degree by an INS agent at the airport, so I carefully planned how I'd handle the situation.

In preparation, I mulled over how best to present myself to achieve my objective: getting back to the United States without sending for the passport and waiting a day or two for it to arrive. I decided I should act deferential, respectful, apologetic, and remorseful, which I was. The INS agent had the power either to cause me unmitigated grief or to send me on my way back home. I wanted to make sure he knew I respected that power, so he wouldn't feel the urge to exercise it. I also presumed that he would be more inclined to cut me some slack if he knew I took my transgression seriously. I apologized for my forgetfulness and assured him that next time I'd remember my passport. I didn't enjoy having to behave like a naughty schoolgirl in the principal's office—but I did get back into the country.

What Should I Say?

The spoken word is the easiest way for people to learn about you. They'll listen to what you say and usually take it at face value, especially if they're not alert to the many people-reading techniques. For that reason, whether you'll be speaking to one person or a thousand, the words that pass your lips are of critical importance. Don't blurt out whatever comes to mind at the time and live to regret it later.

Not long ago I was at a symposium with about a hundred lawyers from Los Angeles. There were both women and men of every race and national origin. The only thing they had in common was that they were all attorneys. During one presentation, the speaker made what could only be interpreted as a blatantly prejudiced remark about immigrants. I felt the air sucked out of the room as he spoke. I'm sure he would have given his eyeteeth to erase that moment.

Most verbal missteps aren't quite as public or catastrophic, but we've all made them. There's no way to ensure that you'll never again put your foot in your mouth. But it's less likely if you think through what you want to say beforehand, particularly if you'll be speaking to strangers. Before you enter any situation where you'll be speaking with people you don't know well, briefly consider the following:

- What do I know about their background?
- Is there anything I might say that could be considered offensive or controversial?
- If I intend to bring up controversial issues, can I frame them in a reasoned, tactful manner?
- Am I certain I want to bring these issues up with these people?
- What are the possible reactions to what I have to say, and have I developed some responses to those reactions?

With slight modifications, these suggestions can be applied to any discussion, even one with a close friend. After you've come on too strong, made an offensive or embarrassing comment, or revealed too much of yourself, you'll almost always replay the encounter and imagine how you *wish* you had handled it. Usually there's no reason why you can't mentally rehearse the encounter beforehand. Think about what you want to say and how you want to say it—before you say something you'll regret later.

READ, REACT, AND READ SOME MORE

Even our best-laid plans don't always work out. We may think we'll be speaking to an audience of experienced middle-aged sales reps, only to find the room filled with twentysomething trainees. We may assume our neighborhood association will greet our suggestion for a July Fourth block party with whoops of delight, only to find that most of them just want some peace and quiet.

Preparation is important, but sticking to a game plan that isn't working is a sure way to disaster. Never become too attached to your agenda. I've seen the consequences of that approach a hundred times in trial. Sometimes an attorney will have made up his mind to examine a witness in a particular way and will persist in that approach even when his client is being crucified by the witness's answers at trial. A good trial lawyer is flexible. He listens and reacts. If he anticipates that a particular witness is going to need to be questioned very aggressively but the witness turns out to be a lamb, he knows it would be a mistake to keep attacking. First, the witness might well lose her cooperative attitude; second, the jurors would wonder why the mean attorney is badgering a perfectly friendly witness.

This same concept applies to the salesperson making a pitch to a customer or the parent making a fund-raising proposal to the local PTA. *To be read favorably by other people, you need to be flexible and responsive, to roll with the punches.* I've found a few techniques to help you do just that.

Don't Think Like an Old Walkie-talkie

The toy walkie-talkies they sold when I was a kid had a button on the side, which you pushed to speak. When you were done, you released the button so you could hear what the other person had to say. You couldn't hear the other person while you had the button pushed. You could either send or receive, but never both at once.

If your receiver is off when you're speaking to other people, you won't know how they're reading you. But if you pay attention while you speak, people will reveal how you're coming across. As you watch them, apply the skills you learned earlier in this book in the chapters on body language, voice, communication techniques, and actions.

- What is their body language telling you? Are eyes rolling? Is there eye contact? Are there signs of boredom or attentiveness? Are they coming closer to you or moving farther away?
- Is the tone of the communication changing? Are there awkward pauses or silences? Are the members of your audience listening as intently as they were at first? Are they starting to make noises, whispering, or talking to one another? Are people starting to join in the conversation, or are they withdrawing from it?
- Are people staying longer than anticipated? Or are those who gave no indication they had to leave early now clamoring to go?
- Are you and your audience starting to make contact? Is the communication developing between you and the audience better or worse than you had hoped? Are people starting to self-disclose, or are they pulling back?

You'll be able to read how others are reading you and to respond productively if you are alert to these and other clues you learned earlier. If you ignore these signs, you may fail to make the most of a good opportunity, or you may make a bad situation even worse.

I can illustrate the point with one of my own pet peeves: the person who comes into my office while I'm very busy and insists on talking to me then and there. At times, I need to focus on my work without interruption. On those occasions I don't want to be rude, but I want people to be sensitive to my needs.

Yet there always seems to be someone who doesn't get the message. Even if I tell them, "I'm really busy now—can't this wait?" they'll respond, "Well, this will just take a minute." As their monologue drags on, I invariably start shifting impatiently in my chair, shuffling papers, or glancing down at my work. It shouldn't take much to pick up on these clues, but they'll drone on even after I've pointed out that I need to make a phone call or simply have to get back to work. Unless I forcefully evict them, they will say their piece come hell or high water. As the minutes tick by, I become more and more offended at their insensitivity to my needs.

Ironically, the worst offenders are the ones who leave my office seemingly most pleased that they were able to have the "discussion" they wanted to have with me, when they wanted to have it. Despite the many signals I was sending, they never realized that I considered their behavior thoughtless and rude. They were so intent on sending their message, they never received mine.

Test the Water Slowly

Planning an approach means knowing your audience, but sometimes you don't have much advance information. You can still prepare what you think will be the best presentation, but don't launch into it at full throttle—begin somewhat cautiously and speed up only once you're sure you're making a positive impression.

For instance, injecting humor into a business setting can be very beneficial. But funny stories or puns that are badly timed or whose audience doesn't understand or appreciate them can freeze things up rather than break the ice. It can be risky to start a sales presentation with too much humor: you could be seen as a jokester, but not a competent professional. Some people appreciate a good pun, while others may think you're weird or nerdy. A romantic remark made on a first date might be considered flattering, or it could offend.

It's almost always possible to test the water one toe at a time until you're sure people are reading you the way you want them to. For example, if you're unsure how humor will play in a meeting, you can start with an underplayed joke. If the response is positive, you can weave more humor into your presentation as you go along. If it's not well received, you can scuttle it altogether.

Shortly after the O. J. Simpson trial I was asked by a women's auxiliary club to come and talk about the American justice system. I wasn't sure what to expect, but I was well aware that many people were un-happy with the verdict and critical of me for working with the defense team. I didn't want my presentation to turn into a debate on the Simpson case, so I decided not to bring it up, at least not at the beginning of my talk.

I correctly assumed that my audience would consist mostly of elderly white women. As a group, elderly white women were upset with the ac-quittal. So I stuck to my plan. Toward the end of my speech, however, I opened the discussion up to questions, and found these ladies were fas-cinated by the Simpson trial. Somewhat hesitantly, I began to answer their questions, carefully watching their faces for signs of disapproval or anger. They listened attentively as I talked about O.J., Johnnie, Judge Ito, and the jurors. And, contrary to my concerns, they were not at all hos-tile. I saw from their smiles and lively interest that I was not being read critically, but rather they were responding to me with interest and en-thusiasm. In spite of their dismay at the verdict, they respected my role in the process and wanted to hear all about it.

LEARNING TO LOOK IN THE MIRROR

There are a number of ways you can improve your ability to see the image you project. These techniques are simple but you need to be ob-jective about yourself, which is no easy task. As discussed in the "Read-ing Readiness" chapter, lack of objectivity is the single biggest obstacle to effectively reading *other* people. It's even harder to recognize our *own* shortcomings. But if you don't, you'll misread how others are reading you.

Using all your people-reading skills as objectively as possible, try the following techniques next time it's particularly important to make a good impression.

The Mirror Never Lies

Candidly look in an imaginary mirror and pretend to be someone else who's reading you. Look at your hair, your clothes, your posture, your body language. Run through the lists in Appendices A and B. Evaluate the tone and volume of your voice, and the manner and content of your speech. Think about how you would interpret your actions if you were someone else. Ask yourself, "If I were a person with the background and beliefs of the person who will be reading me, how would I view someone who looks, talks, and acts as I do?"

Open Your Ears

Listen carefully to what others say about you, whether they're delivering the message in apparent jest or with utmost sincerity. If people comment on your appearance or occasionally mention one of your mannerisms, ask yourself why. Don't casually dismiss what may have been efforts to politely tip you off to your offensive habits. As my mother used to say, "Never turn down a mint. You never know why it's being offered." And don't ignore others' comments just because they're made casually or in jest. As we said earlier, when someone says, "Just kidding," they probably aren't.

This point was brought home early on in jury selection for the O. J. Simpson trial, when Marcia Clark asked a juror if she had said or done anything to offend her. The juror, a conservative, older Italian-American woman, responded, "Well, your skirts are too short."

Given the juror's age and cultural background, this objection wasn't surprising, but it was a small shock to hear it spoken so directly. Some people in the courtroom suppressed a giggle or two, and in general the comment wasn't taken very seriously at the time. I thought about that juror later, however, when the media seemed obsessed with the length of Ms. Clark's skirts. Apparently, that elderly woman's opinion wasn't so far off the mark after all.

Ask the Opinions of People You Trust

Your friends and family can tell you a great deal about the impression you make—if from past experience or your sincere assurances they believe you won't be offended by their advice. But be selective. The critical point is to ask people whose opinions you trust and respect. If it's important for you to look professional, ask someone who regularly deals with professionals to evaluate your demeanor and attire. If you want to look more attractive, find an honest and trusted friend to tell you whether your clothes, makeup, and hairstyle further that objective.

Videotape Yourself

Golfers, skiers, and tennis players watch videotapes of themselves to identify what they may be doing right or wrong, and you can do the same. A salesman can videotape his presentation to see if his posture, eye contact, gestures, and intonation are effectively communicating his sincere belief in his product. A recent grad can videotape a mock job interview, with a friend playing the role of the prospective employer.

The video camera can be a tremendous help even if you have no particular objective except to improve your overall image. If you don't own one, borrow a friend's. Set it up in a room, point it at the two of you, and turn it on. Talk about anything you like—your childhood, your job, your plans for next summer. The result will probably surprise you, pleasantly or not. For those people too shy to ask other people for advice, the video-tape method of self-discovery provides a view very different from a mirror's, and more objective. Even if you're pleasantly surprised with the way you come across, you'll probably find some room for improvement.

BE CAREFUL WHAT YOU ASK FOR— YOU MAY JUST GET IT

If you consciously shape your image and tune in to how people are responding, you will increase the control you have over most relationships and situations. Sometimes these efforts may seem unnatural or manipulative. The cry of the 1960s, "Be true to yourself," is taken very literally by some people. For them, being true to oneself means presenting an unchanging appearance and demeanor no matter what the occasion. Anything else is seen as selling out. But most people have more than one side to their personality, and each facet deserves our conscious attention. What's wrong with putting your best foot forward?

Still, there is no question that learning to project yourself in a certain way can help you manipulate others. The salesman who learns to appear more honest will sell more, even when selling a defective product. The selfish, self-centered man who pretends to be generous and kind will attract more women than the one who reveals his true nature on the first date.

There are undoubtedly people who will take whatever knowledge they've acquired from this book and devote it to manipulating others. But if you want these techniques to improve your relationships, and your life, keep in mind that using these skills to transform yourself into something you aren't will provide only short-lived and shallow successes.

In many instances creating a false impression can backfire badly. A woman who pretends she is interested in sports only to attract a man she knows to be a sports junkie may be making a huge mistake. She'd better be prepared to watch a lot of ball games, or else to have a very upset boyfriend when he finds out she deceived him about her interests. Likewise, a job applicant who claims to have skills he doesn't may get the job, but how good is it going to look on his résumé when he gets fired two weeks later? And how long can the man who pretends to have a lot of money in order to attract a woman keep up the façade? At some point he'll have to pay the piper.

Creating a false image may even have negative consequences you never anticipated. For example, I know single male attorneys who routinely wear a wedding band during trials because they believe jurors who think they are married will find them more credible. Their attitude is "What does it hurt?" Well, for one thing, when I hear them boast of this ploy I read them as less than honest and ethical. Perhaps the jurors will never know, but their colleagues will. Is it worth it?

When I prepare witnesses for trial, I always try to help them project the best possible image. I pay attention to personal appearance, body language, voice, and, of course, the manner in which they testify. I also consider the impression the lawyers' appearance and behavior will make on the jury. But I've learned that the clients, witnesses, and lawyers who make the best impressions act naturally and honestly. A jury will see right through a witness who is precise and analytical at heart but tries to be jovial and casual at trial. A quiet, reserved lawyer who tries to adopt an aggressive, attack-dog style will almost invariably fall flat on his face.

There is a distinct difference between making the best of what we have and putting on a false front. The former is a praiseworthy goal; the latter, a recipe for disaster. As Abraham Lincoln said, "You may fool all the people some of the time; you can even fool some of the people all of the time; but you can't fool all of the people all the time."

KEY POINTS

Prepare to be read: Before any encounter, ask yourself:

- Who will I see?
- What's my objective?
- How should I look?
- How do I get there and back?
- Where should I go, and what should I do?
- How should I act?
- What should I say?

Don't think like an old walkie-talkie: As you present yourself, read your audience, react to them, and read them some more. Be flexible enough to respond if you're sending the wrong message.

When in doubt, test the waters slowly: As hard as it is to make a great first impression, it's even more difficult to recover from a bad one.

Learn to look in the mirror: It's not easy to take an objective view of ourselves. Some techniques which will help are:

- Look in a real or imaginary mirror and pretend you're someone else reading you.
- Listen to what others say about you—even if "in jest." They may be sending subtle messages.
- Ask the opinions of people you trust.
- Videotape yourself. If you think hearing your voice on a tape recorder is eye-opening, just wait until you see your first "screen test."

Be careful what you ask for, you might just get it: Don't pretend to be someone you're not. Put *your* best foot forward, not someone else's.

The Need for S.P.E.E.D.:
Making Snap Judgments
That Make Sense

I was driving with my family along the central California coast. It was getting dark and we were running low on gas. I saw a small convenience store and gas station off the freeway, so I took the exit and slowed to pull in to the lot. One car was parked in front of the store. There weren't any cars getting gas. I took in the rest of the scene: a young man in a baggy jacket was just entering the store, while two others wearing similar clothing stood at opposite ends of the building. They were not speaking to one another but were glancing nervously up and down the street.

Call it intuition or simply the result of years of involvement in criminal cases, but I had a very uncomfortable feeling. Something wasn't right. Should I pull in? Should I stop and watch to see if something was amiss? Or should I pull back on the highway and drive a few miles to the next town to get gas? I had just a few seconds to make up my mind. At the time, I felt I was probably overreacting, but I decided to drive on anyway. The next morning I read in the newspaper that the convenience store had been robbed at gunpoint by three young men.

In a perfect world we would have all the time we need to size up a situation, read the people involved, and make our decisions. And we usually do. But in real life, situations sometimes unfold in a matter of seconds and snap decisions must be made. In the courtroom, I've become accustomed to making these rapid-fire judgments. Every case doesn't involve days, weeks, or months of jury selection, as most of the high-profile ones do. Sometimes I have only a few minutes to watch and listen to a juror before making a decision that may mean the life or death of a client. After years of practice, I have developed a method that substantially increases the odds of reading people accurately on the fly. I use it whenever I need to read with S.P.E.E.D.

Reading with S.P.E.E.D. isn't foolproof, but if you memorize the technique and practice it carefully, you'll greatly improve the quality of your decisions—no matter how quickly they're made. There are five steps to the process of reading with S.P.E.E.D.: Scan, Pare, Enlarge, Evaluate, and Decide.

The approach I use when I need to read with S.P.E.E.D. is essentially an abbreviated version of the people-reading techniques discussed in the previous chapters. But don't use it unless time is of the essence. Reading with S.P.E.E.D. is not as reliable as a thoughtful, patient analysis that allows time for patterns to develop more fully. Always remember: *The less time you have to evaluate someone, the more likely it is that your evaluation will be faulty.* Don't rush to judgment unless you absolutely have to.

While understanding people and predicting their behavior is not a process that lends itself to shortcuts, you do need some method of making snap judgments or you'll be unprepared for real-life emergencies. Reading with S.P.E.E.D. works for the taxi driver who must decide each night which fares are safe to pick up, the foreman who must decide whether a heavy-equipment operator returning from a long lunch has been drinking, and the father who must decide whether to leave his child at a pool party, trusting people he hardly knows to be vigilant enough to avoid a tragedy. It's equally effective whether you're buying an item at a flea market or stopping at an ATM while someone is loitering nearby.

Even when you've been forced to read a situation with S.P.E.E.D., stay alert for additional clues that may warrant a reevaluation of your snap judgment. If you quickly accept a ride home from someone and three blocks later you realize that he's drunk, don't hesitate to reverse that decision. Remember, few decisions are irreversible. Keep testing your impression against any additional information that is revealed over time.

SCAN

Literally hundreds of pieces of information were available to me as I began turning in to the gas station in central California, among them: the time of day; the weather; the location of the convenience store on the lot with respect to the gas pumps; the position of the three men; whether they were talking; how they were acting; how they were dressed; and how their behavior compared with what I would expect from three young men who'd stopped for a snack or something to drink while they were out together for the evening. I couldn't possibly evaluate all that information in the few seconds in which I had to decide whether or not to stop. In order to quickly decide what information was critical and what was irrelevant, I needed to view it in the broadest possible way.

When faced with such circumstances, first *scan* the entire picture, then work your way from general impressions to more specific ones. Begin by taking in the backdrop: the environment, location, weather, and other physical aspects of the scene. It's as if you're looking at a stage and noticing the set and props. Then move on to the actors on the stage. How many people are there? What are they doing? How are they relating to one another?

After you get a general sense of the backdrop and the entire cast of players, focus on the individuals. Consider their physical appearance and body language, such as their eyes, movements, and speech. If you're speaking with them, watch their facial expressions and try to gauge how they're relating to you. As you do all this, *be alert to anything peculiar or unique*—anything that might define the person or the moment. Gather as much information as you can as quickly as you can, from the general to the specific. Make a first pass through all the information available to you.

PARE

Once you have scanned the stage and the actors, noting their appearance and behavior, *pare* the information so you can get a handle on it. To do this, *identify the items or traits that stand out*. When you're in a hurry, you will usually need to limit yourself to no more than five or six traits. If you focus on more than that, you probably won't have time to complete your evaluation before you need to react.

If you don't have a clear idea of what you need to decide about someone, you won't be able to quickly select the handful of critical traits. So before you decide on your short list of important traits, consider for a moment what question you need to answer. For example, assume a woman goes to a party with friends who are available to drive her home, but toward the end of the evening a man she met there offers her a ride home. Before she accepts, she should focus on her concerns and identify the information she needs to evaluate him.

If she wonders whether the man is sober enough to drive her home safely, she should focus on signs of intoxication. Is his speech slurred? Has he been acting in an exaggerated or inappropriate fashion? Is his conversation coherent? How much did he drink? Does he show any signs of poor balance or impaired motor control?

If her concern is whether his intentions are honorable, she should focus on an entirely different set of facts. Has he been a gentleman toward her thus far? Has she noticed how he's treated other women at the party? Is he a friend of someone she knows, who can reassure her that he's not the next Ted Bundy? Was there anything suggestive in his body language, voice, or words when he offered to give her a ride home?

When you must make a decision quickly, you need to identify what your primary concerns are and then focus on the most distinctive traits that pertain *directly* to those concerns. You won't have time under these circumstances to look carefully at everything.

ENLARGE

Once you've pared down the hundreds of bits of information available to you, the next step in the process when reading with S.P.E.E.D. is to *enlarge* those few traits that are most important and bring them into clearer focus. Think of it as if you were looking through a telescopic lens. As you scanned the environment, you saw a handful of features that you want to view more closely. You now focus on those, and zoom in.

You'll need to concentrate if you expect to be able to enlarge the key traits quickly and clearly. Eliminate any distractions. If you know you'll have only a short period of time to read someone in a meeting, then before it begins, turn off the phones, radio, or TV. Clear your mind of what you'll be having for dinner or whether you need to stop off at the cleaner's on the way home. Close the door so no one will enter the room and tear your attention away from where it needs to be. When the meeting starts, maintain that same focus.

This is exactly the process I used when I made that critical decision not to pull in to the gas station. I had only a few seconds to increase my awareness of the key events unfolding before me. Once I scanned the entire environment and identified my concerns sufficiently to be able to pare down hundreds of pieces of information to just a few, I focused on the most important ones. I focused on the two young men standing outside the convenience store. I watched them carefully and saw they were not looking at or speaking to each other. Instead, they were looking nervously up and down the street—and at my car as I drove in. I noticed their body language, which reeked of anxiety. And I tuned out my children, the noise of the car radio, and every other distraction. It was as if the rest of the stage, the props, and even the other members of the audience disappeared, leaving only the actors, who became the exclusive focus of my attention. In the process, the minute details of their behavior emerged even more clearly.

EVALUATE

Now that you've focused on and enlarged the most important pieces of information, you need to *evaluate* them. To do this, use the tools we've discussed throughout this book—but consider this the lightning round. You must continue to concentrate. The more focused you are, the more accurate your evaluation will be.

Look for deviations from normal behavior. Does it make sense that three young men out for the evening would visit a convenience store and not go in together, but instead have one enter the store while the other two position themselves like sentries? Does it make sense that the two young men who stayed outside would not be speaking to each other? Wouldn't you expect them to talk, laugh, and joke, rather than stand quietly, looking nervously up and down the street?

Look for extremes. How far apart are the men? Do they talk a little, or not at all? Do they seem particularly nervous or vigilant? Is there any other logical explanation for their behavior?

Always ask yourself whether a pattern has developed that points in a particular direction. There was nothing unusual about three men pulling in to a convenience store–gas station and not getting gas. It happens all the time. Likewise, it may not mean much that only one of the three men went inside. Maybe the other two just needed some air. It might not even be that unusual that the two men outside were not speaking to each other—perhaps they weren't getting along. Even the fact that they were looking up and down the street didn't necessarily mean they were up to no good. Conceivably they could have been watching for friends who were supposed to meet them there. But when I put all these clues together, a pattern became clear. This particular pattern told me that there was a reasonable chance something was wrong, and I should be careful.

DECIDE

You have scanned, pared, enlarged, and evaluated; *now you need to make a decision. If you don't decide, and decide quickly, you run the risk that the decision will be made for you.* Had I delayed too long at that gas station, one of the armed men might have gotten jumpy and demanded that I get out of my car, or worse.

When you're reading with S.P.E.E.D., there's always the chance that you'll make the wrong decision. That's true in any situation, but in cases where snap judgments are required, the margin for error is a lot greater. That's why I always follow one rule: *If you must err, err on the safe side.*

One of the reasons I've had such a good success rate as a jury consultant is that when in doubt, I take the path least likely to have adverse consequences. I'm sure that among the people excused on my say-so because I was uncertain of them were a number who would have been wonderful jurors. If I make a mistake and excuse someone who would have been a good juror, it doesn't matter, as long as I am confident in the one I pick as his replacement. On the other hand, if I have concerns about someone and we leave him on the jury anyway, rather than search for someone about whom I feel better, the consequences could be catastrophic. Better safe than sorry.

Engineers use the term "fail-safe design," which means that products are designed so that if they fail, they do so in a way that ensures no one will get hurt. A machine that malfunctions automatically shuts off. A bolt that breaks will drop into a location where it won't do any serious harm. The concept of fail-safe design should be applied to the decision-making process—especially when you're reading with S.P.E.E.D.

At the gas station, I quickly considered my options and their consequences. If my concerns proved well founded and a robbery was under way, I would expose myself and my family to potentially serious harm if I pulled in to the station. But if I chose to drive to the next town and it turned out the men were not robbing the station, at worst I'd waste a few minutes. My decision was easy. I knew the next town was just a few miles down the road and I had plenty of gas to get there. If I had been driving on fumes, and passing up that gas station meant we might be stranded on the roadside at night, the decision would have been more difficult.

Weighing the consequences of a decision is crucial. The dad who takes his child to a pool party may wonder whether there will be adequate adult supervision, especially if his child can't swim. As he evaluates the scene, he might look to see how many other parents are around, and if the adults seem attentive. He could ask whether the kids will be playing unattended near the pool, and whether the adults will be drinking alcohol. After he's gathered and weighed all the information, the final decision should hinge on the consequences of his decision. If he is concerned that the environment presents a risk that his child may drown, he may choose to stay at the party himself, especially if there's no compelling reason for him to be elsewhere.

The more important the decision, and the more devastating the consequences could be if you are wrong, the wiser you are to err on the side of caution. If you don't have enough time to eliminate the risk, take the safe course.

PRACTICE MAKES PERFECT

Reading with S.P.E.E.D. gets easier with practice. As you become more attentive, focused, and perceptive, you'll be able to identify and understand important traits more quickly. And you'll become more confident of your ability to make sensible snap judgments as your decisions improve and you begin to trust your people-reading skills.

Don't be surprised if you feel a bit overwhelmed at first by all the information you'll have to scan, pare, enlarge, evaluate, and decide. The process may seem unwieldy at first, but after a while it will become second nature—like driving a car. I remember how completely overwhelmed I felt by all the things I had to keep in mind when I first got behind the wheel. It was all I could do to handle the clutch, accelerator, and gear shift—how could anyone expect me to use my turn signals, check my rearview mirror, and watch for oncoming traffic, too? Yet within a few months I no longer even thought about shifting. It just happened.

As you practice reading with S.P.E.E.D., you'll become as proficient at it as you are at driving. Whatever you do, *don't give up*. While reading people in everyday circumstances when you have plenty of time will greatly enhance your relationships, it's perhaps even more important to be able to make the right decisions when time is short. Both skills require the same tools, and both will help you gain control over your life. Whenever I think of that gas station, I thank the fates that I was able not only to read those young men, but to read them with S.P.E.E.D.

KEY POINTS

Take your time if you can: But if you must decide about someone quickly, remember to use the acronym S.P.E.E.D.

- SCAN. Start with the big picture—the entire stage upon which the events unfold—and work your way down to the subtle clues projected by the individual actors.
- PARE. Keep in mind the issue you need to resolve as you identify the five or six elements of the whole picture that stand out most.
- ENLARGE. Zoom in on those five or six key elements as if you were a telephoto lens, until your concentration is focused on them alone.

- EVALUATE. Look for a pattern within those key traits, and for deviations or extremes within the patterns.
- DECIDE. When you're in the lightning round, if you don't decide, and decide quickly, your decision will be made for you by others or by the haphazard manner in which events unfold.

When in doubt, take the safest course: Err on the side of caution. You may miss a few golden opportunities, but you may also avoid disaster.

Most important, practice, practice, practice: It may seem difficult at first, but with practice, reading people accurately will be as automatic as driving your car.

Physical Traits and What They Reveal

To sharpen your observational skills, the next time you meet someone new imagine you're taking a snapshot of her. Freeze her for a moment, then mentally step back and look her up and down. You'll be scanning her for physical characteristics and noting consistent traits, as well as the one or two that may stand out. What follows is a list of the types of things you should notice. It may seem long, but in reality you can take in most of this information very quickly. And it gets easier with practice.

PHYSICAL CHARACTERISTICS

Body
height
weight
proportion/shape
overall size
physical condition (muscular, wiry, soft)
posture (slouched, potbellied, erect, stiff)
body hair

Face
eyes (open, squinty, red, dilated, watery, droopy)

lips (open or tight; smile, frown, grimace)
teeth (crooked, white, clean, false, missing; braces)
nose (red, bulbous; broken capillaries)
ears
head hair (bald; thin; color, style, cut, condition, cleanliness)
facial hair (beard, mustache, eyebrows, nose and ear hair)
complexion (pale, red, blushing, sweaty, dry)

wrinkles (smile lines, crow's-feet, furrowed brow, bags under the eyes)

Extremities
hands (callused, clean, wrinkled, tanned)
fingers
fingernails and cuticles (length, condition, color; manicured)
feet
toes
toenails

Skin
pigmentation
birthmarks
moles
warts
scars
acne
pallor
wrinkles
rashes
hives
sweatiness

Physical Irregularities/Disabilities
physical deformities
prosthesis
body braces (back, leg, neck, ankle, knee)
scars
unusually thick glasses
hearing aids
bandages
casts

Ornamentation/Jewelry
earrings
necklaces/chains

bracelets (wrist, ankle)
rings (toe, finger, nose, eyebrow, pinkie; college, high school, sport, fraternal organizations)
cuff links
tie tacks
watches
watch fobs or chains
ornamental pins
lapel pins
fingernail jewelry

Makeup
foundation
lipstick
lip liner
eye shadow
eyeliner
eyebrow liner
blush
mascara
powder
fingernail polish
toenail polish
fake eyelashes
body makeup

Accessories
hats
belts
purses
scarves
gloves
socks
stockings/nylons
garters
ties (bow, regular, bolo)
suspenders
pocket scarves
hair adornments (bows, barrettes, pins)

glasses (type, style)
headbands

Clothing
shirt/blouse
pants/slacks
dress
shoes
jacket
coat
cape
sweater
vest
shorts
bathing suit

*"Bodifications" (Elective
Alterations of the Body)*
body piercing—whether or not
   any jewelry is currently in the
   holes (ears, nose, eyebrow,
   tongue, navel, nipple, cheek;
   holes)
plastic surgery, if noticeable
   (eyes, face, ears,

breasts/pectorals, other
   implants, tummy tucks, fanny
   lifts, liposuction, face peels,
   nose jobs, tattoos [both
   decorative and eyebrows],
   collagen injections)
manicures
dyed hair
lash/brow tinting
eyebrow plucking

Hygiene
hair
face
ears
nose
hands
fingers
nails
feet
teeth
breath
body odor
clothing

Once you have armed yourself with information by noticing the various traits on this list, you can begin to interpret them. The following are twelve common characteristics and what they *may* mean. The only way to accurately interpret the meaning of these physical traits in any particular situation is to view them in context with other physical characteristics as well as mannerisms, environment, voice, and actions.

COMPLEXION

Complexion may reveal much about someone's behavior and values, particularly if he or she tries to change it.

Tan   A tanned face may reveal that the person's job or hobbies put him outdoors for considerable periods. A tan may also indicate that someone is vain and appearance conscious, or only that he just returned from a vacation in a sunny location. To figure out which, you'll need to look at other clues. For example, if a man is very tanned, deeply wrinkled, and has calluses on his hands, he has probably spent a lot of time working outdoors, since few outdoor hobbies would leave heavy calluses. On the other hand, if you saw a man who had manicured nails and an immaculate suit along with bronzed skin, the odds are he thinks he looks better that way and has the time to pursue a dark tan, either outdoors or at a tanning salon. This much attention to skin tone indicates vanity and image consciousness.

Pale skin   People whose skin is very pale generally have few outdoor hobbies and don't work outdoors. There are, as always, exceptions: someone may protect her skin out of health consciousness, or she may be ill, or she may be from the Pacific Northwest, or somewhere else where there are extended periods of overcast weather. In years past, I found that light-complected people with softer, paler skins tended to be less physically active and health conscious than those who showed at least some exposure to the sun. But as people become more aware of the harmful effects of the sun, this conclusion is sometimes off-base.

Irregularities   Facial irregularities such as moles or warts, particularly if they're conspicuous, are significant because today most people can afford to have such blemishes removed. But remember, there have been famous actresses and models known for their "beauty marks." More frequently, these irregularities point to a socioeconomic background in which physical appearance was, by necessity, a very low priority. But often someone's reasons for retaining a facial blemish are more complicated. If someone doesn't bother to remove a large, dark mole from the tip of her nose it may mean she is very comfortable with herself, moles and all. Or it may show she doesn't want to cater to our image-conscious society, in which case it may also reveal rebellious leanings.

HYGIENE

Hygiene is one of the most significant and noticeable traits. Poor hygiene reveals a wealth of information about a person, but it's essential to make the distinction between people who are unkempt and those who are dirty. People who are messy but clean fall into an entirely different category. The rumpled look is covered in the "Dowdiness" section later in this appendix.

Hygiene can speak of a person's education, social class, perception of himself and others, intelligence, organization, laziness, carelessness, self-image, rebelliousness, cultural background, consideration for others, desire to please, and desire for social acceptance.

The signs of poor hygiene include

unkempt, greasy hair or scalp
dirty hands, face, and/or body
dirty fingernails
dirty, stained, or missing teeth
bad breath
body odor
dirty, smelly clothing

People with poor hygiene may be

- *oblivious to the effect they have on others.* This indicates a high level of self-centeredness; a lack of common sense; and inability to read the reactions of those around them. They are out of touch.
- *insensitive.* They might know but not care about the effect they're having on other people. This may indicate a lack of education or uncaring attitude toward others as well as, again, self-centeredness.
- *mentally ill or drug or alcohol abusers.* People who are depressed often neglect their personal hygiene. Those with other chronic mental illnesses, including drug and alcohol abuse, also frequently ignore personal hygiene.
- *unable to care for themselves because of a chronic medical problem.*
- *from a very poor socioeconomic background.* Few people can't afford to be clean. But some people raised in poverty were never taught the basics of personal hygiene. They never got into the habit of bathing regularly or putting on fresh underwear each morning, and never pick it up later in life.
- *lazy.* Some people just don't want to make the effort to keep clean.

Personal hygiene, like all traits, must be viewed in light of other traits. My first case, fifteen years ago, involved a man charged with the kidnap, rape, and murder of a ten-year-old. The Los Angeles media called him "the Ice Cream Man" because he enticed the young girl into his truck while selling ice cream. He had a long, scraggly, unkempt, filthy beard and mustache and long, dirty fingernails. His fingers were stained yellow because he smoked and didn't wash. His eyes were frequently encrusted. This complete inattention to hygiene signaled the worst type of socioeconomic background. Indeed, he had been abused as a child and was uneducated. He had no goals in life, and even less self-esteem. He wanted to die, and the jury gladly accommodated him. He remains on death row today.

On the other hand, an isolated lapse in the hygiene department doesn't warrant too much consideration, especially if you can identify a reason for it. I know a fabulous trial lawyer who speaks several languages and is a model of professionalism. He also has a passion for rebuilding old cars. As a result, scrub as he may, he frequently has grease under his fingernails. His dirty fingernails are inconsistent with the rest of his pattern and don't indicate poor hygiene. Instead, they provide insight into his hobbies and, perhaps more important, his practical and unpretentious nature.

FASTIDIOUSNESS

Fastidiousness can be reflected in a perfectly trimmed beard, freshly pressed clothing, a precisely positioned pocket scarf, and any similar trait. Like all traits, it varies in degree. I've known people who press their T-shirts and even their sheets. Others constantly straighten and re-straighten their clothing or their desks. This degree of fastidiousness is unusual. When it reaches an extreme, it may mean the person is suffering from obsessive-compulsive disorder.

Except for the few people who suffer from this clinical disorder, I've generally found that the more fastidious a person is, the more he'll tend to be egotistical, structured, inflexible, unimaginative, vain, and concerned about the opinions of others. Almost invariably, fastidious people have acquired the trait from their parents, so fastidiousness also usually reflects a strong parental influence.

Those on the opposite end of the spectrum may wear shoes that are heavily scuffed and worn-out, shirts with holes, torn seams, or missing buttons, or pants with an unraveling hem. My first consideration is whether this lack of personal maintenance is anything more than an indication that money is tight. If someone's clean and any items that can be maintained inexpensively have been, I can usually conclude little more from this feature alone. But if money doesn't seem to be the issue, I look for characteristics of the dowdy person, described later.

WRITING, LOGOS, AND PICTURES ON APPAREL

Words or images displayed on clothing are virtual advertisements for someone's lifestyles and values. They may reflect the person's employment, hobbies, religious preference, cultural background, politics, and more. They may also provide clues to his or her personality. The sleeping cat worn by the elderly grandmother is a symbol of nature, serenity, compassion, warmth, and contentment. It is hard to imagine a young, macho Marine picking out that shirt at the department store. He'd probably favor a picture of a bulldog or a pit bull—symbols of power, aggression, virility, and confidence. Sexually suggestive statements should be noted, as should humorous and intellectual ones. Most people do not randomly put on clothing with particular words, logos, or pictures. Rather, they choose what embodies their personality, depicts their interests, or reflects an image they want to present. For example:

- Prominently featured designer logos can indicate someone who is image conscious and perhaps lacks confidence. She may be trying to buy credibility with a designer label.
- Souvenir T-shirts from other cities and states, national parks, and so forth may tell you the person is a traveler or outdoorsman.
- T-shirts or polo shirts with sports insignias can indicate someone who is either a fan or a player. His haircut and degree of athleticism will often tell you which. Interestingly, some team logos have even been adopted by certain gangs as a type of uniform.

Many of these inferences are fairly obvious, but remember that seeing a pattern is the key. Everyone owns a few T-shirts with insignificant pictures or logos, but someone who consistently wears a certain label or logo is consciously trying to broadcast a personal priority.

TATTOOS AND OTHER "BODIFICATIONS"

When we actually alter our bodies, I call the changes "bodifications." Like clothing and jewelry, many bodifications are temporary, just like the states of mind they may reflect. For that reason, I give traits such as severely plucked eyebrows and false nails the same analysis as other ornamentation. But sit up and take notice when someone makes an affirmative decision to *permanently* alter her body with tattoos, implants, or dramatic body piercing.

Tattoos, for example, are revealing on many levels. The subject matter alone may be telling. A small flower or butterfly may indicate that its wearer is artistic and is trying to add beauty or interest to her life. Someone in the service may get a tattoo that symbolizes his branch or unit. Regardless of their subject, large, obvious tattoos may demonstrate

- a need to be different
- rebelliousness
- nonconformity
- an artistic or bohemian nature
- membership in a peer group, such as the military or a gang
- lower socioeconomic or educational background (you'll seldom see a wealthy person with tattoos)

If someone has chosen to get a noticeable tattoo it usually indicates that she's individualistic and nonconformist. You can expect original thinking and spontaneity. You may also encounter a bit of an "I don't give a damn what other people think" attitude. The bigger, brighter, bolder, and more outrageous the tattoo or tattoos, the more revealing of these personality traits they become.

Other elective bodifications, such as implants, are also very important clues about someone. Each of the many ways we can change or enhance our bodies will point toward what a person values, in herself and others. Someone who elects breast implants usually wants to enhance her sexuality. She is vain and concerned about what others, particularly men, think of her. A man who has liposuction to remove his love handles is also conscious of his appearance and attractiveness. He is vain and usually financially secure enough to afford to be. As with tattoos, it's important to note the degree of any surgical enhancement. A little tuck around the eyes isn't the same as a dramatic facelift, and small breast implants don't say what huge ones do. Such extremes emphasize the traits we've already discussed. If the surgical alterations are what most people would consider outlandish, I also can't help but think the person's self-centered and emotionally needy nature is clouding her judgment and ability to accurately understand how others perceive her.

TASTEFULNESS

Taste is a slippery concept. Every culture has its own definition of good and bad taste—*don't misjudge a person by mistaking cultural preferences for poor taste.*

For example, I've occasionally heard people comment that skimpy bikini-style swimsuits on men are tacky and inappropriate. But these swimsuits are standard fare in Europe. American men may feel uncomfortable in, or around, such revealing garb, but Europeans do not, and it doesn't reflect at all on their tastefulness.

You can learn a lot from someone's taste in clothing and other physical trappings if you're familiar with his background and culture.

In fact, whenever someone's choice of clothing and accessories clearly identify him or her with a specific region I always ask myself if people from that area are more likely to have particular values and characteristics. In some cases I can't draw any significant conclusions. In other cases I can, since regional origin is often indicative of cultural influences, and cultural influences can be very important as discussed in chapter 9, "Spotting Exceptions to the Rules."

Good taste can reveal

- good judgment and awareness of societal norms.
- a sensitivity to image and the opinions of others.
- sophistication. Those who have learned to dress tastefully also tend to act and think with equal social sophistication.
- prosperity. Tastefulness, like trendiness, can be expensive.
- parental influence. Taste is typically learned from one's parents, along with manners. You usually won't see one without the other.

Poor taste tends to reveal just the opposite of these traits. But taste is such a tricky category that any guidelines I give you come with a warning: be careful to look at all the other traits before passing judgment, particularly if cultural preference may be an issue.

REGIONAL STYLE

Southwestern jewelry, African clothing, a European-style bathing suit, cowboy boots, a fisherman's hat—any distinctive clothing, jewelry, or accessories—is often a tip-off to where someone was raised. If not, it probably signals that the person either lived in the area and enjoyed that period of her life, or identifies with the location for some reason. Keep your eye out for items with a distinctive regional style. They almost always have special meaning.

Not long ago, I pulled in to a gas station in Beverly Hills behind a brand-new, bright red Jaguar convertible. A fiftyish woman stepped out, holding a small, white, immaculately groomed poodle with red bows carefully placed in its fur. The bows matched the color of the car perfectly. The woman's makeup was flawless. She had platinum-blond hair and was wearing high heels and a royal blue formfitting velour pantsuit. If ever I saw a woman who had cultivated the wealthy Beverly Hills image, here she was. Apparently it was important to her to project an image of youthful sexiness, wealth, and success. In Beverly Hills, her appearance may have caused others to see her as she intended. But what would they think in Little Rock or New York City?

More importantly, her obvious association with the "Beverly Hills lifestyle" revealed her vanity, materialism, and image-consciousness.

CULTIVATED IMAGES

A distinctive image that someone intentionally tries to cultivate can reflect his true nature or simply his attempt to look a part. Some of the more common images people adopt are Country, Hollywood, Punk, Hippie, Grunge, Jock, and GQ. In general, it is more likely that a younger person has chosen a particular style to reflect a role, rather than his true nature. But old or young, it usually takes time and additional information to know whether someone is playing a part or is the real thing.

I recently conducted a focus group in which one of the mock jurors was a fifty-five-ish white man. He had a neat, long, gray ponytail, and his tanned, wrinkled skin showed the effects of years in the sun. His socked feet were clad in Birkenstock sandals, and he wore a T-shirt emblazoned with a hand-painted butterfly. This man exuded the image of a diehard hippie.

I wondered at first whether he truly held the liberal, creative, artistic, nonconformist views epitomized by the hippie movement, or whether he was just a middle-aged man who wanted to look hip. It turned out that he was a sociology professor at a local university, lived in a rural area outside of town, and drove a ten-year-old pickup truck. Since his lifestyle matched his hippie persona, I believe the nonconformist appearance was probably an accurate reflection of the inner man.

On the other hand, country bars all over America are packed with urban cowboys decked out in Stetson hats and snakeskin boots. To tell how much of their appearance is a conscious effort to adopt the Marlboro Man image—strong, macho, independent—requires more information. So watch out. Though you're looking for a rough, tough he-man with down-home manners and small-town values to match, you may find nothing more than a big-city boy in costume, unless you look behind the façade and examine their actions.

FLAMBOYANCE VERSUS CONSERVATIVENESS

Flamboyance is characterized by bright colors, shocking or distinctive styles, eye-catching jewelry, and the like. Conservatism is reflected by classic styles, subdued colors, and careful, meticulous grooming. Almost all of the many traits listed earlier in this chapter can range between the extreme ends of this spectrum. It's in where someone's traits lie in the spectrum—gaudy earrings, a toe ring, a flashy belt—that you'll find clues about whether she is more flamboyant or conservative at heart. But remember: to be flamboyant at heart, you don't need to dress like Liberace or Elton John.

The most clear-cut difference between these two types is their desire for attention. *Those who are flamboyant generally want to stick out. Those who are conservative usually want to blend in.* I've found that extremely flamboyant people are sometimes insecure, lonely, needy, and bored and dissatisfied with their life. But flamboyance is one of those traits that can reflect polar opposites. Flamboyant people can also be confident and self-assured.

Whether they are lonely or confident, flamboyant people generally share a few characteristics. They

- are creative, artistic, and imaginative.
- usually have at least some money, since flamboyant clothing and jewelry are generally fairly expensive and not very practical.
- themselves are not very practical.
- are nonconformists. They may not care much about what other people think of them, as long as they've got an audience.
- are independent, and maybe even a bit flaky.

Conservative people, on the other hand,

- are likely to care about the opinions of others and want to fit in and be accepted.
- are conformists who feel most comfortable when they meet social norms and expectations.
- are often practical, authoritarian, and analytical.
- are less creative or imaginative than flamboyant people. They tend to be more conventional thinkers.
- are more judgmental

Someone may dress very conservatively out of insecurity, in an effort to be accepted or to fit in, or they may be very secure and confident. To uncover their motive, you'll have to examine other clues. It usually takes some careful observation and questioning before you can tell if your conservative friend is confident or afraid to stand out. The same goes for flamboyant people—it requires more than a snapshot to determine whether they are lonely and needy, or gloriously liberated. But in either case, careful attention to someone's appearance will be an excellent place to start to develop the pattern that ultimately will reveal the answer.

PRACTICALITY VERSUS EXTRAVAGANCE

Many people are simply middle-of-the road in their fashion statements, neither flamboyant nor conservative. But most fall into one of two distinct camps with respect to practicality and extravagance.

Anything that emphasizes comfort, cost, or utility over style will point toward the practical person. It usually takes me very little time to determine whether someone is more interested in comfort and practicality than style and image. Many different features of most people's appearance help place them in one category or the other.

Does a woman

- wear matching accessories with her outfits, or prefer basic blacks and browns that are easy to coordinate?
- have long, carefully painted, manicured nails, or are they short and functional?
- wear flats or high heels?
- have a high-maintenance haircut?
- wear large jewelry that can easily snag her nylons, or get in the way generally?
- wear a lot of makeup, which is expensive and time-consuming to apply?

Does a man

- wear color-coordinated ties, pocket scarves, socks, or other clothing?
- wear a lightweight running watch or a heavy Rolex?
- wear walking shoes or Italian loafers on his morning stroll to work?
- have his nails manicured?
- get frequent haircuts, or allow his hair to grow a bit long before having it trimmed?

The nature of someone's toys also says something about whether he is practical or extravagant. Someone who golfs only rarely but owns an expensive set of clubs, or who plays tennis infrequently but has several tennis rackets, is probably extravagant, not practical. The same can be said of someone who chooses an expensive, high-maintenance car.

I can make some generalizations about someone once I have determined how practical or extravagant he is. People who are interested in comfort and practicality are usually

- at ease with themselves and their position in life
- not self-centered

- willing to be nonconformists, if that's what it takes to be comfortable
- frugal

Extravagant people often

- are image conscious
- suffer from poor self-esteem
- desire acceptance and approval and need the respect and admiration of others
- genuinely enjoy "the gift of giving." Giving people presents brings them pleasure.

Before you assume that someone will have traits typical of the extravagant person, take a good look at where he spends his money. If he spends it where it will be very much in the public eye—on clothing, jewelry, cars, big parties, and so forth—then he probably fits the extravagant profile. But someone can spend a lot of money without having the typical extravagant personality traits. The normal rules won't apply if he usually spends money where few people will see it—for instance, on vacations, a summer house only his family will visit, or quiet contributions to his favorite charities.

SEXUAL SUGGESTIVENESS

Some people wear clothes and accessories that are exceptionally sexy, even in the context of our very sexualized culture. The man or woman who wears sexually suggestive clothing may be tremendously confident or very insecure. What is consistently true, however, is that he or she is trying to get attention.

The confident man or woman dressed in revealing clothing will tend to mingle freely in groups. He or she will have good, upright, posture, move gracefully, and approach members of the opposite sex, rather than wait to be approached. They will normally have no significant affectations or unusual body motions. Such an individual is often outgoing, self-centered, and vain.

The less confident will often slouch or shuffle as they move. They will generally wait for others to make the first move. Their body motions and voice will tend to be tentative.

Revealing garb worn at inappropriate times also indicates a lack of good judgment. It's also likely, although not a given, that the wearer is sexually liberated, though he or she may also just be a confident tease.

DOWDINESS

Dowdiness is yet another of those categories that can signify polar opposites. Men and women who seem dowdy (men like this are usually called rumpled or unkempt) tend to be out of the social mainstream and insensitive to most issues of appearance.

Common signs of dowdiness include

- wrinkled but fairly clean clothing
- shapeless, outdated, or bland clothing and accessories
- messy, uncombed hair
- an unflattering or out-of-date hairstyle
- well-worn shoes

Dowdiness can signify

- *lower socioeconomic background.* Good grooming is often a reflection of financial status. Obviously there are exceptions. Many people who grew up without much money are stylish dressers. But if a person consistently wears rumpled clothing, there is a good chance she was never taught otherwise. This occurs in lower-class or lower-middle-class homes more often than in families that are well off, but it can exist at any socioeconomic level.
- *the artistic, intellectual, or "absent-minded professor" syndrome.* Some dowdy dressers simply don't pay attention to the way they look. These are typically people whose intellectual or creative life eclipses all other concerns. Engineers, scientists, inventors, and artists often fall into this category.
- *preoccupation elsewhere.* Some people have decided their true passion in life is travel, or dog breeding, or record collecting, or surfing the Internet. They just don't put much time or energy into their appearance, and they don't care what the outside world thinks. They often associate with others with similar interests who look and dress just as they do anyway.
- *sloppiness.* There are those who aren't obsessed with their computer or lost in an effort to find a cure for cancer or put a man on Mars. They're just slobs—pure and simple. Their house is a mess. Their car is a mess. Their locker at work is a mess. And yes—they're a mess. Appearance just isn't high on their list of priorities.

Body Language and
What It Reveals

There are as many body movements to pick clues from as there are people and moments in the day. Like the list of physical characteristics in Appendix A, the list that follows, long though it is, does not include all the potentially revealing aspects of someone's body motions. But it does contain those you will see most often. Review it with a mind toward broadening your vision. No one notices all these possible clues all the time. But you'll start picking up more and more if you at least think about them from time to time.

WHOLE BODY MOVEMENTS

Walk
slow/fast
bouncing
tentative
striding
pacing

Positioning
in groups
in couples
alone
closeness to people
erect

chest out
slouching
sitting on edge of chair, or lying
   back

Motion
shaking
trembling
rocking
shifting
twitching
wiggling
strutting

skipping
running
swaying
still
dragging
rapid jerky motions
stepping away
stepping forward
leaning forward or back
turning away

HEAD

nodding
shaking
hanging down
tossing
circling
looking down or up
looking around
looking in mirrors
nose in the air

FACE

Eyes
open or shut
staring
moving back and forth
moving up and down
blinking
winking
closing frequently
wincing
squinting
smiling
rolling
looking over eyeglasses

Mouth/Jaw
lips open
lips tight

smiling (toothy grin, smug,
   relaxed)
lips pursed
frowning
yawning
turned-up corners
licking lips
biting lips
teeth clenched
mouth twitch
grimacing
set jaw
grinding jaw
dry
running tongue over teeth

Eyebrows
moving up or down
furrowed

Miscellaneous
wrinkling of nose
facial tics

EXTREMITIES

Touching
handshakes (fishy, firm, two-
   handed, held)
poking
petting
backslapping
leaning

Arms, Hands, Legs, and Feet
tapping fingers or feet
touching fingers together
twiddling thumbs
obscene gestures with
   hands/fingers
hands over mouth

hands on chin
hands to temple
hands on hips
hands in pockets
hands on lap
wringing hands
clenching fists
scratching face or ears
twisting hair
flipping hair
stretching
scratching head
crossing and uncrossing
flailing

Fiddling
biting nails
picking at nails
twirling hair
rubbing beard or mustache

touching or picking at clothes
twirling glasses
playing with watch
clicking pens

VOCALIZATIONS

breathing (deep, shallow, short,
   rapid, slow, rapid exhaling
   "whew")
burping/belching
sighs
swallowing
gulping
coughs (nervous, deep, dry,
   clearing throat)
humming
whistling
becoming quiet
becoming loud

Each of the traits or emotions discussed in the next sections is revealed most clearly through a combination of many different body motions, as well as environment, voice, and actions. Don't be overwhelmed by the fact that the same body motions can mean many different things. If you look at the whole pattern, you will almost always arrive at the right conclusion.

Arrogance/Humility

A would-be king holds himself above the masses. A true prince walks among them.

The essence of arrogance is an attempt to exalt oneself above others. The core of humility is the recognition that no matter what one's status may be, one person is no better or worse than another.

Not surprisingly, arrogant people try to separate themselves from the masses, whereas people who are humble opt for unpretentious contact and communication with others regardless of their "rank." Those who are arrogant are not necessarily secure, whereas humility usually reflects a certain deep-seated security. As a result, humble people are much less likely to be overcompetitive, particularly with friends or family. They are more forgiving, understanding, and compassionate.

In placing someone on the arrogance/humility scale, appearance may be telling. The arrogant person's attire, grooming, and behavior often reflect his effort to set himself apart and above. He may wear expensive, pretentious, or impractical clothing, or dress more or less formally than others. And he'll often act aloof, bored, or pretentious. Humble people tend to dress and act in a more down-to-earth style.

Arrogant people frequently

- preen
- glance at their reflection in mirrors and windows
- attempt to be the center of the discussion
- make grand, flamboyant gestures
- keep greater than average physical distance from others (although some arrogant people feel entitled to invade others' personal space and do so inappropriately)
- bore easily and quit listening (arrogant people don't really care what others have to say)
- make sexually suggestive movements and postures
- boast
- adopt affectations and put on airs

Signs of humility are

- focusing on others rather than oneself
- good listening skills
- self-deprecating humor
- a quiet demeanor
- courtesies such as giving up a chair or opening a door for someone

It's important to make certain there is a *pattern* of arrogance. A loud, boisterous woman may also be considerate, and a quiet man might not be listening to a conversation simply because he's tired. Look for more than one symptom.

Confidence/Leadership

A politician sits quietly, back straight, eyes forward, hands still in his lap, a slight smile on his face, as he waits for the debate to begin.

Not surprisingly, leaders tend to be confident, and followers tend to be insecure. Consequently, identifying leaders requires sensitivity to the traits shown by anyone who's confident, and vice versa. And spotting followers is the same as identifying those who are passive and insecure.

Leadership and confidence do not have to entail an outgoing, domineering, aggressive personality. There are quiet and confident leaders, and there are loud and aggressive ones.

Leaders and others who are confident may

- typically lead (and often control) conversations
- usually have a number of people around them as a result of their personality
- position themselves at an appropriate distance from people when talking (although a "control freak" will usually invade someone's personal space)
- volunteer for unpleasant tasks
- be good listeners
- have a self-assured smile, not overstated or toothy, but sometimes almost smug
- walk with confidence, almost striding, frequently with their arms moving rather significantly
- have a firm handshake
- be better-dressed
- have good hygiene
- dress conservatively and appropriately for the occasion
- dress in more expensive and more tasteful clothing
- seldom follow any faddish trends
- be willing to engage in conversation
- be physical and athletic
- make good eye contact
- have a conservative haircut or hairstyle
- have erect posture
- square their body to the person they're speaking to
- carry the trappings sometimes associated with responsibility, such as a briefcase, calculator, cellular phone, pager, calendar, or Day-timer

People often expect leaders to be outgoing or aggressive, and overlook quiet, confident ones. Not all leaders and confident people strut like bantam roosters. Quiet, reserved leaders will still usually have a firm handshake and engage in direct eye contact. In conversation, they will be attentive and good listeners.

Leaders usually settle into a position of power in any room. If there is a table, they will tend to gravitate toward the end of it. If there are people scattered throughout the room, the leader will usually be more centrally located. Leaders usually don't show signs of nervousness and frequently take good care of their health and bodies.

Confusion

Visualize the windup toy, scurrying in one direction until it hits the wall, rebounding and heading off in another direction. The movement is random, not orderly.

You'll seldom see confusion in complete isolation from other basic emotions. Frequently, someone who is confused will also be frustrated or indecisive and will show signs of those emotions. But even when coupled with other emotional states, confusion can usually be spotted. When someone is confused, she has lost her bearings and is trying to find them.

Symptoms of confusion include

- verbal repetition
- repetitive motion
- picking items up and putting them down
- conflicting or inconsistent behavior
- shifting or shuffling
- signs of indecision
- signs of frustration

The important thing to watch for when trying to distinguish confusion from other traits which have similar symptoms is whether the person's physical movements and vocal variations tend to be random. Repetitive but structured or orderly movements or speech is more likely the result of nervousness or indecision than confusion. The confused person will tend to career about, both physically and verbally.

Defensiveness

Picture a cat cornered by a dog. It's backed against a wall, hair standing on end. It's looking for a chance to run away, but ready to attack if necessary.

Most defensive gestures are instinctive ways of protecting ourselves. Feeling defensive is extremely unpleasant. It's a product of feeling attacked. At the very least, someone who's feeling defensive will also be feeling awkward and vulnerable. As a result, his behavior usually reflects a desire to avoid the situation, either by physically or verbally moving, or by deflecting the attack.

Most people detest confrontation, and when we feel defensive it's usually because someone has confronted us. Sometimes we also feel defensive if we fear a confrontation is about to erupt, or if we mistake a neutral comment for a challenge. Not surprisingly, many symptoms of defensiveness resemble the symptoms of anger, but you may also see signs like those of nervousness or secretiveness.

Symptoms of defensiveness may include

- crossing arms, legs, and/or ankles
- clenching teeth, jaws, or lips
- averting the eyes
- body squared, not turned away (confrontational)
- hands on hips
- quick exhaling
- closing the mouth tightly and refusing to talk
- leaving the awkward situation

Usually the best way to tell if body language that could result from several different emotions in fact reflects defensiveness is to reevaluate it in conjunction with the person's words. As we mentioned when discussing "Defensive Behavior" on page 167–170, people will often give themselves away by the communication they chose to employ.

Drug and Alcohol Use

Denial is the biggest problem. Don't ignore the obvious symptoms.

Drug and alcohol abuse extends across all socioeconomic boundaries, cultures, income levels, occupations, and ages. The signs are fairly obvious and well publicized. What's more difficult than seeing them is admitting to yourself that you're seeing them, especially in a loved one. Once you're aware of the symptoms of substance abuse, don't refuse to acknowledge them.

Look for signs of intoxication not only in chronic abusers but also in people who indulge only occasionally. You don't want to get in the car with a drunk driver even if he gets drunk only once a year. No matter how responsible and reliable someone is when sober, drug and alcohol use can turn Dr. Jekyll into Mr. Hyde, altering behavior in both obvious and subtle ways.

Symptoms of drug and alcohol use include

- slurred speech
- extremely rapid speech
- inappropriate behavior, especially if exaggerated (too close or intimate, too loud, too quiet)
- red eyes

- partially closed eyes
- bags under the eyes
- mood swings (animated/depressed behavior)
- loss of inhibitions
- shaking
- bulbous, red nose
- odor
- inconsistency, particularly dramatic inconsistency, of appearance and behavior between one occasion and another
- poor hygiene
- withdrawal from normal social activity
- a large torso and thin legs, or a potbelly on a thin person (both body types are typical of alcoholics)
- frequent failure to fulfill committments or keep appointments.

Embarrassment

Think of a young boy strutting into the cafeteria. He trips and falls in front of everyone. His face turns red. He brushes himself off, awkwardly trying not to show his embarrassment, and slinks off to a table in the corner.

Symptoms of embarrassment are generally well known. They include

- nervous laughter
- avoiding eye contact
- shaking of the head
- turning away
- flushing
- avoiding people; leaving the room

Even though the symptoms are usually obvious, embarrassment is often missed, since people who are embarrassed invariably try hard to conceal it. Many people react to embarrassing situations by going away quietly and hoping the awkward moment will be forgotten. Others will try to laugh it off. It's important to be able to recognize the signs of embarrassment, because unless you're attuned to them you can easily mistake embarrassment for anger, defensiveness, or even nervousness. Or you might miss the signs altogether and assume someone is insensitive or antisocial, when in fact he might be deeply ashamed of his embarrassing actions and just not know how to apologize for them.

Fear

Visualize a deer, frozen in its tracks in the middle of the road, eyes wide, body stiff.

The deer in the headlights is a perfect metaphor for how people frequently look in the initial stage of fear. Surprise is the main emotion at that point, but if the fright continues, defensiveness and nervousness also kick in. Fear is, of course, one of our most basic emotions. Only rarely do most of us experience fright—as distinguished from anxiety—but it's worthwhile to know the symptoms.

Symptoms of fear include the signs of surprise:

- wide-open eyes
- screaming
- hands over the face
- being frozen or paralyzed
- flushing
- gulping and swallowing
- looking around (looking over one's shoulder)
- clutching hands together or gripping another object tightly (white knuckles)
- placing hands in front of the body
- leaning or shifting backward
- turning away (especially the upper body)
- quick, jerky flailing or stretching out of the extremities
- grabbing other people
- shaking
- heavy breathing
- quick, shallow breathing
- holding one's breath
- walking quickly
- rigidity or stiffness
- licking lips
- taking small, tentative steps (as in searching a dark room)

Different people respond differently to fear. When I visited France two years ago with my friend Denise, we found this out firsthand. While we were at a stoplight, a man jumped into the back of our car and stole some of our luggage. Denise began screaming uncontrollably, while I became paralyzed. Social scientists have found one of two reactions kicks in when most people are confronted with such an aggressive and hostile act: "fight or flight." Denise and I are living proof that the menu of possible responses is much broader. We did neither.

Resentment

Picture a high school girl who wasn't picked to be a cheerleader, watching as the squad practices. Her arms are folded, her eyes are slightly closed, her body stiff.

Resentment is usually a by-product of anger or jealousy. *Whatever its origin, resentment usually shows itself in a cluster of mannerisms designed to put distance between a person and the one she resents.*

Symptoms of resentment include

- crossing the arms
- stiffening of the body
- grimacing
- pouting
- avoidance
- looking or turning away
- signs of anger

Lawyers can be an egotistical bunch. That's what gives them the drive to succeed, but it can also lead to a competitiveness that can turn to resentment overnight. I've been involved in many trials where two or more lawyers represented a single defendant. Each lawyer usually brings different talents to the table, but almost invariably one will emerge as the lead counsel. Who that is may even vary from day to day or week to week. As this ebb and flow of courtroom supremacy takes place, I often see classic signs of resentment develop. The lawyers' chairs will slide slightly farther apart. Their arms will be folded. One lawyer's gaze will be fixed in the opposite direction as the other speaks. I'm sure if you were to ask the players in a scene like this whether they were aware of their body language, they would say no. But like so many mannerisms, those of resentment can creep in unnoticed, especially by the one displaying them.

Secretiveness/Openness

Think of a poker player, expressionless, peering over his cards, which he is holding tightly and close to his face.

People who are open expose themselves to you in their manner and speech. Secretive people reveal very little of themselves and carefully guard personal information. Often they prefer to keep the various areas of their life compartmentalized, and are open about one or more of their worlds—work, play, school, the dating scene—but secretive about others. Secretive people may literally keep their distance, as if afraid that if they get too close you will be able to size them up more effectively.

Symptoms of secretiveness include

- whispering
- a "guarding" posture, with shoulders hunched
- covering mouth with hand
- body turned partially away from the other person
- tightly closed lips
- set jaw
- seldom invading the personal space of others, since they don't want others in *their* space
- avoiding social interaction or other circumstances in which they might be expected to reveal something of themselves
- revealing little emotion
- brief, almost mechanical handshake
- frequently glancing down during a conversation
- looking around the room when being addressed, rather than returning a gaze
- instinctively and routinely covering or removing any personal material from view
- seldom volunteering an opinion or belief until they have everyone else's.

Signs of openness include

- body fully facing the person to whom one is speaking
- standing fairly close to the other person (although not within personal space)
- frequent and prolonged eye contact
- warm, relaxed smile
- kissing or embracing when greeting
- firm, sometimes prolonged handshake
- enjoying social interaction
- self-disclosure

When gauging whether someone is secretive, consider whether specific behavior is an isolated trait or part of a slew of secretive habits. *The truly secretive person will generally exhibit many secretive traits, not just one or two.* If someone who is normally outgoing won't say much about why she was on the phone all day, don't jump to conclusions—who knows, maybe she's planning your surprise birthday party. And the person who habitually locks his desk drawers before he goes to lunch each day but is otherwise outgoing and open may be hiding something, or he may have been the victim of a lunchtime burglary. You won't know without more information. Look for a pattern of several of the symptoms listed above to develop before you draw any firm conclusions.

Sexual or Romantic Interest

A seductress from a 1940s detective movie rubs her palms slowly down her sides to straighten her jacket. She slinks into the room, looking the gruff detective up and down, then sits slowly on his desk and crosses her legs.

Sexual attraction usually spurs people to make contact. *Any action that reveals, emphasizes, or draws attention to someone's sexuality can be seen as a sign of sexual interest.* There are scores of behaviors that are well-known tip-offs to sexual interest, and many books have been written on the subject. What follows is just a brief list of the most obvious traits.

Sign of sexual interest include

- making eye contact
- exaggerated smile
- laughter
- staring
- winking
- blinking
- wetting lips
- crossing and uncrossing legs
- thrusting out the chest or hips
- walking with a swagger or wiggle
- primping
- lounging back
- coy smile
- flipping of the head or hair
- entering someone's personal space
- any revealing clothing (particularly if not appropriate for the occasion)

- touching oneself (smoothing nylons or playing with shirt buttons)
- touching the object of one's affection (even if just briefly on the hand, arm, shoulder or back)
- excessive makeup, perfume, or cologne
- overdressing for the occasion
- whispering or other attempts at intimacy
- intent listening
- intently looking the other person up and down
- trying to isolate the target of one's affection by getting him or her alone

Surprise

The lights go on and everyone yells, "Happy birthday!"

Surprise may be the result of fear, excitement, or pleasure. *The response is usually the same regardless of the reason for the surprise: quick body movement and a temporary loss of control over the smaller muscles.* Usually someone will quickly resume his "presurprise" posture.

Symptoms of surprise include

- stepping backward (if standing) or leaning backward (if seated)
- mouth opening
- eyes widening
- extending the arms and legs
- jumping upward
- gasping or screaming

The symptoms of surprise usually don't vary much, whether the news is good or bad. The last day of the O. J. Simpson criminal trial proved this point in many people's minds. The media frequently replayed the physical reaction of Mr. Simpson's friend and attorney Robert Kardashian to the not-guilty verdict. Pointing out that Mr. Kardashian's mouth dropped open as the verdict was read, commentators suggested that he was surprised. The writer Dominick Dunne was also seated in the gallery. Mr. Dunne firmly believed that Mr. Simpson was guilty. For Mr. Kardashian, the acquittal was good news; for Mr. Dunne it was terrible news. Yet Mr. Dunne's facial expression, while slightly more extreme, resembled Mr. Kardashian's very closely.

Suspicion/Disbelief

Visualize an elderly English judge, peering down from his bench, fingers sliding his glasses down his nose just enough so you can see his eyes over the top of them, as he slowly shakes his head back and forth.

Classic symptoms of suspicion include

- furrowed brow
- a squint in the eyes
- turning the head slightly down and looking slightly upward (the peering-over-the-glasses look) or tilting the head slightly
- tightening of the lips
- the signs of pensiveness

Once disbelief has set in, the symptoms may be

- eye-rolling
- head-shaking
- grimacing
- turning up the corners of the mouth
- exhaling quickly "through the teeth"
- those of frustration

The difference between suspicion and disbelief is a matter of degree. To suspect is to have doubt but not yet to have formed a firm opinion. *The suspicious person is still thinking about what to believe, and consequently the characteristics of suspicion include those of pensiveness.* Suspicion most often arises when someone doubts the truthfulness of a statement. When he makes up his mind that the statement is in fact false, the characteristics of pensiveness give way to those of disbelief.

Worry

Think of a nervous father pacing back and forth as he awaits news from the delivery room.

When someone is worried, he is also normally anxious, nervous, or afraid. Consequently, whenever I see signs of anxiety, nervousness, or fear, I associate them with worry.

Symptoms of worry include

- repetitive action, such as pacing
- biting nails
- wringing hands
- shaking
- fidgeting
- rubbing the face
- running hands through hair
- lack of mental focus

The hand-wringing, pacing, fidgeting brand of worry or anxiety isn't hard to spot. But the same can't always be said of the dull, constant anxiety we feel at times. Someone watching the last few minutes of her daughter's basketball game with the score tied 50–50 will probably show many of the classic signs of worry or anxiety, but how about the woman who has been fretting constantly for days that she may fall victim to the cutbacks at work? She may look anxious, but just as likely she will show signs of attentiveness and pensiveness, as she concentrates on her problem and how she can handle it. Or she may have lapsed into depression over the thought of being laid off and what that might mean to her family, in which case symptoms of depression would dominate her emotional picture. The important point to keep in mind is that worry, like almost every emotion, can take many forms, and vary from person to person and situation to situation. You need to be alert to all of the possibilities if you want to be certain not to overlook any of them.

Send Us Your Best Tips
for Reading People!

We all have a favorite story or two about how we could tell our friend was lying, our child was upset, or our boss was in a bad mood. We want to hear yours!

While we were writing *Reading People* and discussing it with our friends and families, they often suggested that our next book should be a collection of tips from our readers about reading people. We thought it was a great idea, and we're planning to publish just such a collection. Your real-life stories and words of wisdom will be grouped by category (how to tell if someone is lying, how to distinguish between the blowhard and the true leader, et cetera), followed by our comments and impressions. It will be fun and informative.

If you'd like to see your story in print, just send us your favorite, along with your name and address, to:

Reading People
P.O. Box 305
Bonita, California 91908-035

Fax to:
(619) 475-7122

E-mail to:
Tips@ReadingPeople.com

Or visit our website at:
www.ReadingPeople.com

ABOUT THE AUTHORS

JO-ELLAN DIMITRIUS, PH.D., has consulted in over six hundred jury trials, including the Rodney King, Reginald Denny, John DuPont, McMartin Preschool, and O. J. Simpson cases. She has appeared on *Oprah, Good Morning America,* the *Today* show, *Larry King Live, Face the Nation,* and *60 Minutes,* and she has consulted with many Fortune 100 companies. MARK MAZZARELLA has been a practicing trial lawyer in San Diego for twenty years. He is a past chairman of the twelve-thousand-member litigation section of the California State Bar, and he writes and lectures extensively.